How to Do Everything with

Podcasting

Shel Holtz

with Neville Hobson

SUBSCRIBE

UPDATE

McGraw Hill

New York   Chicago   San Francisco   Lisbon
London   Madrid   Mexico City   Milan   New Delhi
San Juan   Seoul   Singapore   Sydney   Toronto

The *McGraw-Hill* Companies

Cataloging-in-Publication Data is on file with the Library of Congress

How to Do Everything with Podcasting

1234567890 FGR FGR 01987

ISBN-13: 978-0-07-226394-7
ISBN-10: 0-07-226394-6

Sponsoring Editor Roger Stewart	**Copy Editor** Mike McGee	**Composition** International Typesetting and Composition
Editorial Supervisor Jody McKenzie	**Proofreader** Ragini Pandey	**Illustration** International Typesetting and Composition
Project Manager Arushi Chawla, International Typesetting and Composition	**Indexer** Steve Ingle **Production Supervisor** Jean Bodeaux	**Art Director, Cover** Pattie Lee
Acquisitions Coordinator Carly Stapleton		**Cover Illustration** Jason Cook

To the worldwide listenership of *For Immediate Release:
The Hobson and Holtz Report*. Much more than just an audience—a vibrant
community.

To my wife, Michele, whose endless patience makes my involvement in social
media—and book-writing—possible. It's even better when she shares the same
passions. Because she is a podcaster herself, this is one of those happy times.

—Shel Holtz

My personal dedication is to Shel and to our agent, Yvonne DiVita. Shel is a
powerhouse and I stand in awe of his ability as a book writer. My contributions
pale by comparison. Thanks to you both for your energy and your leadership.

—Neville Hobson

About the Authors

Shel Holtz is a U.S.-based communicator, blogger, and podcaster. With more than 30 years of professional experience, Shel has focused on online communication since the late 1980s, concentrating on social media, including podcasting, for the last several years. He works with organizations to help them apply online strategies and tactics to their organizational communication efforts. He is the author of four previous communications-focused books and numerous articles for magazines and journals. He has also written several manuals. He lives in Concord, California, with his wife and their two children.

Neville Hobson, a U.K.-based communicator, blogger, and podcaster, is a leading early adopter in new-media communication for business. He helps companies use effective communication to achieve their business goals. He is passionate about business communication and technology, and also about new ways to develop organizational communication to enable people to connect more easily and openly.

Contents

Foreword

It was in December 2004 that my world shifted. I had just celebrated my birthday and Christmas was quickly approaching when a knock came at the door and the mailman delivered my first iPod. Little did I know that this small device that I planned to use to play music was about to change everything I knew about entertainment and content, or that it would also completely change my life.

You see, on that day as I searched the Web for more information on my new toy, I came across a term I didn't recognize: "podcasting." I kept seeing the term in various forums and other posts in relation to MP3 players, blogs, and the production of shows. I wasn't quite sure what it was all about yet, but it seemed to make sense.

I have been a blogger for years and the concept of an audio blog was not foreign to me, but it never really appealed to me for some reason. What I quickly discovered was this was taking that old idea and adding a new spin to it. People could actually subscribe to content and it would appear on their computer or MP3 device to listen to whenever they wanted. This was different—and in a big way! I knew that I had to try this and try it soon.

I started recording random thoughts that came to me with the microphone on my computer. I was playing around with no long-term goal in mind. I wanted to play music and quickly realized there were legal issues to doing so. I found the community of podcasters out there through sites like Podcast Alley, which floored me when I first visited because I discovered others who were excited by this as well. What had I stumbled into? I knew it was going to change the rules, but I didn't think it was going to happen as fast as it did. Apple would wake up months later and the landscape would shift again.

My good buddy, Mike Branum, got a call from me saying, "You have got to check this out," and soon we were producing a show together called *Reality Bitchslap Radio*. Almost overnight we had people commenting back to us, sending us audio comments to play on the show. We would reach out to artists to ask about playing music, and they would get excited by our requests. We were having fun, and people were listening. It was cool.

That show faded away, and Mike and I both started doing our own things. People told me I had great taste in music, so I started *Accident Hash* as a show to highlight independent music. Two months into it, I got a call from PodShow to help them manage the development of what is now The PodSafe Music Network, which makes it easier for artists to get their music heard on podcasts. For podcasters, it's an easy outlet to find cleared music.

2005 also saw Apple get into the game, the first major Podcast Expo, and the explosion of the podcasting realm as a whole. It was a strange year for lots of us because suddenly there was talk of money from advertisers, the need for better equipment, and overall a lot more focus on the content rather than on the fun. To me, it's important to keep a happy balance between it all. I firmly believe that if you are not having fun doing something, then why do it? I also believe that you can make money and not have to sell your soul. The key is that it's up to you what you do and don't do when you hit the Record button.

The true power of podcasting is that it gives anyone a voice that the world can hear. The cost of entry is extremely low, and, while you can spend thousands of dollars on setting up a full blown studio, I'm a huge fan of not doing that unless it's really necessary. I'm still using the $200 worth of audio equipment I bought back in the beginning. My podcasts are heard by thousands of people around the globe every week. If you have a voice and something to say, podcasting enables you to share that.

Companies are beginning to wake up to all of this, but they certainly don't understand it fully. Yes, it can be used to push your brand out to more people, but at the same time it can be used to improve corporate communications, share information with stockholders, or give another level of transparency to a company. Podcasting isn't a one trick pony and you need to be sure you work with people who can tell you all the angles and options before you just throw all your time, money, and energy in a single direction.

Podcasting is just one piece in the big new media puzzle. It's an important piece, but still just a piece. The best thing is that we have yet to see what the puzzle looks like all together. There is no box cover to look at so we know if we are doing it right or not. That causes a mix of both fear and excitement. If you lean more towards the excitement side, then welcome to the fun! This is what led me to create *Managing the Gray*, my podcast that focuses on all of new media. I like to stress that both companies and individuals need to play in the whole space and have at least a basic understanding of all the pieces. Books like this are a great way to start heading down that path.

Every day technology is changing. The tools, sites, and resources that have come about since podcasting first entered my vocabulary are amazing.

I've traveled the world speaking to a wide spectrum of interested parties: from large corporations to soccer moms. Every fresh excited face I see only adds to my sense of accomplishment. The community continues to grow every day, and, right now, *you* are becoming part of it as well. Remember that this is a community and there will be bumps in the road. Remember your passion and your drive, and be sure to have fun! I know I will.

Catch ya on the flipside.

C.C. Chapman
www.cc-chapman.com

C.C. Chapman is a podcasting pioneer. The host of the award-winning music podcast, Accident Hash, *Chapman is the host and producer of two other podcasts (*U-Turn Café *and* Managing the Gray) *and the developer of the Podsafe Music Network. He speaks regularly on podcasting and is widely known in podcasting circles.*

Acknowledgments

The initial idea for writing a book about podcasting came in an e-mail to Neville from Yvonne DiVita in mid-2005. That idea—the seed, really—led to Neville talking to Shel and both of them speaking with Yvonne. From those conversations came a plan to create a source of information and help about podcasting that would draw on the experiences of two of the pioneers in business podcasting. The result is the book you are reading now.

We especially want to thank Yvonne for her unwavering support and encouragement. The same acknowledgment is also due to Roger Stewart at McGraw-Hill.

Thanks also go to podcasters who have helped us—wittingly or not—learn our craft, including Adam Curry, Craig Patchett, Tim and Emil Borquin (the Podcast Brothers), Eric Rice, P.W. Fenton, Leo LaPorte, Rob Walsh, Todd Cochrane, and Michael Butler.

We would not be able to produce our podcast over two continents without Skype, the brilliant Voice over IP solution; therefore, it would be inappropriate not to acknowledge the company and innovators who created and continue to develop Skype.

Paul from Guitar Center and Christopher from Spitzer Music, both in Concord, California, lent invaluable assistance with the technical sections of this book.

And special thanks to Jerry Back from The Nielsen Company, who was able to track down some statistics we just couldn't find.

Introduction

I first became aware of podcasting when I read about it on a few blogs—mostly blogs by people working in the public relations/organizational communications business. It sounded interesting, but I wasn't quite sure I got it. What kind of audio files would people want to subscribe to?

I finally found a few minutes to download a podcatching application and tap into a podcast or two to try. I don't remember which podcast was the very first I listened to, but it was either *Geek News Central*, a twice-weekly roundup of goings-on in the world of podcasting technology with Todd Cochrane; *Evil Genius Chronicles*, a mixture of personal commentary, observations, and music with radio veteran Dave Slusher; or *Daily Source Code*, the very first podcast ever produced, by former MTV veejay Adam Curry.

As the number of podcasts—and podcast listeners—grew, it became clear this was more than a passing fad. A few things struck me about podcasting:

- Some listeners got actively engaged; others felt like they belonged to a community. There was definitely something going on, some kind of vibe between listener and podcaster that was radically different from radio.

- The subject matter of podcasts was unique. It's tough to fit a podcast like *Evil Genius Chronicles* into a category, and to call *The Rock and Roll Geek Show* a music podcast is doing host Michael Butler a disservice. Unlike radio shows, podcasts are not interchangeable.

- Podcasts fill niche needs that alternative media cannot. The audiences interested in knitting or the TV series *Firefly* or the experiences of airline flight attendants are passionate but small. No mainstream media channel could produce a return on the investment in such a show. But the barriers to entry have vanished. Anybody can produce a show on these topics for global audiences—and even generate an income doing it.

These factors, and some others, convinced me that I needed to pay close attention to podcasting. Since my business requires me to be able to advise my clients on new communication technologies, I knew I would probably be getting some inquires about it. I figured the best way to learn about podcasting was to do it. After all, that was the same reason I began blogging.

My podcast would be about public relations (the field in which I work) and technology. I wanted it to have global appeal, and I didn't want to do it by myself—so I asked Neville Hobson if he would be interested in co-hosting a show with me. A Brit living in Amsterdam at that time, Neville would bring the European perspective to our listeners. (Neville and I go back about 20 years, to the days of CompuServe and its Public Relations and Marketing Forum.) He agreed, and we began podcasting *For Immediate Release: The Hobson and Holtz Report* on January 3, 2005.

What's Special about This Book

In the two-plus years since then, we have learned a lot about podcasting. We have learned to build a community with our show, how to get high-quality sound over a free Internet telephone service when we are an entire continent and ocean apart, how to work with a sponsor, and how to edit a waveform file. Plus a lot more. And none of it is anything we would have *thought* we would know before podcasting came along.

This book is our way of sharing the knowledge we have accumulated over 230 shows. Of course, a lot of that knowledge was shared with us by other podcasters and social media experts. The rest was a combination of research, trial and error, and dumb luck.

We went into this knowing there are already some good podcasting books out there. However, there didn't seem to be a comprehensive book that covered all the various aspects of podcasting. Some focus more on the technical aspects of podcasting, while others look mainly at content. A few offer tips and secrets, one is focused entirely on promoting your podcast, but none looked at podcasting for business.

So we decided our book would cover it all, telling you how to do *everything* with podcasting. How lucky for us there's a series of books out there dedicated to doing just that!

Who Needs This Book

Probably *you* need this book. You've picked it up, you're reading the introduction…it seems you already have some interest in podcasting. Our goal in writing *How to Do Everything with Podcasting* was to provide a resource to anybody engaged with podcasting, from casual listeners to independent podcasters to businesspeople looking for a new communication channel.

If you're not sure what a podcast is, you'll soon find out. If you've downloaded a few but want to become a more engaged and savvy listener, this book will help. If you're ready to do your own podcast, you'll find a step-by-step guide to getting started. If you're been podcasting for a while, you'll learn about equipment, software, and techniques that can help you improve your show, build your audience, and engage your listeners.

There's also information for podcasters ready to make the leap from hobbyist to paid professional through sponsorship, advertising, and other means of profiting from your passion for podcasting. And this book is definitely for you if you're thinking of reaching customers or other business audiences with a podcast.

There is one audience this book is *not* for, however: video podcasters and those wanting to produce a video podcast. It is said that a podcast is a podcast, whether it's audio or video. I agree, and some of this book would be useful to any podcaster (such as the audience identification chapter and the business uses of podcasting). But video production and audio production are entirely different beasts, and our experience is in audio podcasts. There *are* great books out there on video blogging and video podcasting, though.

How This Book Is Organized

The structure of this book parallels a basic learning curve, from the basics to more complicated topics. We cover practical matters before getting theoretical. We focus first on matters of interest to most people, then get into topics of interest to segments of readers.

Chapters 1 to 5 serve as Podcasting 101, a primer on podcasting. You'll learn everything you need in order to find podcasts that interest you, download them, subscribe to them (so you'll never have to download one again), and listen to them.

The nuts-and-bolts production of podcasts is covered in Chapters 6 through 10. This is a soup-to-nuts review, covering hardware and software, the recording process, editing, and production of a podcast audio file.

Chapters 11 through 14 get more strategic about the nature of podcast content. Then, in Chapters 15 to 19, you'll find advice on enhancing your podcasting experience through networking with fellow podcasters and tapping into some of the resources and services that have emerged alongside the burgeoning podcasting community.

Finally, Chapters 20 to 26 explore the potential for podcasts as a business communication tool. The various business audiences to which podcasts can be directed include customers, business-to-business customers, investors, and employees, among others. Each of these audiences is covered in these chapters.

How to Use This Book

This book is divided into sections that should make it easy to use. For example, if you've had a personal podcast for a while and already know how to produce one, but now you've been asked to produce one for your company, you can jump right into the section on podcasting for business. On the other hand, if you want to produce a personal podcast and have no interest in the business aspects of it, you can put the book down when you get to the business section.

How to Contact the Authors

You can reach Shel at shel@holtz.com. Neville is at neville@nevillehobson.com. Let us know if we can answer any questions that arise from the text of this book. You can also find us on our podcast at http://www.forimmediaterelease.biz. We also have a web site dedicated to this book at http://www.everythingwithpodcasting.com.

Get Ready...

For all the many and varied reasons people podcast, the one thing they share in common is passion. They love podcasting and they love listening to podcasts. So prepare yourself. If you're new to podcasting, you're about to get hooked on a whole new medium. If you've been a listener who's ready to get his feet wet, you'll find yourself completely enthralled with being a podcaster. And if you're already podcasting, you already know what I'm talking about...that's why you're ready to dig into some tips and techniques for enhancing your show. So dig in and have fun!

Part I

Get Started with Podcasting

Chapter 1 — What Is Podcasting?

How to...

- Find topics in this book
- Understand the history and characteristics of podcasting
- See the benefits of the "long tail" in podcasting

Timing is everything.
So it was for podcasting. A variety of factors converged at just the right time to give rise to a new channel for the delivery of everything from music and comedy to news and commentary. The stars were aligned. The fates were kind. And podcasting was born.

Podcasting Defined

But just what is podcasting?

At its core, a podcast is a sound—or audio—file. These are recordings of just about anything—music, talk, or any kind of sound—that has been saved in a format that a computer or other digital media device (like an MP3 player) can recognize and play. These audio files are stored on a computer called a server somewhere on the Internet and made available for people to listen to online or download so they can listen later at their convenience.

But the download of audio has been an Internet capability for nigh on a decade. There must be more to these audio files to account for the growth of podcasting— from one podcast in August 2004 to more than 20,000 independent podcasts in early 2006 (and thousands more repurposed from radio and other mainstream media broadcasts), from zero listeners to 10 million, according to some estimates.

It's true. There is more to podcasts than simple downloadable audio. Let's take a look at the main ones, the characteristics on which most of those in the podcasting world agree.

You Can Subscribe to a Podcast

The primary distinction between a podcast and downloadable audio is the ability to subscribe to them. Subscription is handled through a paradigm-changing technology called RSS, which stands for "Really Simple Syndication." (We'll dig into RSS in detail in Chapter 4.) Using any of a variety of applications or web sites, you can ensure that every new episode of a podcast will automatically be delivered to your computer as soon as it's available. There's no need for you to remember to check a podcast web site to see if a new episode has been uploaded, and then stop whatever you're doing to download it. Software called "podcatchers" let you manage your subscription. Or, you can use a popular multifunctional tool like Apple's iTunes, which makes subscribing to a free podcast as easy as buying a 99-cent song. (Chapter 5 covers the nitty-gritty of subscribing and listening to podcasts.)

Podcasts Are Episodic

Downloadable audio can be just about anything: a speech, a rant, a recording of a meeting, a piece of music, an investment analyst call, you name it. Podcasts, on the other hand, are recurring shows. Many of them adopt the format of radio programming, with introductory music, idents (those brief interludes where an announcer reminds you what show and station you're listening to), sweeps (musical transitions used to transition between segments of the show), listener call-in lines and other radio conventions. You wouldn't subscribe to a podcast that consisted of a single episode. You would subscribe with the expectation that you'll get future installments.

There are no rules in podcasting. You can commit to a daily show or one that will be uploaded every Thursday. You can also produce a show whenever you get around to it. Your show can go on forever, or it can consist of a limited number of episodes for a defined period of time. Part III covers the wide variety of formatting and frequency decisions you'll need to make when you start podcasting.

Podcasts Are Detachable

The dominant file format for podcasts is MP3. Unfortunately, there is a critical drawback to MP3 files: Audio fidelity is not as good as it is with some other files that do not compress the audio, an approach known as "lossy." Files like WAV are called "lossless" because no data is removed in the creation of the file. But because MP3 files do remove data during compression, they are smaller, which means they download faster. And most people have a hard time detecting the reduced quality, even in music.

This has led a number of manufacturers to develop devices on which you can store your MP3 files so you can listen to them anywhere. Apple's iPod dominates the MP3 player market. In fact, the popularity of the iPod accounts for the name "podcasting" (along with the fact that it rhymes with "broadcasting").

But the simple fact is, you do not need an iPod to listen to a podcast. You can listen at your computer. You can burn MP3 files to an audio CD. And you can play them on any MP3-compatible device, made by companies like iRiver, Samsung, Creative Labs, and a host of others.

The idea of taking a digital audio file with you opens up a world of possibilities. Instead of being chained to your computer, you can listen while you drive your car, walk your dog, work out at the gym, wait for a plane or do chores like housework. Looking at this another way, you can listen to audio while you're doing something else. You can't say that about any other content format. Text and video—and even face-to-face communication—require your full attention. (We have seen people reading while they drive, but it terrifies us to be on the road with these people! Conversely, we have no issue sharing the road with someone listening to a podcast over their car stereo speakers.)

Given the phenomenal adoption of portable digital media players like the iPod, people are hungry for content. Initially, most people settled for music, but the more time they spent with earphones pressed to their ears, the more content they needed. Sure, you can rip your CD music collection and buy online music. But at some point, most people want to listen to more than just music. News, commentary, humor, and other forms of content were missing from the mix.

You Can Listen to a Podcast Whenever You Want

While traditional terrestrial radio offers some good content, you're limited to listening to your radio at the time the show you want to hear comes on. Digital video recorders (DVRs) like TiVo (also called personal video recorders or PVRs) have solved this problem for television. Podcasts, on the other hand, solve the problem for radio. This concept is called "timeshifting," and it explains why so many shows produced originally for broadcast over the radio are being repurposed as podcasts. In the United States, National Public Radio (NPR) has embraced podcasting as a means of distributing its content and that of its affiliates. NPR offers over 250 podcasts, and has recently introduced some shows not originally broadcast. For example, fans of *Morning Edition* and *All Things Considered* often wonder about the music played between segments. NPR has introduced a podcast that showcases that music.

Podcasts Can Target Niche Audiences

To get a show on the radio, you have to offer content of interest to a broad enough audience for advertisers to want to buy commercial time. A radio show hosted by a paramedic that offers news, information, and features of interest to other paramedics may have value to its audience, but that audience is not nearly large enough to attract the advertising dollars necessary to support it.

On a podcast, however, you don't need big numbers to be successful. The fact is, if you're having fun and enjoying podcasting, your audience can number in the single digits. Because the barriers to entry are so incredibly low—practically nonexistent—you can podcast just for the heck of it.

For those seeking to reach a targeted audience, podcasting is an ideal medium. Podcasting offers an alternative to the sea of text in which most people are drowning. The authors of this book, for example, produce a twice-weekly podcast aimed at people working in public relations and organizational communications (our area of expertise and the focus of our professional passion). Not only can we be satisfied with an audience that numbers in the thousands, we can even attract sponsors and advertisers anxious to reach this highly targeted audience.

Podcasting fits nicely into a popular concept known as "the long tail," which refers to a simple graph, initially used to represent music sales. Here's the idea: a traditional brick-and-mortar music store, with limited shelf space, carries only those CDs that most people are likely to buy—in other words, hits. It makes no sense to stock CDs that might sell only one copy every few years. Online music stores, on the other hand, can carry the entire music catalog since there are no shelf-space restrictions. Now, imagine a chart that depicts sales of CDs. Along the left-hand side of the chart are the mega-hits with lots of sales. But as you move along to the right-hand side of the chart, the numbers dip precipitously. These are songs from the back catalog. Online, however, people are spending as much on the back catalog as they are on the hits! For every thousand copies of a hit song purchased and downloaded, one thousand songs from the back catalog are being purchased once or twice. That's the idea of the long tail—that numbers don't matter—and it applies to blogs and podcasts and other online content as much as it does to music sales. In other words, you don't need as many listeners as a radio show to have an impact in the world of the long tail.

The Barriers to Podcasting Are Very, Very Low

Producing a traditional radio show requires a huge investment. The equipment alone can quickly deplete a strong bank account. You can acquire all the technology you need to produce and distribute a podcast for less than 20 dollars. While you will need to learn a thing or two about recording a podcast, along with a few Internet tricks dealing with file storage and bandwidth consumption, which we'll cover thoroughly in Part II, there is nothing so daunting that you won't be able to figure it out pretty quickly. (This book should help considerably!) That's why you'll find 13-year-old podcasters and others (like your authors) who are over 50—as well as all ages in between.

Of course, you may find yourself so enamored of podcasting that you'll want to explore the equipment and technology to take your show to another level. It's easy to get carried away with high-end microphones and other recording equipment. More sophisticated recording and editing software lets you employ special effects. You may want to figure out how to conduct interviews over the phone or use a Voice over Internet Protocol (VoIP) service like Skype. Plus, if your show becomes really popular, you'll have to deal with bandwidth issues as well.

But even if you go whole-hog, you'll spend far less on a podcast than a radio station would invest to produce a simple talk show, and the technical end of a radio show requires an engineer certified by the Federal Communications Commission (the FCC in the U.S.). Podcasting effectively puts radio into the hands of the individual.

You Have Far Fewer Restrictions in a Podcast

A few years back, singer Janet Jackson made headlines and became the subject of jokes that continue to this day when she experienced a "wardrobe malfunction" during a Super Bowl halftime show. Ultimately, the television network that broadcast that glimpse of Jackson's breast paid a massive fine to the FCC for violating public broadcast rules. On radio, talk show host Howard Stern was fined repeatedly for his language.

Because podcasts are delivered over the Internet, no such restrictions exist. If you want to talk trash, you're free to do so. Explicit sexual podcasts share the Internet with other shows where the hosts freely spew invectives. Certainly not all podcasts are only for mature audiences, but if that's your bag, you're free to pursue it.

While you can curse a blue streak that will offend a sailor on a podcast, you still need to pay attention to other laws that do apply online. For example, you cannot play licensed music unless you have all the required rights. (We'll cover the issues surrounding licensed music in Chapter 14.) You cannot slander people. (Well, you can, but you'll probably be sued and lose in court.) In other words, except for the rules that govern broadcasts on the public airwaves, all the laws that apply in the physical world also apply online—and in podcasts.

Where Did Podcasting Come From?

Podcasting has its origins in three distinct areas:

- Technological innovations that made podcasting possible

- Cultural demands that made listening to podcasts desirable

- The desire of individuals to create and distribute audio content

Each of these elements came together, like a perfect storm, to create the current podcasting phenomenon.

Two capabilities were required to launch podcasts: the means by which producers syndicate their content (that is, make it available for listeners to subscribe); and the software listeners use to manage their subscriptions.

The first of these capabilities turned out to be an enhancement to RSS, a technology that had been around for several years, designed to allow people to subscribe to text "feeds" of web content. (RSS is the tool that underlies the explosion in blogs, the personal online journals that put the ability to publish web content into the hands of the average individual.) An author and entrepreneur named Tristan Louis first proposed the notion back in October 2000. One of the principal innovators of RSS—a driven technologist named Dave Winer—implemented the idea, delivering the first multimedia file (a song by the Grateful Dead) in early 2001.

Winer incorporated RSS multimedia enclosures into his company's blogging tool, Radio Userland. Some subscribers to the blogging service began using the capability to deliver "audioblogs," audio versions of their weblogs. (Blogs [short for "weblogs"] are online personal journals that address everything from politics to business, music to movies. Because of the ease of creating and maintaining a blog, their presence online has exploded, with one blog search engine monitoring more than 30 million blogs!)

The final piece of the puzzle came when a former MTV veejay and longtime computer enthusiast named Adam Curry devised the software individuals would use to subscribe to podcasts. (Originally called iPodder, that first podcatcher is now called Juice, the result of a cease-and-desist order issued by Apple's attorneys. Apparently, Apple didn't like the software incorporating the name of their best-selling digital media device.) This wasn't the first software to accomplish the task, but it was the first that would work outside the Radio Userland environment. An important element was the ability to transfer files from iPodder to media player software like Apple's iTunes application.

The term podcasting itself was among the list of labels *Guardian* writer Ben Hammersley suggested in an article on February 12, 2004: "…all the ingredients are there for a new boom in amateur radio. But what to call it? Audioblogging? Podcasting? GuerrillaMedia?"

The Growth of Podcasting

A number of drivers are fueling podcasting's phenomenal growth. The popularization of portable MP3 players (led by the market-leading iPod, which sold some 14 million units in the final quarter of 2005 alone) is creating a hunger for content beyond the music downloaded from online music services or ripped from CDs. The niche nature of many independent podcasts is also creating demand since shows targeting these audiences have never been available before. The ability to find new music from unsigned artists is another factor, as is access to mainstream radio content without the constraint of having to listen at the time the show is initially broadcast.

The speed of podcasting's adoption has been staggering. On September 28, 2004, author Doc Searls undertook an effort to track the number of references in Google to the term "podcasting." Searls found Google registering 24 hits. (The popular search engine also asked, "Did you mean broadcasting?") One short year later, Google would return one hundred million hits for the same word. The *New Oxford American Dictionary* named "podcast" its word of the year for 2005; the 2006 edition would be the first to contain the word.

Podcasts are even in the *Guinness Book of Records,* with "The Ricky Gervais Show" earning the honor for the most popular podcast, averaging over 250,000 downloads for each weekly episode. (Gervais, the star of the popular UK comedy "The Office," would decide later to charge a monthly fee for access to his podcast, setting another new precedent.)

Several podcasting directories have now emerged where podcasters can list their shows. On one directory, "Podcast Alley," listeners vote for their favorite shows, leading to a ranking system. As podcasting became more popular, Apple added a directory to its iTunes music store, allowing users to subscribe with a single click; nearly one million subscriptions were recorded in the week following the June 2005 launch of the podcast section of the iTunes music store. To this day, iTunes remains the dominant means of subscribing to podcasts.

Mainstream media was also quick to jump on the bandwagon, repackaging content produced originally for traditional distribution and making it available as podcasts. "Web Talk Radio," a radio show syndicated in the United States, became the first to add podcasting as a distribution channel, followed quickly by shows from KOMO, a Seattle, Washington–based news station, Los Angeles station KFI, and the NPR station in Boston, Massachusetts, WGBH.

Today, a review of the key podcasting directories on iTunes and at Yahoo reveal a dominance by mainstream media, with the most heavily promoted shows coming from sources like NPR, *Slate, The New York Times,* and ESPN. NPR and the British Broadcasting Corporation (BBC) have embraced podcasting wholeheartedly—NPR offers in excess of 250 podcasts—but other mainstream media outlets are also churning out podcasts. The American television network, ABC, for example, offers a podcast focusing on its hit series, "Lost."

Still, the directory Podcast Alley, which lists only "independent" podcasts (those produced by individuals or companies, but not the mainstream media), offers nearly

1

16,000 podcasts. By some accounts, as many as 20,000 shows are available, with more added every day. A few are produced by businesses like Purina, Whirlpool, IBM, and BMW (although businesses have been slow to embrace podcasting as a channel for delivering their messages into the marketplace). Podcasting for business is the subject of Part V of this book.

As for listeners, estimates vary, but 10 million listeners worldwide seems to be a commonly accepted number. Various studies (including one released in early 2006 from eMarketer) project the number of listeners by the end of the decade to be around 50 million.

The growth of podcast networks is another sign of the medium's growth. These networks leverage cumulative listener statistics to generate advertising for the shows that participate. The largest of these networks is Podshow, a venture of podcast veteran Adam Curry and his partner, blues guitarist and businessman Ron Bloom. Podshow got several million dollars in venture capital. Several smaller networks are also out there, too, including the Podcasters News Network, The Tech Podcasts Network, and others. We'll explore podcast networks in depth in Chapter 17.

Products and services continue to emerge at an accelerated clip. These include hardware and software tools for recording, sites that host podcasts, and search engines that let listeners find podcasts based on their content.

The projection of 50 million podcast listeners by the end of the decade could be low, though, given the recent addition of video podcasts into the mix, spurred on by Apple's 2005 launch of an iPod that plays videos. Independent music may well be another source of new listeners, as musicians seeking exposure offer their music to podcasters. Music directories like the Podsafe Music Network make it easy for podcasters to find such music to play on their shows, offering a wide spectrum of choice for music fans who have grown weary of computer-programmed top-40 lists typical of the terrestrial radio market.

Without question, this is an exciting time to consider podcasting!

Chapter 2

Who Is Podcasting and Why

How to…

- Understand the size of the market
- Find a subject for your podcast

Today, you can find podcasts that cover almost any subject you can imagine. Do you support the Red Sox, or have an interest in Australian Rules football? Do you have an ear for opera or hip hop music? Several podcasts might interest you. Perhaps you make your own wine. Or you'd like news and analysis on the oil and gas industry. There are podcasts. Want small business advice in the United States or United Kingdom? Fringe comedy from the Edinburgh Festival? Adult entertainment? Some insight into the Catholic church? Yes, there are podcasts on topics and themes such as these, too.

As we saw in Chapter 1, podcasting's rapid and steady growth as a communication medium and, most importantly, its low barriers to entry combine to offer anyone, whether an individual or an organization, an opportunity to share their thoughts, ideas, and opinions on virtually any topic imaginable with, literally, the world.

Research from the Pew Internet and American Life Project in 2005 showed that more than 22 million American adults own iPods or MP3 players, and 29 percent of them have downloaded podcasts from the Web so they can listen to audio files at a time of their choosing. That amounts to more than 6 million adults who have tried this new feature, allowing Internet "broadcasts" to be downloaded onto their portable listening device.

According to Forrester Research, an IT industry research firm, podcasting will see significant growth by 2010, reaching 12.3 million households, as portable digital audio player adoption climbs and broadband Internet reaches 62 percent of households.

In July 2006, the Internet media and market research firm Nielsen/NetRatings published research showing that 6.6 percent of the U.S. adult online population, or 9.2 million web users, have downloaded an audio podcast.

In Europe, Forrester Research conducted a study in 2004 that showed 14 percent of consumers have MP3 players and 61 percent have Internet access. About one-third of consumers with Internet access also have an MP3 player. Many popular mobile phone brands also support MP3, and as European consumers replace their mobiles on average every 24 months, the number of mobile MP3 devices will grow rapidly. Indeed, Forrester says that 20 percent of all European consumers already download free content via the Internet.

The Drivers of Change

To get a real sense of who is podcasting and why, let's take a step back and look at a broader and deeper picture of the world at large and the forces at work that are driving changes in our society as to how people want to access their news, information, and entertainment, as well as create it.

Findings from research firms like Pew Internet, Nielsen/NetRatings, and Forrester Research clearly suggest that while the forces of change have largely to do with developments in technology and the ease with which ordinary people have become empowered, they also have to do with changes in many people's attitudes and expectations concerning how they wish to obtain content via the Internet.

There is more to it than just accessing and consuming content, though. It's also about who the creators of that content are.

First, though, consider the following numbers:

- Internet penetration in the United States and Canada had reached over 68 percent of the population of both countries by 2005.

- The biggest growth areas for Internet usage are in the Latin American/ Caribbean area (over 300 percent growth from 2000 to 2005), the Middle East (nearly 400 percent growth), and Africa (nearly 430 percent).

- Take-up of broadband Internet—the fast, always-on connectivity that lets you do things like discover and download audio, video, and other large files—in North America and Europe is expected to double in the next five years, according to a study by the Leichtman Research Group released in June 2006. It's estimated that 60 percent of consumers in the U.S. now have fast Internet access.

- When Apple launched podcast support in its iTunes Music Store in mid-2005, over one million subscriptions to podcasts were made during its first few days of operation.

- Over 800 million mobile phones, many with large storage space for content like audio and video files, were sold worldwide in 2005. By 2009, it's estimated this figure will be more than a billion. Most of these so-called smart phones will have built-in support for the MP3 file format—the favored format for podcasts, as well as music. Many of them will have wireless Internet connectivity in addition to their normal functionality with cellular networks, which makes finding and retrieving audio files as easy as it is on your desktop or laptop computer.

Advances in technology mean that access to information, and the sharing of it, is now global and immediate. The tools we have at our disposal now—from wireless laptops and tablet PCs you can take anywhere, to the latest camera phones that work everywhere—enable anyone to find and share information with anyone else, literally anywhere on the planet. With all those MP3 players and MP3-enabled phones and other devices, there is a growing hunger for content.

The other side of the coin concerns the changing attitudes and expectations of people across the globe, which have turned the traditional business models of who creates and distributes content upside down.

In the context of our discussion about podcasting, this refers to who the "broadcasters" are—or more aptly described, "the creators."

A primary driving force behind changes in these attitudes and expectations first emerged in the United States where traditional radio content, whether music or talk, has become increasingly homogenized and bland. Much of the programming you encounter on radio stations across the country offers listeners little to get excited about in between frequent advertising and disc jockeys with the same playlists.

It will come as little surprise, then, to learn that radio audiences across the United States have been in steady overall decline for the past several years.

This scene-setter is but a prelude to Act One of a theater play that could rival Agatha Christie's *The Mousetrap* as the world's longest-running play.

The drivers of this radical shake-up in traditional ideas of radio broadcasting are led by technology, which can now let anyone operate like a radio broadcaster.

As we saw in Chapter 1, the barriers to entry have plummeted, meaning that anyone with a PC, some free recording software (such as Audacity), a microphone, a bit of imagination, and a place from which to deliver the audio MP3 files, can effectively compete for the hearts, minds, and souls of listeners who want more than they're getting from traditional broadcast radio.

Today you can be your own program-maker, creating and mixing the music and talk you enjoy, and sharing it with your friends and anyone else interested.

Behind all of this is a bigger change in society as the age of mass media (newspapers, television, and radio) rapidly evolves into a new age of social media—what some commentators describe as personal or participatory media, which chiefly uses the Internet as its means of distribution.

One significant difference, however, between this new age and the mass media age of old, is today's emphasis on the word *social,* meaning that control of the creation, distribution, and consumption of news and information in their varied formats (written and spoken words as well as images) is no longer the exclusive domain of the few. It is now in the hands of the many.

The "many" are transforming the traditional model of one-way distribution into genuine two-way engagement through the new equivalents of newspapers, television, and radio—weblogs, video, and podcasts—that give people what they crave: unfiltered news, information, and opinion to which they can directly relate, and consequently interact with by offering their own opinions.

They are now participants—no longer simply passive consumers.

Such disintermediation (which cuts out the middlemen: the mass media) is opening a floodgate of opportunity for individuals to experiment at little to no cost.

It should come as no surprise then to see that podcasts have sprung up everywhere the past two years, starting in the United States and spreading across North America, Europe, Asia and elsewhere, covering all sorts of niche markets that the majority of broadcast radio stations, with their need to attract mass audiences to satisfy advertisers (or license payers in the case of the BBC in the UK), simply cannot economically cover, or have no interest in doing so.

So Just *Who* Is Podcasting?

The answer is thousands of ordinary people around the world, as well as hundreds of organizations—and the numbers are growing.

Podcast directories like iTunes, Podcast Alley, Yahoo! Podcasts, The Podcast Network, and many others list thousands of podcast episodes produced by thousands of individuals. (We'll look more at how to find podcasts in Chapter 3.)

In 2006, podcasting communities began to emerge that went beyond merely being "podcast Yellow Pages." One of the earliest such communities is Blubrry (www.blubrry.com), which is rapidly developing into an online place where individual podcasters and listeners can meet, interact, and learn from each other.

Increasingly, organizations large and small are paying close attention to this communication medium. Some have started experimenting with it, while others have already embraced podcasting as an effective business communication tool. (In Chapter 20, we take a detailed look at business podcasting.)

Which brings us to *why* people are podcasting.

Motivations for Podcasting

For many people, the reason they broadcast is—because they can. In less time than it takes to watch a prime-time soap, or listen to a comedy show on the radio, you can create your own piece for the new social media landscape, and make it available to anyone via the Internet.

In reality, the reasons for why you might want to get into podcasting are literally as varied as the diversity of the podcasts themselves.

Do any of these situations resonate with you?

- **Your hobby:** You are a passionate golfer. Each weekend, you're out there on the fairway trying to get that handicap into the lower single digits. You have a keen appreciation for the fine art of playing golf. You talk to your friends about your pastime and you share your knowledge. What if you could record your thoughts and opinions and share them with your friends in a way that lets them listen to you when they want and where they want? With a podcast you can.

- **Your profession:** As a volunteer with the local chapter of your professional association, you like to get involved in helping others learn and expand their professional networks. You have some ideas about recording some of the professional development seminars and workshops, perhaps even interviewing speakers and attendees, so that others may benefit as well. But how could you do that without hiring costly professional services? With a podcast you can.

- **Your workplace:** Your company has just launched an exciting new product. You want to help employees understand its features and benefits in a way that's different and imaginative. How can you do so without wading through organizational approvals and chains of command that can stifle such initiative? Well, imagine easily producing a series of short podcasts yourself—for your department, office, or its various branches—on key aspects of the new product that would support and complement other communication channels. Depending on your communication objectives and specific content, the series might also be used in external communication.

- **Your place of worship:** Each week, your priest delivers a sermon to members of your religious community. You wish such words could be made available to wider audiences. How? With a podcast you can.

- **Your band:** So you're not signed with a big record label. Perhaps that's not in your thinking anyway. You're happy making the music you do with your friends, perhaps playing a gig here and there in local clubs. What if you could record some of your songs and make them available to others, just as if you had a record deal but without that big infrastructure, loss of control, and costs? With a podcast, and a place like iTunes or the Podcast Music Network, you can.

These are but a few simple examples that illustrate how simple and easy it can be to create and produce an audio recording of a topic or theme that interests you, and that might interest others. Those low barriers to entry we discussed in the previous chapter mean you can liberate your imagination and creativity and communicate with others—whether it's 5, 50, 500, or 5000 others. With podcasting, the world can be your oyster.

2

Chapter 3

Find Podcasts that Suit Your Interests

How to…

- Find podcasts on iTunes
- Find podcasts on Podcast Alley
- Find podcasts on Blubrry

Now it's time to discover and subscribe to some podcasts you can enjoy listening to.

As there are literally tens of thousands of podcasts covering thousands of different topics, how do you find a podcast that interests you? Where do you go and how do you search?

One easy way is to use a search engine like Google.

For instance, if you were looking for podcasts about golf, you could simply type "golf podcasts" in your web browser, click the Search button, and see what shows up.

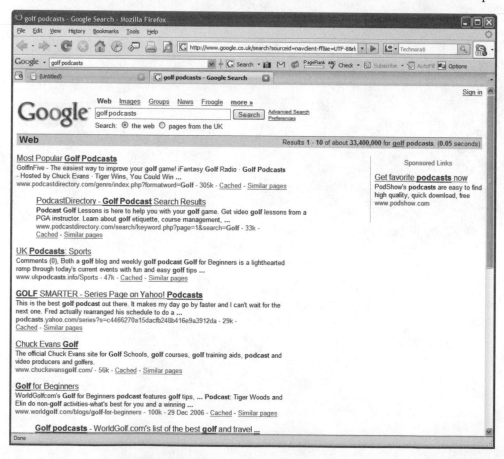

Then you'd review the results and try to determine which ones might be worth visiting to learn a little about what's on offer. Once you find something you think might be what you're looking for, you'd go to the web site and locate the podcast file to download.

While you might consider this an acceptable way to find podcasts of interest if you're a casual podcast-searcher, it's hardly the best way if you want to discover the rich breadth and depth of content that's available out there.

To start with—if you're using Google—all you have is a search engine results listing based purely on the keywords you searched for. If your search produced lots of results, it's hard for you to know which result to pay attention to, nor do you know anything about the individual podcasts, who the podcaster is, what other listeners think of it, and so forth.

Thankfully, there is a much smarter way to find podcasts that requires little effort on your part: directories of podcasts.

As podcasting has developed over the past few years, many enthusiasts, individuals, and organizations have set up web sites that list, tag, and rank podcasts. Nearly all these directories have reviews of podcasts and enable listeners to vote on their favorites, thus providing you with more meaningful information about podcasts that might interest you.

While many of these resources include listings of the same podcasts— especially the more popular podcasts—they all offer you a wide range of choice and usually have detailed information about the podcasts, the podcasters and individual episodes, plus easy ways to get hold of podcasts, both as direct downloads as well as via RSS subscription.

Thus, podcast directories are easily the best way for you to discover what's out there.

iTunes

In June 2005, Apple introduced a new version of its popular iTunes digital media player application that included support for podcasting and introduced a podcast directory in the online iTunes Store.

The addition of podcasting functionality to a mainstream audio application like iTunes greatly helped bring podcasting to a much wider global audience.

Podcasters rapidly embraced the new iTunes and, within months, nearly every major podcaster had submitted his or her podcast for categorization and inclusion in the iTunes Podcast Directory.

This literally changed the podcasting landscape overnight, where you could suddenly obtain your favorite podcasts with just a few mouse clicks on your computer.

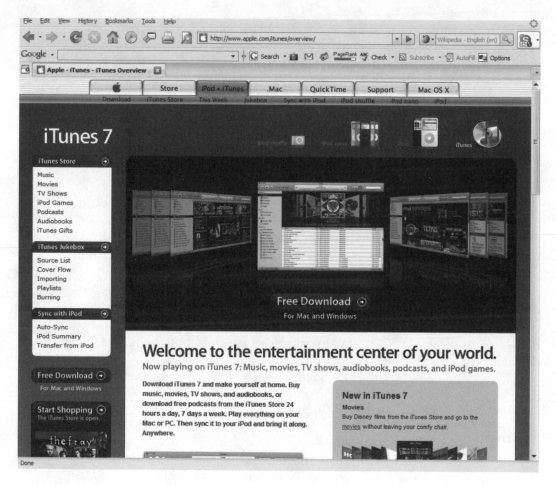

With iTunes, you can select podcasts to download from the Podcast Directory, to which anyone can submit their podcast for placement.

The vast majority of all podcasts in the iTunes Store are free of charge—you pay nothing to subscribe and download.

Doing so is as easy as 1-2-3:

1. Launch the iTunes program on your computer, go to the iTunes Store, and click Podcasts in the top-left menu.

2. You'll then be in the Podcast Directory where you can either select a category in the left menu or use the search box at the top right of your screen to find a podcast that interests you.

3. Once you find a podcast and click the Subscribe button, iTunes displays your podcasts list and starts downloading the podcast, showing you the download progress. From now on, every time a new episode or edition of a podcast you've subscribed to is available, it will be automatically downloaded to your computer whenever you launch the iTunes program and you're connected to the Internet. (You also have the option to manually download a podcast instead.)

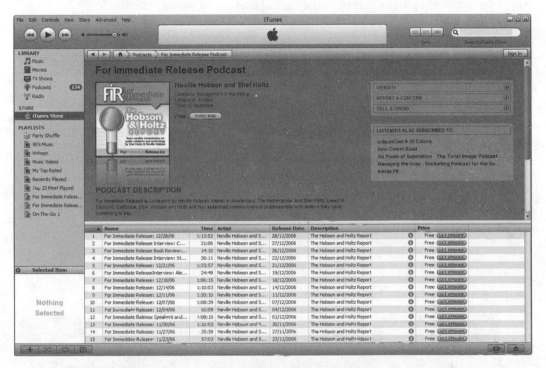

It's that easy to get a podcast from the iTunes Store!

The main screen of the Podcast Directory also displays popular podcasts from commercial broadcasters and independent podcasters. In addition, you can browse podcasts by category or popularity.

One of the major appeals of iTunes to serious podcast listeners is the ability of the program to automatically synchronize downloaded podcasts with an iPod portable digital player—just as many of you do with music purchased at the iTunes

Store—every time you connect it to your Windows or Macintosh computer. In addition, recent versions of iTunes for Macintosh computers running the OS X operating system support other portable digital players as well as the iPod.

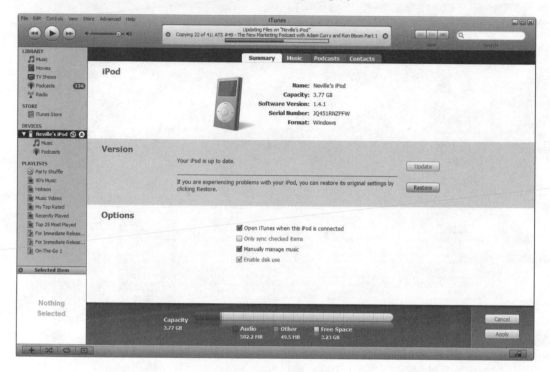

In 2006, based on a number of reports, the iTunes Podcast Directory accounted for 70 percent or more of all podcast subscriptions in the U.S. But it's not the only game in town.

As mentioned earlier, there is a rich array of resources you can use to find and subscribe to podcasts that interest you. While iTunes offers arguably the easiest way for you to do this—especially if you have an iPod, and auto-synchronization is important to you—other directories can offer a more granular selection of choices.

There's the fact, too, that some people don't want to use Apple's software or one-stop-shop approach, preferring to use a podcatcher or RSS aggregator of their own choice. (In Chapter 4, we discuss different podcatchers—programs you run on your computer that download podcasts and manage your podcast subscriptions—and how to set them up.)

We're going to cover two such directories here, with a listing of others at the end of this chapter. You can access a regularly updated listing of podcast directories at the companion web site of this book.

Podcast Alley

One of the pioneering early adopters, founder Chris McIntyre, has built Podcast Alley into a formidable resource with over 27,000 different podcasts and more than one million episodes (as of December 2006), categorized by genre.

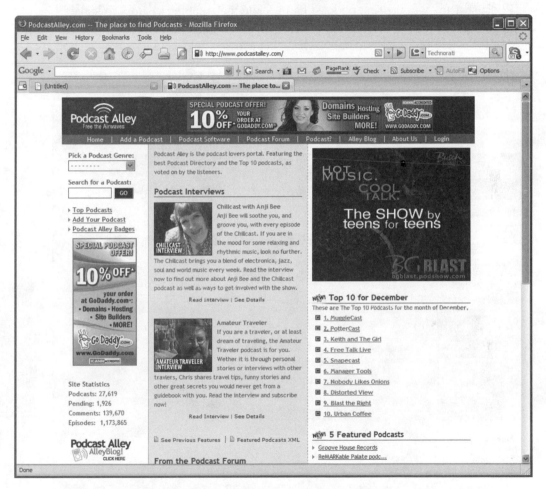

Founded at the cusp of podcasting in early 2005, by September 2005 Podcast Alley has grown to be widely regarded as a premier online community for podcasters as well as podcast listeners. (Podcast Alley is now owned by Podshow, the podcasting network started by podcast innovator Adam Curry and his partner, Ron Bloom.)

In addition to podcast listings, Podcast Alley offers a vibrant discussion forum where more than 18,000 people from around the world are registered users.

The site include tips from leading podcasters, reviews of podcast production software, podcast reviews, the Top 10 Podcast list as voted by site visitors, online podcaster discussions, and member-contributed articles.

Podcast Alley was the first podcast listings site that enabled visitors to leave comments with their opinions about podcast episodes—a great help when you're looking for podcasts and want to know what other people think about a particular show.

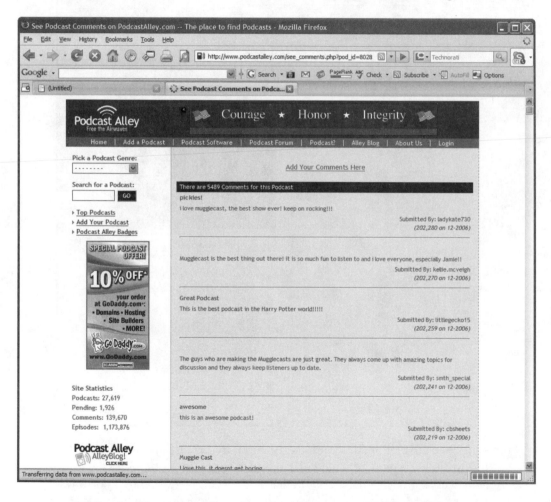

Adding to this sense of listener participation, the site also enables you to vote once each month for your favorite podcasts. As you discover and listen to podcasts, you'll undoubtedly encounter episodes where the presenter urges listeners to "go vote at Podcast Alley."

Finding and subscribing to a podcast at Podcast Alley is a simple process, and there are two ways to do it.

In both cases, you start at the www.podcastalley.com home page, which you access with your web browser.

1. Choose by genre:

    ■ Select a podcast category from the drop-down genre list at the top left of your screen.

    ■ The resulting page presents a list of links to subcategories in the genre you selected, plus a listing of podcasts.

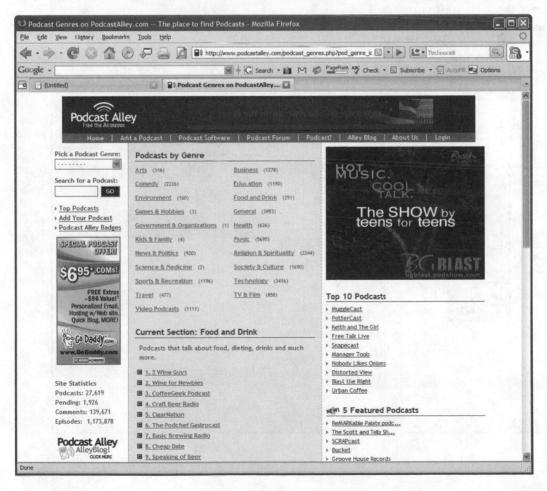

■ Either click a subcategory link to see what podcasts are listed, or click a specific podcast link to see detailed information about that particular podcast, including listener comments.

2. Search for a podcast:

■ Type your search keyword into the search box at the top left of your screen.

■ From the search results page, click a specific podcast link to see detailed information about that particular podcast, including listener comments.

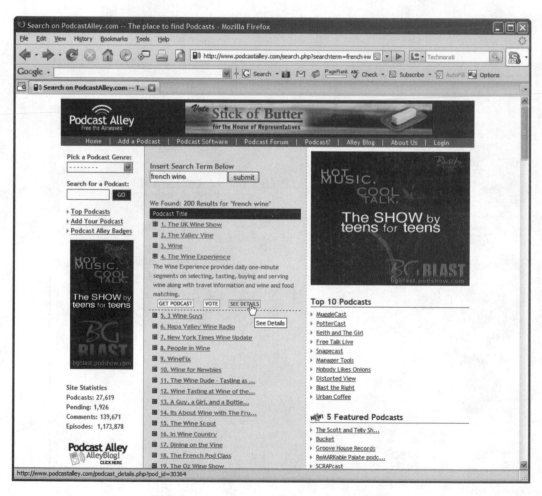

Blubrry

Blubrry is a social podcasting community that was established in June 2006. It is the first of a new breed of online resources that its founder Todd Cochrane—presenter of the popular *Geek News Central* podcast—points out should not be regarded as a directory.

Cochrane intends to develop Blubrry into a one-stop place to connect podcast producers, advertisers, and listeners looking for independently produced content.

In December 2006, Blubrry was listed as a "Hot for 2007" site in the Mashable.com *Social Networking Awards 2006* (we talk more about Blubrry as a social network in Chapter 17).

However you want to describe Blubrry—as a directory, community, or both—it offers podcast listeners a growing and wide choice of podcasts to discover and enjoy.

The site provides a number of features that many listeners will find helpful, and which some podcast directories currently lack:

■ A single RSS feed allows you to "catch" podcasts in many popular podcatchers and services such as iTunes, Juice, My Yahoo!, or Google.

■ Integrated search functionality and tags allow you to easily find podcasts or individual episodes related to the topics you're interested in.

■ A Hot List feature lets you share your favorite content.

■ The MyCast feature allows you to manage multiple podcast subscriptions online.

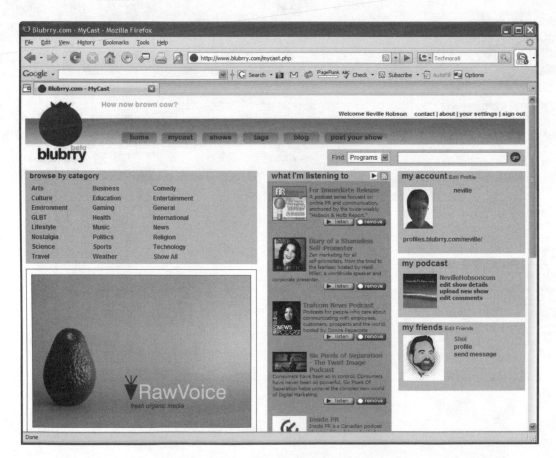

While you can listen to many podcasts directly from the Blubrry web site as streaming audio via the site's built-in audio player, you must join Blubrry (it's a free sign-up) if you want to download podcast files onto your own computer.

Once you've joined, though, you then gain access to all the podcasts made freely available by Blubrry members who are podcasters, which you can aggregate into your subscription with the MyCast feature.

Searching for podcasts is a simple exercise using either the category search or the tag search.

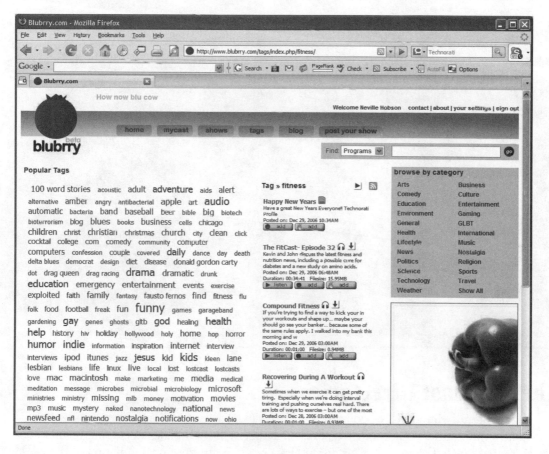

In either case, just click a category name or a tag keyword to see listings of podcasts. Once you spy the one you're looking for, click its title to see detailed information about the podcast as well as any comments listeners have left.

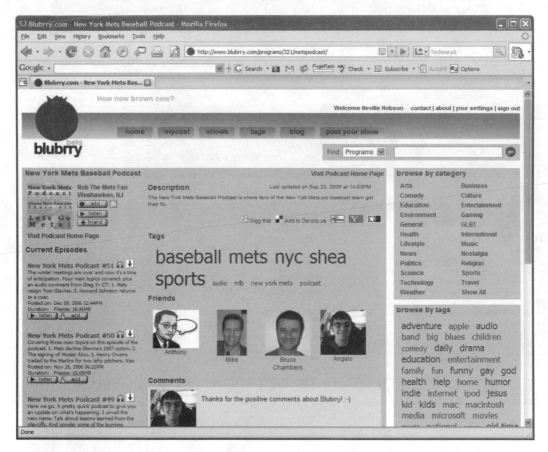

Other Podcast Directories

Today, literally hundreds of podcast directories exist. Many of them serve small, niche communities; others, such as those listed here, have broader depth and reach. Note that this list is by no means comprehensive. A regularly updated listing of podcast directories can be found at the companion web site of this book.

IndiePodder: Originally known as iPodder when it was started by Adam Curry in 2004, this was the first podcast directory launched. Very much a bare-bones, tech-oriented site, it contains lots of direct links to podcast RSS feeds. (www.ipodder.org)

Yahoo! Podcasts: Launched in late 2005, this Yahoo! service lets its members easily find and subscribe to mainly music podcasts. (podcasts.yahoo.com)

Podcast Bunker: A directory designed to find and promote "only the best podcasts." (www.podcastbunker.com)

Podcast Pickle: One of the oldest podcast directories, the site offers a My Favorites feature that lets you save your favorite podcasts on the site to give you quick and easy access to the podcasts you visit most often. Podcast Pickle is a pioneer in Second Life, building a community in the popular three-dimensional virtual world, also known as a "metaverse." (www.podcastpickle.com)

The PodLounge: Based in Australia, this directory includes a growing number of podcasts produced in Australia, as well as "casts from other countries," and has a strong community forum. In September 2006, the directory launched The PodLounge Mobile, a podcast directory built specifically for mobile phone users to find, listen, and subscribe to their favorite podcasts on their mobile phones. (www.thepodlounge.com.au)

Britcaster: The first directory and community forum for British podcasts. The community forum was disbanded in December 2006, but the directory lives on. (www.britcaster.com)

3

Chapter 4

Download and Subscribe to Podcasts

How to...

- Download podcasts to your computer using a podcatcher
- Download podcasts to your computer using Apple iTunes Music Store
- Download podcasts to your computer using alternative sources

If you followed our advice in Chapter 3, you have compiled a list of podcasts you can't wait to listen to. Before you can listen, though, you have to get the audio file of the podcasts from the server where they're hosted to your own computer's hard drive. (There is one exception to this rule—the ability to play podcasts directly from their web pages [which we'll cover in more detail in Chapter 5].)

You can get podcasts to your computer in two ways:

- Manual downloading
- Subscription

Downloading Podcasts to Your Computer

As we've already said, your computer is most likely already equipped to play podcasts, and once you have retrieved the file, playing it is a simple matter. In fact, according to some studies, more people listen to their podcasts at their computers rather than transfer it to some kind of device to take away.

But before you can listen at all, you have to get the podcast onto your computer. As with most things digital, there is more than one way to accomplish this.

On most podcast web pages, you'll find some kind of icon you can click to start a download. A few examples of icons are shown in Figure 4-1.

Some sites simply offer a text link that reads, "Download."

| FIGURE 4-1 | Download icons typical of those found on many podcast web pages |

Most of the time, simply clicking these links doesn't actually start a download (although in some cases, depending on the browser you're using, it might). Instead, it begins streaming the file directly from the server. To download it, right-click your mouse (in Windows) or hold the mouse button down over the icon (on a Mac) to bring up the context menu. Depending on your computer type and operating system, the option you want could say any number of things, including "Save target as source," "Save file," or "Save link as."

Once you make this choice, what happens next depends on your browser. For example, if it's Internet Explorer, you will be asked where you want to save the file. You might have a folder set up just for your podcasts, so you can navigate to that folder. If you use Firefox, the file just downloads to your desktop (you'll need to move it to your preferred folder after the download completes).

This is the same process you would use to download *anything* from the Web to your computer. Though it works just fine, there is a better way: you can *subscribe* to the podcast. Subscription capability is, after all, the distinction that makes a podcast a podcast, as opposed to just a plain old downloadable audio file.

You can subscribe to a podcast in a couple of ways. Behind the scenes, all podcast subscriptions are enabled by the same technology: RSS. Every podcast has an associated "feed," a text file that contains information the software on your computer needs in order to get the files for you.

Once you have gone through the relatively simple process of subscribing to a podcast, you don't have to do anything else. The shows to which you subscribe will just show up whenever a new episode appears, all ready to play in your computer's media application.

Let's examine two ways to subscribe to podcasts.

Using a Podcatcher

Podcasting came into being (as discussed in Chapter 1) thanks to two technical innovations. One was the coding required to contain a multimedia file in an RSS feed.

RSS stands for *Really Simple Syndication*. It's a way for people to subscribe to content they want to check regularly without having to visit each associated web page individually. Using a piece of software or a web site called a "news reader" or "news aggregator," you can subscribe to the RSS "feed" for the blogs, news sites, and other web pages you want to check. Whenever new items are published, your news reader will retrieve them. An example of a regular RSS news reader called FeedDemon is shown in Figure 4-2.

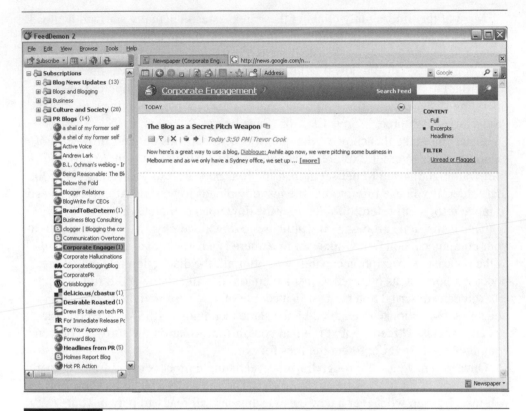

FIGURE 4-2   FeedDemon, an RSS news reader for Windows

Subscribing to RSS feeds is getting increasingly easy. Several browsers—like Firefox, Safari, Opera, and Internet Explorer 7—have subscription functionality built into the software.

Originally, RSS feeds retrieved only text, but the development of a new RSS component called an "enclosure" changed that. By "enclosing" a multimedia file in a feed item, it was now possible to subscribe not only to text updates but to multimedia files as well. With this, the first half of the equation was in place.

The other innovation required to make podcasting work was the development of software that could manage those feeds. That software, which resides on your computer, is generally called a "podcatcher." Several podcatchers, such as Juice, have appeared on the scene, with names like Doppler Radio, Nimiq, and Podcast Ready. Additionally, some RSS news readers (such as FeedDemon) have been upgraded to accommodate podcasts.

Here's a rundown of how to use Juice to subscribe to a podcast. (While the other podcatchers may work differently, the fundamentals are all the same.) The process begins by getting the address—or URL—of the feed for the podcast to which you want to subscribe. P.W. Fenton's *Digital Flotsam* (shown in Figure 4-3) is a terrific podcast, so we'll use it as an example.

It should come as no surprise at this point that there are two ways to get the feed's URL. One is to right-click (on a PC) or hold the mouse button down (on a Mac) on the link to the feed. When the context menu appears, select the option that says something like, "Copy link." The other way is to click the link to the feed, which will bring up a page that contains the actual feed. How the feed looks depends on a number of factors. It could be confounding source code or it could be a pleasant looking page you can actually read if you wish. Which type of page you see doesn't matter, because all you want to do is highlight the URL in the address bar, as shown next.

FR http://www.forimmediaterelease.biz/rss.xml

Another alternative is to write down the URL to type in later, but that seems a bit old-fashioned, doesn't it?

```
<?xml version="1.0" encoding="UTF-8"?>
<!-- must include xmlns:itunes tag-->
<rss version="2.0" xmlns:itunes="http://www.itunes.com/dtds/podcast-1.0.dtd">
  <channel>
  <title>For Immediate Release Podcast</title>
  <itunes:author>Neville Hobson and Shel Holtz</itunes:author>
  <link>http://www.forimmediaterelease.biz/</link>
  <description>The Hobson and Holtz Report is a twice-weekly podcast covering the intersection of organizational communication
  <itunes:subtitle>At the intersection of PR/communications and the online world.</itunes:subtitle>
  <itunes:summary>For Immediate Release is co-hosted by Neville Hobson, based in Amsterdam, The Netherlands, and Shel Holtz, b
  <language>en-us</language>
  <copyright>This work is licensed under a Creative Commons License, http://creativecommons.org/licenses/by-nc-nd/2.0/</copyri
  <itunes:owner>
    <itunes:name>Shel Holtz</itunes:name>
    <itunes:email>shel@holtz.com</itunes:email>
  </itunes:owner>
  <itunes:explicit>no</itunes:explicit>
  <image>
    <title>For Immediate Release</title>
    <url>http://www.forimmediaterelease.biz/images/logos/fir-itunes-art.jpg</url>
    <link>http://www.forimmediaterelease.biz/</link>
    <description>Conversations and content from the intersection of public relations and the online world.</description>
  </image>

<category>Business</category>

  <category>Business</category>
  <itunes:category text="Business">
  <itunes:category text="Management &amp; Marketing"/>
  </itunes:category>

<item>
  <title>For Immediate Release: 11/09/06</title>
  <itunes:author>Neville Hobson and Shel Holtz</itunes:author>
  <link>http://www.forimmediaterelease.biz/</link>
  <description>Leesa Barnes is guest co-host; Shel's in Atlanta, Neville's speaking at a conference; One-Minute News: SEC chai
  <itunes:subtitle>The Hobson and Holtz Report</itunes:subtitle>
  <itunes:summary>Leesa Barnes is guest co-host; Shel's in Atlanta, Neville's speaking at a conference; One-Minute News: SEC c
  <pubDate>Thu, 09 Nov 2006 18:15 GMT</pubDate>
```

FIGURE 4-3   The RSS feed for For Immediate Release, our podcast.

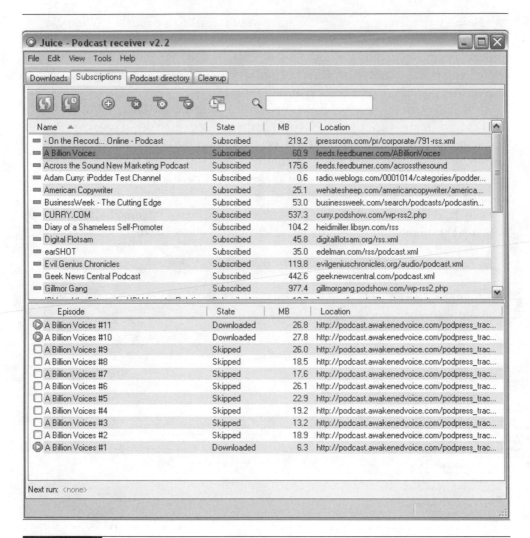

FIGURE 4-4   Juice, a free podcatcher for Mac and PC

Now that you have the feed URL, it's time to open Juice. The following images are from Juice for the Mac, but Juice for Windows looks and works just the same. Figure 4-4 shows what you see when you first open Juice (which you can download at http://juicereceiver.sourceforge.net).

1. Click the button with the plus sign (+) to subscribe to a podcast. Paste the URL you just copied into the field labeled URL. Don't fill in the Title field—the software will do that for you. Click the Save button. You are now subscribed to that podcast!

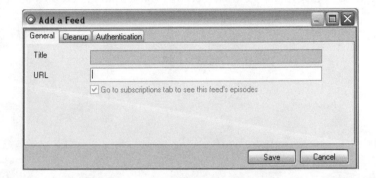

Check to make sure you have subscribed to the show by finding it in the main Subscriptions window.

2. Tell Juice how often and what time to retrieve new podcasts. In the Tools menu, select the Scheduler. You can have Juice check for new episodes up to three times each day, or at regular intervals (lasting anywhere from 12 hours to 30 minutes).

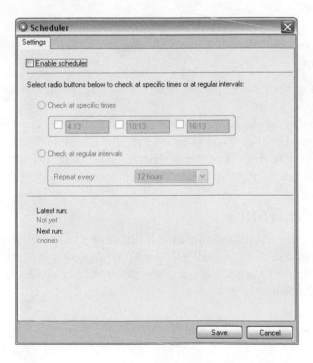

3. Designate which media application to use to play your podcasts. In the Preferences window, select Player and choose from among the available options. You will be able to select only players installed on your computer.

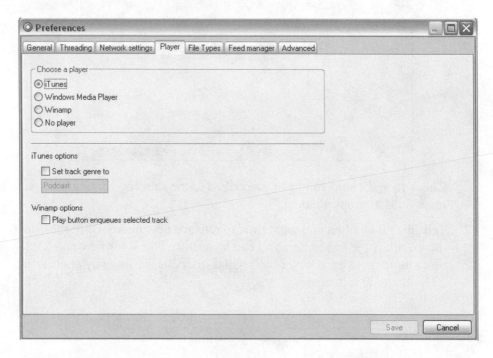

That's all there is to it. Now, each of your podcasts will automatically be delivered right to your media player—and even organized into playlists—so all you have to do is listen!

By the way, if you just can't wait for your podcatcher to get your podcast, you can force it to check for new shows by clicking the Check For New Podcasts button (the button farthest to the left on the toolbar; it's green with two arrows on it). Click it and Juice will run through all your subscriptions and get any new episodes.

Using Apple iTunes

In mid-2005, Apple added podcasts to its wildly popular iTunes store. During the first week, podcasts were available, yet Apple recorded more than a million subscriptions. The reason? Apple made it easier to subscribe to and manage subscriptions than any other service.

iTunes has its drawbacks, however. For example, if you want to save your podcasts to a device other than an Apple iPod, iTunes won't work for you; it is designed to function exclusively with the iPod. If you're just planning on listening at your computer though, iTunes works great. The software is free and there are versions for both Windows and Mac computers.

Start by downloading the software from apple.com/itunes. Once you have installed it, go ahead and launch the application. In the listing of options on the left-hand side of the window, select Music Store. You'll see a screen similar to the one shown in Figure 4-5.

On the Inside the Music Store menu, select Podcasts. Now you'll see a similar screen, but the focus is completely on podcasts. In the center of the screen are some of the shows Apple is hyping. These are usually mainstream podcasts—content from radio and TV stations (much of it previously broadcast) that has been converted into podcasts. On the right appears the most downloaded podcasts for

FIGURE 4-5   The Apple iTunes Music Store

Tools for finding podcasts at the Apple iTunes Music Store

the day. On the left-hand side, down the page a little, are the two most important parts of the screen: podcast categories and a search engine (as shown in Figure 4-6).

Use the search engine to find podcasts whose title or host's name you already know, or to find one you're reasonably certain contains a particular word. For example, if you're looking for a podcast about Harry Potter, you could just type "Potter" into the search engine to find matches. The results would look something like the following.

As you can see, plenty of Harry Potter podcasts are available! Many podcasts have nothing to do with Harry Potter, but of course the search engine returned every one with the word "Potter" somewhere in the listing. The host's name might be Earl Potter, for example.

If you want more information, you can find it in the podcast's listing—like that shown in the following for PotterCast.

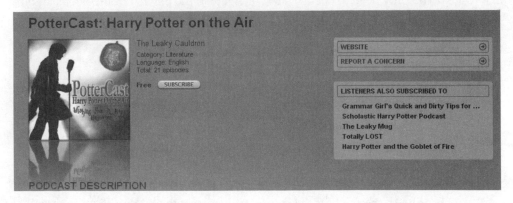

FIGURE 4-7   Playlists and episodes ready for listening in Apple iTunes

Subscribing is as easy as clicking the Subscribe button. The software handles all the rest, so you only need to open iTunes, navigate to the playlist of the podcast you want to hear, and click the Play button. Figure 4-7 shows podcast playlists on the left and the available episodes of C.C. Chapman's *Accident Hash* in the main window.

Alternative Subscription Methods

Innovative web developers and podcast enthusiasts have developed a dizzying array of alternative ways to subscribe to podcasts. The following are a few examples:

■ **Gigadial (www.gigadial.com)**   You have a friend who listens to all the best sports podcasts. He has set up a free account at Gigadial and created a "station" that contains all the shows he listens to. All you have to do is subscribe to the feed for the station he has created and you'll automatically get all those shows. Or, you can create your own station.

■ **Podcaster News Network (www.podcasternews.com)**   Dozens of news updates under five minutes each make up the Podcaster News Network, as shown in Figure 4-8. You can assemble your news mix from categories like sports, entertainment, business, science-tech, health, travel, and weather. From within each category, select the update you want added to your mix. Now paste the URL for your customized news mix into your podcatcher and you'll get each new episode of every one of the shows you indicated.

4

Now that you have some podcasts on your computer—either by manually downloading them or subscribing to them—it's time to actually listen. Details on your listening alternatives are covered in Chapter 5.

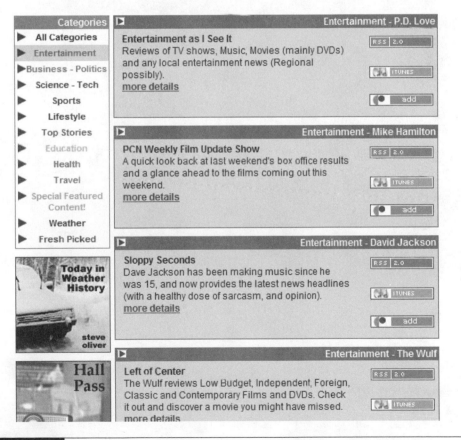

Chapter 5

Listen to Podcasts

How to...

- Listen to podcasts on your computer
- Burn podcasts to a CD-ROM
- Transfer podcasts to a portable player

Now that you have some podcasts on your computer's hard drive, it's time to listen! Let's celebrate, because that's actually why you want to get podcasts in the first place! The next step is to figure out *how* to listen. This may sound like a simple enough question, but it's not. We've already explained that podcast formats include all those most commonly used on computers, mainly MP3. You can play MP3s in iTunes, Windows Media Player, Real Player, Winamp, and any number of other players, one of which you're probably accustomed to using. So what's the big deal?

To begin with, there are other—and perhaps easier—ways to listen. You can listen at your computer or away from your computer, or even make your podcast enjoyment mobile. In other words, there is enough to cover to justify an entire chapter, even if it's a short one.

Listening Live

Your first option is to listen directly from the web page where you found the podcast. That's right, after dedicating an entire chapter to downloading podcast files, we're telling you that you don't have to.

This feature is growing increasingly popular with podcasters, thanks largely to the availability of web-based players built on the Macromedia Flash platform. The software that lets a podcaster put the player on his page is extremely inexpensive. Some are even free. One example is the Dew player, shown in Figure 5-1. Anybody can use these, and they have controls just like those on a VCR—play, pause, stop.

The fact that you listen as the show streams from the server is the drawback to using these Flash players. If you leave that web page, the show ends. You have

FIGURE 5-1 The Flash-based Dew player, which plays podcasts directly from a web page, has VCR-like controls.

to stay on the page in order to keep listening. You likely won't use these players to listen to your regular podcasts, but they *are* a nice way to sample new podcasts without having to download the whole file.

Listening at Your Computer

Most people listen to podcasts at their computers. This is really a simple matter, which most readers of this book already know how to do. In Chapter 4, we showed you how to put podcast files in your media player. To play them, open the media player, select the podcast file from the list, and push the Play button. Figure 5-2 provides a look at this function in Apple's iTunes, which is available for both Mac and Windows. Windows comes with Windows Media Player, which will also play podcasts. Some people prefer alternative software like Winamp, QuickTime, Real Player, and Roxio Media Center. All are fine.

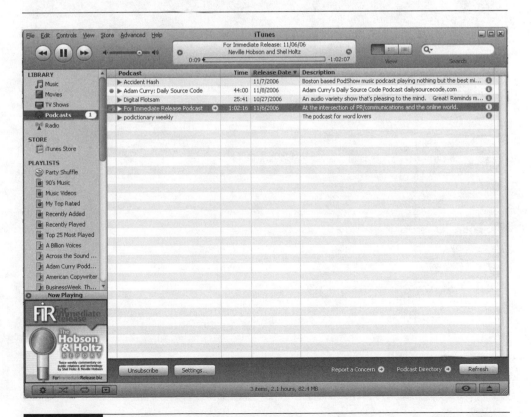

FIGURE 5-2   Playing a podcast file in iTunes

It's a good idea to make playlists for your podcasts. Playlists are like folders for your multimedia files. You can put all your Frank Sinatra in one playlist and all your Nine Inch Nails in another. Or, you can create a playlist for jogging; another for relaxing. It's easier to find podcasts when they are organized into playlists, particularly when you've accumulated several episodes of several shows. You can create playlists manually, but many podcatching applications create them automatically. Figure 5-3 shows a playlist open in iTunes. It works the same in other media players.

There is one other way to listen from your computer. If you are using a podcatcher that includes a built-in player, you never need to use software other than the podcatcher—unless you want to burn the podcast to a CD. Podcast Ready (podcastready.com) is an example of a podcatcher that handles everything from playing podcasts to transferring them to digital media players. The RSS aggregator FeedDemon (feeddemon.com) also lets you play your podcasts.

FIGURE 5-3 A playlist open in iTunes

So many options are available with different configurations and variables, not to mention continual updates, you really should check the software specs to see what it can and cannot do.

Taking Your Podcasts with You

Two ways to get podcasts off your computer (so you can listen wherever you are) include the following:

- Burn them onto a CD
- Transfer them to a digital media player

Burning a CD

The process of burning a CD of your podcast is exactly the same as burning a CD with any other kind of audio file. Like so many things, the details of burning a CD will depend on the media software you're using. Consult your software's Help menu to learn how to make a CD. Of course, you'll need a CD drive that lets you burn a CD-R or CD-RW disc.

There's one consideration in creating audio CDs: they're limited to 80 minutes of playing time. Given that, it's easy to see how you can go through a lot of CDs!

Another option concerns whether your CD player is configured to allow you to play MP3 data files. If so, you can burn a *data* CD that contains your podcast MP3 files, in which case you'll be able to store podcasts that come to far more than an 80 minutes—the limitation is based on file size instead of the length of the audio, and most CDs let you store 700MB. Since an hour-long podcast can consume 30 to 60MB, it's obvious you can put a *lot* of podcasts on one CD using this approach! Just be certain your CD player can, in fact, play MP3 data files.

Transferring to a Portable Digital Media Player

Your other option—and really the best one—is to transfer your podcast files to a portable digital media player. The iPod from Apple dominates with 70 percent of the marketplace, and the iPod *is* a wonderful device. However, it's not the only one out there. Players are produced by iRiver, Samsung, Creative, RCA, Archos, Toshiba, Microsoft, and a host of others.

Note that if you have an iPod, you *must* use the iTunes software to manage the transfer of files (although other software like Winamp for Windows can also transfer files when the ml_iPod plug-in is installed)—and if you have anything *other* than an iPod, you cannot use iTunes to manage the transfers.

You're most likely getting tired of hearing this, but how to transfer files depends on the software you use. Some require that you tag the files you want to synchronize, others have you drag and drop the files from the media player to the device (both will be mapped in your media player), while some will transfer every file. The iPod (and several others) automatically synchronize your media player with your portable player as soon as you attach it. When in doubt, read the Help files that come with the player.

Using a portable digital player offers many benefits:

- You'll be able to access your playlists right on your media player.

- These devices hold anywhere from dozens of podcast episodes to thousands; the biggest storage disks on portable media players hold up to 60 GB.

- They're small and easy to carry.

- Because you're using digital files, portable players never skip when the player is jarred or jolted.

- They consume less power. You'll generally get more hours of listening on a portable digital player than from a CD player.

Of course, you're not limited to using your portable player only for podcasts. You can also put all the other audio you want on the player, including your CD collection!

Part II

Produce Your First Podcast

Chapter 6

Get the Hardware You'll Need

How to...

- Choose the right microphone
- Select a mixer
- Add other peripheral equipment
- Set up a hardware chain

You're not content to listen to podcasts. You want to produce one. The rest of this book is dedicated to podcast production, starting with the good old-fashioned how-tos. To get us started on the path to creating knockout podcasts, we'll start with the most basic requirement: hardware. Podcasting can cost you a lot of money in two ways. One is if your podcast reaches the pinnacle of popularity, driving your bandwidth costs up. The other is to get carried away with hardware.

The fact is, you can produce a perfectly serviceable podcast without spending more than $15 if you already have a computer. The only thing you need that many computers don't come with (although some do) is a microphone. You can get one that plugs into either a USB port or your computer's microphone line in and be podcasting in no time. Everything else required is software-based, assuming all you want to do is record your own voice and add effects you can store on your computer, such as music, sound effects, interviews, and other audio files.

You can also record a fine-sounding podcast with one of the many varieties of headsets available on the market that combine headphones with a microphone for as little as $45.

The better your microphone, the better your sound quality will be, so the one investment to consider making is in this critical piece of equipment. Again, you can produce a podcast that sounds just fine with an inexpensive mike, but when you're ready to start investing in your podcast, we recommend starting with the microphone.

Since microphones are the most important podcast hardware, we should spend a bit of time explaining the differences between them so you can make an informed decision about what to buy.

Microphones

Technically speaking, a microphone is an acoustic-to-electric converter that turns sound into an electrical signal. It works by detecting sound waves in a diaphragm, wherein the diaphragm vibrates in response to the sound waves.

How the microphone converts those vibrations into an analog signal depends on the type of microphone. Two basic types of microphones are available: dynamic and condenser. Regardless of the kind of microphone you buy, you will still have to select the kind of pickup pattern you want the microphone to have. We'll cover both of these issues in the pages ahead.

Dynamic Microphones

Dynamic microphones offer podcasters a lot of advantages. For instance, they tend to be less expensive than condenser microphones. They can take a lot of abuse because they don't have a lot of moving parts. Among audio professionals, the dynamic microphone is used in live situations on stage and for vocal purposes— great news for podcasters!

These microphones use an induction coil situated in a magnet's magnetic field connected to the diaphragm in order to produce the analog signal, which is created when the vibrations of the diaphragm result in a current running through the coil.

Condenser Microphones

Condenser microphones, also called "capacitor" microphones, are more sensitive, have more moving parts, cost more, and produce better sound under many conditions. Just as dynamic microphones are used most commonly in live, on-stage situations, condenser microphones are used more frequently than dynamic microphones for recording.

One key distinction between dynamic and condenser microphones is the need for power. Dynamic microphones don't need any—just plug it into any recording device and it works. Condenser microphones, on the other hand, require power. In most cases, a battery can be installed in the microphone, which also comes with an on-off switch. These microphones can also be powered with "phantom power," supplied by a recording device, a mixer, or certain other devices to which microphones can be connected. Unless the condenser mike you buy has the capacity for a battery, it won't work if you just jack it into your computer. Generally, condenser mikes draw phantom power only when inserted into XLR inputs. These are rugged three-pin connections found on mixers and some of the larger portable digital recorders. However, this is not universally true. For example, the M-Audio MicroTrack 24/96 provides phantom power through its one-quarter-inch connections. When you purchase your equipment, talk with the store's electronics expert to make sure everything you're getting will work the way you want it to. If you're buying online, use an e-commerce site that lets you make a call or exchange e-mail with experts to get the same level of information.

In condenser microphones, the diaphragm acts as one of two capacitor plates. When sound is produced, the plates vibrate, altering the distance between them. The plates are biased with a fixed charge (hence the need for power), which leads to changes in the voltage maintained by the capacitor plates when sound waves produce vibrations.

Other Microphone Types

As if it isn't confusing enough having to choose between dynamic and condenser microphones, other categories of mikes exist as well. Fortunately, you probably won't have to give them much thought since most podcasters use one of these two primary classes of mikes. For the record, though, the following microphone types are also available:

- **Electret capacitor** Used in high-quality recording environments and lavaliere (lapel) mikes, as well as small sound recording devices and telephones. A relatively new innovation dating only to the early 1960s, these are phantom-powered microphones that use material that maintains a permanent electrical charge.

- **Ribbon microphones** Mostly used in telephone handsets, so they're not of much interest to us!

- **Piezo microphones** Mostly used to amplify acoustic instruments during a live performance, so you won't be likely to need one for podcasting purposes.

- **Laser microphones** New, uncommon, and uncommonly expensive, used mainly in espionage circles.

Pickup Patterns

Pickup patterns are engineered into microphones to manipulate how the mike will draw in sound.

Omnidirectional

Omnidirectional microphones pick up sound coming from all directions equally. You can speak into the top or sides of the mike and it will record your voice at consistent volumes. That makes omnidirectional mikes easy to use, particularly in the field when you're holding it in your hand and possibly passing it back and forth to an interview subject; you don't have to twist and turn it to make sure it picks up your voice. However, on the downside, omnidirectional microphones also pick up ambient sound with the same degree of consistency. If there are other sounds in the room, these mikes will record them at the same levels as everything else.

Cardioid

Also known as "unidirectional," cardioid microphones block sound from the rear. As the "unidirectional" label implies, these mikes pick up sound from only one direction: the front. There's also some sound pickup from the sides. This is the kind of microphone we use for recording in *For Immediate Release* from one of our offices; the microphone is suspended from a mike stand with the recording side facing the person speaking; other office sounds are reduced because the mike is facing away from that part of the office. (We use a dynamic microphone when traveling because they are tougher and stand up better to the rigors of travel.) A popular style of cardioid mike is shown in Figure 6-1.

Cardioid mikes are ideal, then, for studio and office environments, particularly when there is only one person speaking. They do have a reputation for being sensitive to low-frequency audio the closer the source of the sound gets to the mike, creating a bass-like quality to the audio. Most field reporters use omnidirectional mikes not only because the mike doesn't need to be twisted and turned to the right direction during interviews, but because passing the mike back and forth results in a wind-like noise captured along with the rest of the recording.

FIGURE 6-1   The Audio Technica AT3035 is a style of microphone favored by many podcasters

Super-Cardioid and Hyper-Cardioid Microphones

Super-cardioid microphones offer an even tighter pickup pattern than plain old cardioid mikes, restricting more of the sound coming in from the sides. Hyper-cardioid microphones are even more restricted and tend to be limited to highly specialized mikes used by pros. An example is a shotgun microphone that hears only what it is pointing at, picking up nothing from the sides, and little, if anything, from behind. If you were speaking into a shotgun mike and stepped just a bit to the side while leaving the microphone stationary, nobody would hear what you were saying.

Bi-directional

Bi-directional microphones pick up sound from the front and back, but not from the sides. The ribbon microphones referenced earlier are usually bi-directional microphones.

Choosing Your Microphone

A lot of podcasters proudly proclaim their satisfaction with $20 microphones. That's fine. We understand their pleasure at recording with so small an investment, and we continue listening to some of these, despite their excruciating audio quality. However, at some point, even excellent content will suffer at the hands of a cheap microphone.

That's why we advise choosing a microphone with care. More than with any other factor—hardware or software—your microphone will determine the quality of your audio.

When selecting a microphone, you should consider the choice of dynamic or condenser and the pickup pattern. The following are some factors built into each microphone that we think you should also consider:

- **Frequency of response**   Essentially, this refers to the sensitivity of the microphone in decibels over a range of frequencies.

- **Equivalent noise level**   The lowest point of the microphone's dynamic range, this is the sound level that produces the same output voltage as the inherent microphone noise. In other words, it's the sound the microphone records when everything is quiet.

- **Maximum Sound Pressure Level (SPL)**   Higher values are better when assessing SPL, the top end of which is measured for values of total harmonic distortion. Since you can't usually hear sounds at these levels, you should be able to use the mike at this level without affecting the recording.

- **Clipping level**   A better indication of the maximum usable level than SPL, clipping is a term with which you'll become *very* familiar as we move through recording and editing topics. Clipping is the dispensing with sounds that exceed the maximum level a device can accept. In a microphone, clipping occurs when the diaphragm reaches its ceiling, generating harsh sounds at peak amplitudes. Look for clipping levels that are significantly higher than SPLs.

- **Dynamic range**   The difference between the equivalent noise level and the maximum SPL.

- **Output level**   Technically known as "transduction gain," this is a measure of the microphone's ability to convert acoustic sound waves into output voltage. The higher a microphone's output level (or sensitivity), the less you will need to amplify the input at the point where the microphone is connected to a device like a mixer or recorder.

- **Signal-to-noise ratio (SNR)**   Measured in decibels, this—usually an average—assesses the difference between the signal strength a system reproduces compared to the strength or amplitude of background noise.

We realize that's a lot of technical information, but if you devote time to any one aspect of your podcasting rig(s), this is the one. So let's look at some of the microphones embraced by the podcasting community. As we said, any cheap plastic microphone or headset can get you started, but when you decide to get serious, you are going to need to invest at least $100—and ideally about twice that—in a decent microphone.

The Low End: US $100 to US $150

Heil PR-20 is a full-range dynamic microphone available only online from Heil Sound at http://www.heilsound.com. This cardioid microphone was designed for professional broadcast purposes. Heil lists the microphone at around US $160.

KEl HM-1 is a cardioid condenser mike that lists for around US $130.

Audio Technica AT2020 is an electret cardioid condenser mike that lists at about US $170. The microphone has a high dynamic range and a reputation for handling high SPLs.

6

The Shure SM58 is a dynamic cardioid microphone from one of the best-known names in mikes. Tuned to accentuate the warmth clarity of vocals, it can handle a variety of podcasting tasks.

The Next Level: Up to US $300

About the best quality sound for a podcast will be delivered through microphones in the range of US $200 to $300. You can spend more, but at the point where the audio is converted to MP3 and played over devices with limited quality (computer speakers, for example, as opposed to high-end stereophonic equipment, or cheap ear buds versus expensive headphones), the differences will most likely be lost.

Shel uses an Audio Technica AT 3035, which lists at about US $200; the same company makes the AT 4040, which costs another hundred dollars.

From Heil comes the PR-40, which retails for just over US $300 and has become a favorite of many podcasters, including Adam Curry. This dynamic microphone is a cardioid mike that produces sounds which, in tests, have surpassed that produced by comparably priced condenser mikes.

The Studio Projects C1 condenser cardioid microphone has wowed many critics with its large diaphragm, making it a favorite of many professionals who record vocals. It hasn't made inroads into the podcasting space yet, but has a reputation and a price (around $200) that suggest podcasters will discover it soon enough. The C3 costs about US $70 more and accommodates three pickup patterns—cardioid, omnidirectional, and bi-directional.

The High End

You *can* spend more than three or four hundred dollars on a mike, and, to be sure, there are some podcasters who do. After all, what hobby *doesn't* inspire hobbyists to seek the best? Among those recommended by podcasters are the Electro Voice RE20, a dynamic cardioid microphone built primarily for broadcasting. It is available in the $400 range. By doing some research, you could find excellent microphones for podcasting purposes from manufacturers including Heil, Sennsheiser, Shure, Beyerdynamic, Samson, Neumann, RODE, and a host of other companies.

Professional musicians can spend thousands of dollars on microphones. In fact, each time we visit a shop that sells recording gear, we salivate over some of these items. Nevertheless, we resist, not just because of the price tag, but because of the diminishing returns podcasters could realize from such high-priced equipment. Most of these microphones are designed for recording or performing music.

Mixers

Once you have a microphone, you have to have something to plug it into. Yes, with many microphones you can go directly to your computer. We advise against it. The mixer is a piece of equipment that does exactly what the name suggests: It accepts input from a variety of sources—including your microphone—and then mixes them together in a single sample that it sends to the recording device (whether that's your computer or some other device). The key benefit of a mixer is the ability to independently control the settings for each of those inputs.

By way of example, let's look at a recording of *For Immediate Release*, which usually involves three separate inputs. Shel handles the recording on his end in California, so his microphone is one input. Neville's voice, coming over a Skype call from Shel's laptop, represents the second input. The third input is an iPod Nano that contains audio comments, music, and other samples that will be included in the show. If all of these were recorded directly into the computer, their varying levels would be recorded as is, requiring considerable editing after the recording is done to try and get them to roughly the same level. With a mixer, Shel is able to ensure all of the inputs record at the same level, reducing the amount of postproduction work required to get the podcast to sound good.

Even when Neville and Shel record in person, in the same room, Shel tends to be a bit louder than Neville, soft-spoken Brit that he is. Shel can reduce his own "gain" and bring Neville's up enough that in the mix they sound like they're speaking at the same volume.

In addition to volume adjustments, mixers let you control other aspects of each input, including the following:

- **Equalization**   The high, mid, and low frequencies; not unlike adjusting the treble and bass in a car stereo

- **Pan**   Stereo balance left and right

- **Mute**   Temporarily turn off one input

- **Trim**   The volume of the original input

- **Gain**   The increase in signal amplitude produced by a pre-amp or amplifier

- **Pre-amp**   A circuit that amplifies a small signal before sending it to the amplifier for additional amplification

6

Depending on the sophistication of your mixer, it could also feature channel inserts that let you add peripheral equipment to each channel, as well as auxiliary inputs. Auxiliary inputs can be important—for example, if you're producing a "mix-minus" (which we'll address in detail in Chapter 8). Auxiliary inputs let you apply a peripheral piece of equipment but choose its levels and other parameters for each channel rather than simply apply it uniformly to the final mix. For instance, let's say you add an effects processor to your hardware chain in order to create some echo. By using auxiliary inputs, you can give your own voice a lot of echo, while applying only a little to the person on the other end of a phone call, and none to any music you play.

Mixer Considerations

Mixers generally have three types of inputs: XLR inputs for microphones, one-quarter-inch inputs for cables coming from, and going to, other equipment, and RCA jacks for tape inputs and outputs. Your computer most likely has a one-eighth-inch (or "mini") jack, so you'll need to make sure you get the right cables to plug into your computer. The same applies to whatever digital recording device you may choose to use either as a backup to your computer-based recording or as an alternative to recording to your PC.

Some mixers come with phantom power (the power required if you use a condenser microphone), while some do not. If you use dynamic microphones, this is not a consideration, but if you have a condenser mike—especially one that has no capacity for a battery—your mixer will need to send power to the microphone. Make sure you get a mixer with phantom power.

One thing you'll notice on mixer inputs is text that reads "BAL OR UNBAL," which is shorthand for "balanced or unbalanced audio." Balanced audio cables are manufactured to minimize unwanted noise created by interference that can increase the longer the cable is. These work by eliminating the interference where the cable plugs into the mixer. They use three lines: a "hot" line that carries a positive signal, a "cold" line that carries a negative signal, and the "earth" (or "ground") line. The hot and cold lines both carry the audio signal, but the voltage on the cold line is inverted so the signals are 180-degrees "out of phase" with each other. When the signal goes into the mixer, the hot and cold signals are combined—effectively returning to an in-phase state—to produce a stronger signal. This process cancels out the unwanted noise.

Unbalanced cables use two lines to transmit an audio signal. The first is the "hot" line, which carries the signal. The second is the "earth" (or "ground") line. For short distances between the mixer and the computer (or other device), unbalanced cables are fine. For longer distances, though, you should look to use balanced cables.

Mixer Price Ranges

When most people see a mixer, they wonder how many thousands of dollars must have been invested in *that* piece of equipment. The truth is, mixers *can* cost a small fortune. If you've ever been to a live concert, you've probably seen mixers with dozens or hundreds of channels and lights bouncing everywhere.

Of course, you won't need anything like that. For a lot of podcasters, a mixer that costs $40 handles all their needs. The Behringer Eurorack UB802 mixer (shown in Figure 6-2) has two microphone preamps and four channels for other inputs, phantom power, control room and tape outputs (for backup recording), equalization, trim, gain, and auxiliary controls. All it's missing are channel inserts, but if you're not planning on running any external dynamics processors—and any podcaster spending this little on a mixer probably isn't planning to use any dynamics processors—who needs them?

Between this remarkably inexpensive workhorse mixer and the high-end equipment you buy, mixers are available that meet a variety of needs from companies like Yamaha, Tapco, Alesis, and a host of others. Some even offer USB or Firewire connectivity to communicate directly with your computer, a function mainly used when producing multiple tracks from the mixer. (We'll cover computer interfaces in the next section.)

6

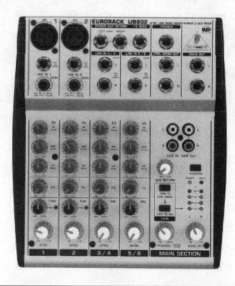

FIGURE 6-2   The Behringer Eurorack UB802 will serve most podcasting needs

FIGURE 6-3   The Mackie 1202-VLZ Pro

Shel uses a Mackie 1202-VLZ Pro (shown in Figure 6-3) in his office. This $300 mixer offers four pre-amps for microphones, 12 total channels, and a variety of other features including channel inserts. Considered a workhorse in the recording industry, the 1202-VLZ Pro is a rugged and fully equipped mixer that didn't set us back too much (only about US $300).

Connections to Your Computer

Whatever audio equipment you use, at some point you need to get your audio into your computer so you can edit it. (We cover software for editing in Chapter 9.) The most common connections for your computer include the following:

- **USB**   Universal Serial Bus (USB) became popular almost immediately when it was introduced in the mid-1990s as a means of connecting just about anything—from mice and keyboards to printers and cameras—to a computer. The popularity grew from the ease of plugging a USB in (versus multiple-pin connections that had to be screwed in) and the fact that a hub could allow you to run dozens of devices through one USB connection. These days, USB ports are standard equipment on virtually any computer, whether it's a desktop computer or a laptop.

- **FireWire**   Also known as IEEE 1394, for the standard set by the Institute of Electrical and Electronic Engineers, this connection was developed by Apple as a means of providing high-speed transfers to the computer. Many non-Apple computers now come with FireWire connections. Those that don't can have FireWire added with the installation of a FireWire card. FireWire transfer rates are higher than USB.

Peripheral Equipment

A microphone and a mixer are all you really need, but you may want more to further enhance and improve the quality of your audio. The following is a list of some of the peripheral equipment most commonly adopted by podcasters.

Headphones

Headphones qualify as peripheral equipment—they connect to the mixer and are not a built-in piece of the mixer or the PC—but they're really not optional. You need to be able to hear the mix that's going into your computer or recording device. Despite all the lights and levels you can see, your ears will tell you how good the sound quality is.

Unlike headphones for listening to music, which take many shapes and forms, these headphones (often referred to as "studio monitors") need to cover your entire ear in order to block ambient noise.

We use the Sony MDR-7506 stereo headphones (shown in Figure 6-4), which list for about US $100. Of course, if you already have a pair of headphones that do a good

Close-up image | Sony MDR-7506

FIGURE 6-4 Sony MDR-7506 headphones

job of blocking out noise, there's no reason you can't use them instead of buying a new pair just for your podcasting efforts. These headphones produce excellent sound and allow you to clearly hear ambient noise the microphone may be picking up.

Pop Filters

For as little as they cost, there is no reason not to buy a pop filter. These circular pieces of fabric, shown in Figure 6-5, are typically held in a metal frame bolted directly to your mike stand and rest between your lips and the microphone. The pop filter softens your "plosives," the sound of a consonant produced by a complete closure of the vocal tract, blocking airflow from escaping the lips. The air is released as the sound is produced. Consider the sound made with the consonant that opens the words "pop," "beer," "tie," "down," "cat," and "gone." These words sound fine in normal conversation, but as the microphone picks them up, they can sound like mini explosions. The pop filter softens these sounds.

In addition to the pop filters that mount on your microphone stand, you can also use windscreens that fit snugly over the microphone itself. While these are designed to minimize the wind that can muck up an outdoor recording, they work on the same principles and serve quite well as pop filters.

6

FIGURE 6-5   Pop filters attached to a studio microphone

Dynamic Processors

Depending on how much you want to manipulate, adjust, and fiddle with your sound, you could invest more of your podcasting dollars into dynamic processors, separate pieces of equipment that connect to the mixer in order to produce various effects on your audio. Each of these can be connected to the mixer in a variety of ways. For example, you can connect a processor to the main mix so it treats all sounds equally; you can connect it to one input; or you can connect it to an auxiliary port so you can manipulate it separately on each input.

Sound professionals use a wide range of dynamic processors, but podcasters need only consider a few of the basics:

■   **Compressors**   Many audio pros will tell you that the single most important thing you can do to improve your audio quality is to "compress" it. You can compress audio with hardware or in the post-recording edit, using the compression feature built into many audio recording and editing software packages. Whether you do your compression with hardware or software, the principle is the same: compression reduces the loudest parts of the audio, narrowing the dynamic range so the sound is more even and, as a result, more pleasing to the ear. If compression reduces the volume too much, you can raise the overall volume in the editing process, which will still leave the peaks more even with the rest of the audio. Hardware compressors can be obtained for $100 and up.

- **Pre-amps**   While many mixers have built-in pre-amps, you may want a separate piece of hardware for the greater control it can give you. What's more, a lot of experts insist a vacuum tube pre-amp produces better quality sound than one that doesn't require those tubes to warm up. The pre-amp's job is to amplify a low-level signal to line-level.

- **Effects processors**   We record *For Immediate Release* from our offices. In Shel's case, this is a spare bedroom in his house he has converted for work purposes. It is about as far from a recording studio as you can get, and sounds like it. To give his recordings more of a studio or auditorium sound, he has added a digital effects processor to his chain. With the processor, he can dial in a faint echo that adds a richness and fullness to the audio that would otherwise sound flat and constrained.

- **Gates**   Known more formally as a "noise gate," the gate ensures there is enough sound to bother recording. Think of a real gate in a yard. When enough wind blows, the unhinged gate opens up, but until there's enough wind, it remains closed. This is the same principle applied to a noise gate, which only allows sound to get into the recording when it's loud enough. Sound that isn't loud enough—perhaps the distant sound of a computer fan—won't be allowed into the recording. If background noise is a serious issue, you may want to consider a noise gate. Gates are often bundled with compressors, handling both tasks in a single piece of equipment, like the $900 PreSonus ACP-88, which includes a limiter as well (see the next item). You may also hear audio experts talk about "expanders," which produce nearly the same result as a gate by reducing sounds recorded below a certain level instead of blocking it altogether.

- **Limiter**   A limiter is a piece of equipment that allows signals below a certain level to pass unaffected, clipping the peaks of stronger signals that exceed that pre-set limit.

Recording Phone Calls

If your podcast includes interviews, you more than likely will need to record the phone calls through which the interview is conducted. Ways exist around this that involve the installation of software on your computer, letting you make such calls online. Skype and Gizmo Project are the two most often used by podcasters, (we'll talk more about these in Chapter 8).

Without one of these services, and the means by which to record them, the phone remains your best option for those interviews you just can't conduct in a face-to-face environment. In order to record a phone call, you need special equipment. Phone recording equipment comes in two varieties:

■ **Inline patches**   An inline patch, such as that shown in Figure 6-6, is a piece of equipment that connects the phone—usually at the handset—to your input device (mixer or recorder). A popular model for podcasters is sold by Radio Shack for less than US $30. One of our favorite podcasters, Donna Papacosta, uses an inline patch called the Telecom Audio Voice Port, which sells for about US $100. We'll reference this item—and Donna—again in Chapter 8.

■ **Digital hybrids**   These more expensive devices cancel out your voice, leaving only the voice of the person on the other end of the line. You would record your voice using a separate microphone. By recording each to a separate channel, you can manipulate the audio levels, noise reduction, and other aspects of postproduction for each voice, achieving the best possible sound—far better than a regular phone conversation. JK Audio sells digital hybrids for as much as $500, while Telos makes one that runs nearly $900! For our money, we'd rather use the popular VOIP software, Skype! Be sure to read Chapter 8 for details on Skype as an alternative to traditional phone recordings.

FIGURE 6-6   The Voice Port in-line patch for recording telephone conversations

Enhancing Computer Audio

You go to all the work of selecting a microphone and a mixer, not to mention effects processors, pre-amps, and what-have-you, and then you record everything directly into your computer, reducing the sound to the capabilities of the audio interface that came with the computer. While that interface may be fine for most of your computing tasks, odds are it's not up to the standards you want your podcast to achieve. For that, you'll need an external interface of some kind that improves the quality of the audio your computer records. You have two choices to make to improve the audio quality above and beyond your computer's built-in capabilities: audio interfaces and external sound cards.

- **Audio interfaces**   Audio interfaces serve as a bridge between your mixer (or other equipment) and your computer. They plug into either your computer's USB or FireWire ports. USB interfaces tend to be less expensive than FireWire. Different interfaces offer different inputs and functionality. Dozens of options are available, at prices ranging from under $100 dollars up to the $300 range for USB, and as much as $1000 for FireWire. These devices, in addition to improving audio quality to the computer, can also preclude the need for a mixer if you plan to only record one or two voices and handle everything else in postproduction. Many come with software that mimics the mixer's functionality.

- **Sound cards**   Talk to any hard-core computer gamer and he can most likely start naming the best sound cards for games. Few gamers accept the sound card built into their computers, unless they've invested in a high-end gaming PC. Instead, they swap out the default card for something that can handle the complexities of game audio. For podcasting, you may also find the built-in audio inadequate and want to swap out your computer's card for a better one, or use an external card. For computers, the card is installed into the guts of the machine, although PC card-based sound cards are available for laptops that override the built-in card. Creative Technology makes the Sound Blaster line of sound cards, the best known products.

The Hardware Chain: The Order of Your Connections

As we noted earlier in this chapter, you can hook up your hardware in myriad ways. Based on the equipment you have and what you're trying to accomplish, one approach will generally work better than others. However, there are so many

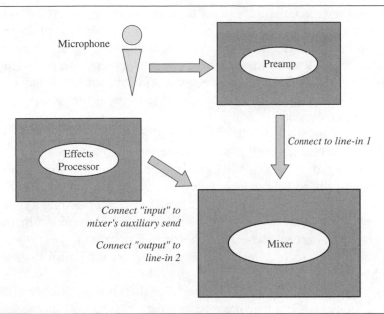

FIGURE 6-7   An example of a hardware chain

permutations of equipment and goals that it's impossible to list all the various chains here. Consider, for example, where an effects processor and a compressor fit into the chain. Each has dials to control volume. So, where do you want to control the volume initially? On the compressor? The effects processor? Or the mixer? The answer, we're afraid, is "It depends." For example, one podcaster we know insists that dynamic processors use a mixer's channel inserts. But what if you want the effect applied to the entire mix? Plus, applying a digital effects processor to a channel insert affects only that channel; using the auxiliary functionality lets you adjust the effects to each separate channel.

Figure 6-7 shows one recommended hardware chain, but you should experiment to see what works best for you. It will pay dividends to spend time talking to the audio pros who sell your equipment to you to figure out the chain that will best suit your needs.

Portable Rigs

There is one last aspect of hardware to address: portable rigs. A mixer, compressor, and other hardware are fine if you're sitting at a desk in an office or a studio. If you're on the road, or recording interviews at conferences or meetings, that represents way too much hardware to lug around with you!

As you might expect, there are many options for portability. At the most basic level, you don't need a specialized piece of equipment at all. One of those digital recorders you can get in any office supply store will do the trick. You can use the built-in microphone, which can be dicey if you're conducting an interview and moving the device back and forth between you and your subject. Many of these devices have a line-in capability, so you can add a microphone. With a splitter, you could add *two* microphones.

The next level up involves MP3 devices with built-in recording capabilities. For example, iRiver makes the iFP-890, a device so small you can carry it in your coat pocket. It records to various MP3 settings you can control, using either a built-in microphone or a hand-held or lapel microphone connected to the line-in jack.

Moving up another step, there are ultra-portable devices designed specifically for recording (whereas the devices like the iRiver iFP-890 are meant mainly as an MP3 player that happens to be able to record). Two examples of these devices (which are about the size of a deck of playing cards) are the Edirol R-09 and the M-Audio MicroTrack 24/96 (shown in Figure 6-8).

Finally, there are recorders professional journalists use that are about the size of an old-fashioned cassette tape recorder or a paperback book. These include the Marantz PMD-660 and 670 and the Edirol R1. These run between $400 and $700. Shel records *For Immediate Release* directly into a Marantz PMD-660.

Microphones for these devices should be rugged enough to withstand the kind of abuse they'll take in the field. Dynamic microphones are nearly always better than condenser mikes because they have fewer moving parts. For interviews, you may also want to consider lavaliere mikes, also known as "lapel mikes," which clip onto a person's lapel.

FIGURE 6-8   The Edirol R-09, left, features built-in microphones and runs on two AA batteries. The M-Audio MicroTrack 24-96, right, charges through the computer's USB interface and comes with a stereo microphone that plugs into the 1/8-inch "mini" input.

Chapter 7

Get the Software You'll Need

How to...

- Choose your recording and editing software

- Find software for making and managing MP3 files

- Select an RSS feeder

Podcasting will involve some software. However, what software, how much you spend, and how you use it will depend on other factors. For example, if you record your podcast on a device other than your computer, you won't need to worry about recording software but may need to edit the file you record. Or, if you don't plan on doing any editing (a technique some people call going "live to the hard drive"), but your recoding device doesn't produce an MP3 file, you'll need to convert your file to MP3.

Therefore, the software configuration you assemble will be based on the approach you ultimately decide to take in producing your podcast. In this chapter, we'll run down the various types of software you may need to consider and point you to some of the more popular options. In the next chapter, Chapter 8, we'll go into excruciating detail about how to use these applications to edit and enhance your podcast.

This is by no means intended to be an exhaustive list. Our intent is to cover what these applications should do and then direct you toward some of the more popular packages. In each category, probably dozens (if not hundreds) of alternatives exist, which you can find by visiting a music or software store, or by browsing the Web.

Recording and Editing

For most podcasters, a single piece of software that handles the recording and editing chores is the only application required. These software applications need to perform a number of tasks to serve your needs. They include the following:

- **Recording**   Unless you're going to record your podcast on a non-computer device (see our discussion of non-computer recording devices in Chapter 6), you need software that will allow you to create your recording on your computer. Most software designed primarily for editing audio also allows you to record.

- **Multiple tracks**   Inevitably, you will wind up needing to use more than just one track in your mix. We'll get more into multiple-track recording in Chapter 9.

- **Settings**   You must be able to control the parameters of the files you create. Look for the ability to control sample rate (measured in Hz, the sample rate refers to the rate at which samples are captured or played back; we'll look at the best sample rates for podcasts in Chapter 8) and sample format (expressed in bits, this refers to the number of digits in the digital representation of each sample; the higher the sampling rate, the more accurate your recording of higher sound frequencies).

- **Sound enhancement**   You should be able to manipulate all or part of your audio file in order to improve the overall sound using techniques like compression, equalization, normalization, and noise removal.

- **Effects**   The ability to create fade-ins and fade-outs, echoes, changes in pitch, and other effects should be part of the package.

- **File formats**   Ideally, your software should allow you to save your file in any number of podcast-friendly formats, notably MP3, but also OGG and AAC (we'll go into detail on these in Chapter 9 when we cover editing your podcast). You can get away with formats you won't use for your podcast, like the uncompressed WAV format, as long as you have additional software that will handle the conversion.

- **ID3 editing**   We'll go into detail on ID3 tags in Chapter 9, but briefly, the ID3 tag contains metadata about the file that displays on both portable and computer media players. It's easier to enter this data while you're editing the file than to do it using third-party applications after your editing chores are done.

Probably the most used application among podcasters is Audacity, shown in Figure 7-1. There are two reasons for this. It's available for both PCs and Macs (not to mention Linux), so the default AUP file format Audacity creates can be moved between platforms. Also, it's free (undoubtedly, the most important reason!). Audacity does everything a recording-editing application is expected to do—although without the amount of control of some of the expensive applications—and is simple to learn. Audacity is available for download at http://audacity.sourceforge.net.

The number of podcasters using Audacity is another good reason to use it. While it may not have the flexibility of some applications, you will be able to turn to the podcasting community with any questions or problems that arise, and odds are you'll find somebody who can help.

Audacity aside, the recording-editing software you select will depend on the platform of your computer. If you use Microsoft Windows, Adobe Audition is one of the most highly touted applications. Originally titled CoolEdit, the technology assets

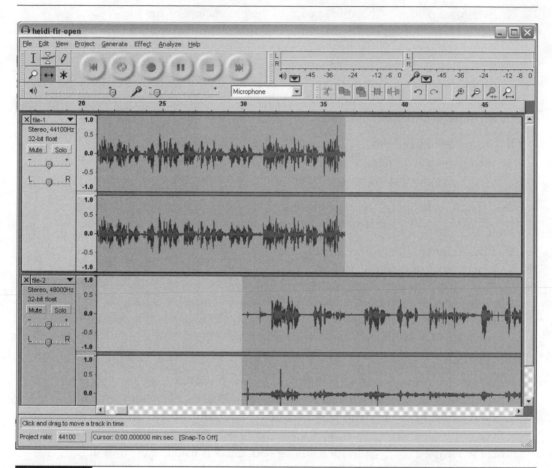

FIGURE 7-1   Audacity, the free recording and editing application, handles multiple audio tracks, stereo or mono, with ease.

of the software's manufacturer, Syntrillium, were acquired by Adobe, which dropped the company's other products and relaunched CoolEdit under its new name. Listing at about US $350, Audition is a fully loaded, highly sophisticated piece of software that is also pretty easy to learn. Complete details on Audition are at www.adobe.com.

Other Windows record-editing software includes the following sampling:

- Sony SoundForge, retailing for about US $300, at www.sonymediasoftware.com

- Steinberg Cubase is somewhat daunting to learn, but is richly packed with features, highly rated, and sells for about US $200. It is also available for the Mac, and can be found at www.steinberg.net.

■ WavePad, from NHC Swift Sound, is free recording and editing software for Windows. If you like it, you can pay to use the Masters Edition that includes additional effects and features. The Masters Edition runs about US $70. You can find both at www.nch.com.au/wavepad.

For the Macintosh, one of the more popular packages is available only over the Net. DSP Quattro Pro is the product of Italian programmers. Selling for about US $150, DSP Quattro Pro is fully featured and well supported (the authors of the program have a terrific reputation for replying directly to customer queries).

A very popular recording package for the Mac is Rogue Amoeba's Audio Hijack Pro. This is *only* for recording, not editing. Designed to allow you to capture any audio playing over your computer (including music, for example, the rights holders may not want you to capture), it has proven adept at podcast recording. You can find it at www.rogueamoeba.com/audiohijack.

Apple makes two of the most popular Mac recording and editing software packages. GarageBand (shown in Figure 7-2) comes with the Macintosh as well as the iLife software package. If you want to spend more—and get more functionality—look at Logic Pro, which is one of the most comprehensive audio packages around,

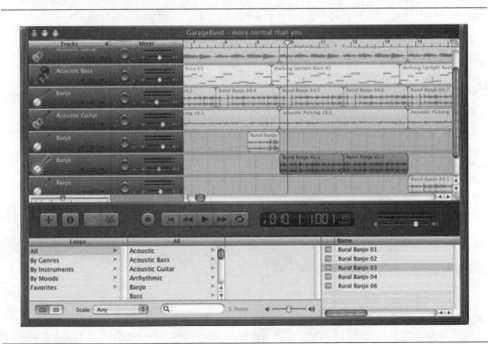

FIGURE 7-2   Apple's GarageBand, software included with every Macintosh, can handle typical podcast recording and editing chores.

7

with a price to match of nearly US $1000. Logic Express is a less powerful version—but perfectly adequate for podcasting—that goes for about US $300.

Plug-ins

Many of the audio recording and editing applications allow you to employ plug-ins, small software applications that perform very specific tasks within the primary program. Plug-ins come in a variety of flavors, including the following:

- Track-based plug-ins affect only the track to which they are applied. These include compressors, limiters, noise gates, and equalizers. (We'll explain what all these are in Chapter 9.)

- Bus-based plug-ins are ones you want to apply to multiple tracks at the same time without necessarily applying them to the entire final mix. "Reverbs" are the most commonly used bus-based plug-ins, but you likely won't need these much in podcasting.

- Mastering plug-ins affect the total mix, applying their effects to the final output. They have the greatest impact on the overall sound of your audio file. Examples of mastering plug-ins include iZotope's Ozone Mastering System, which gives you a complete mastering suite in a single plug-in, including an equalizer and compressor; PSP Audio's Vintage Warmer, which optimizes the bass and treble; and SoundSoap, which cleans hiss and clicks from audio.

Podcast-only Software

A number of companies have figured—correctly—that many podcasters would rather not mess around with a bunch of software intended for audio engineers, that they would much rather use a single piece of software designed specifically to record podcasts.

These packages share a number of features in common:

- Everything you can do is contained in one screen

- Cross-fade sliders

- Countdown timers

- "Cart" buttons, a word that has carried over from long-gone radio practices when sound bits were contained on cartridges, each of these buttons is assigned to an audio sound like a song, a listener comment, or a bumper. Click it and it plays. Carts generally re-cue after they're played so they're ready to play again.

- Decks that also let you assign sounds to them—usually longer files that you'll only use once during a show.

- Waveforms that let you watch the recording levels in real time while you record.

Examples of these programs include...

- **Podcast Station**   www.podcaststation.com (pictured in Figure 7-3)

- **Mixcast Live**   www.mixcastlive.com

- **Castblaster**   www.castblaster.com

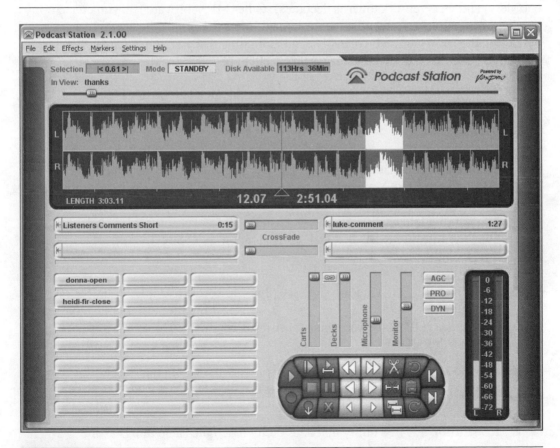

FIGURE 7-3   Podcast Station. The various buttons store the audio clips and files you'll play, so as you're recording, all you have to do is push the button when you're ready to add a new sound.

These kinds of applications have a drawback—but it won't apply to many podcasters. If you're using a mixer to produce the "mix-minus" audio to accommodate a co-host or a guest recorded via Skype, these one-in-all applications simply won't work since you *have* to record directly to your computer.

MP3 Software

A variety of software is available to let you create and manage MP3 files. Several of the applications used for recording and editing require an MP3 encoder, the most popular of which is the LAME MP3 encoder. If an application you acquire asks you to install the LAME encoder, you can get it at www.free-codecs.com.

Most MP3 software is designed to let you convert other files to MP3 (known as encoders) and vice versa (known as decoders). Other MP3 software lets you create playlists, normalize or standardize the volume of MP3 files, and "tag" MP3 files by editing their ID3 tags, which we'll spend more time discussing in Chapter 9.

Daily MP3 (www.dailymp3.com) is an excellent resource for finding MP3 software.

RSS Editors

In order to distribute your podcast, you need to offer an RSS feed. If you're not using software that automatically creates the feed, you'll need to find some other way to assemble the feed. You could learn to code XML, but our guess is that most podcasters are more interested in getting audio content on the Net than they are in learning a scripting language.

Fortunately, software exists that makes the creation of RSS feeds drop-dead easy. These include

- **Feed for All**   For Windows and Mac, this $40 software guides you through wizards to create your feeds. It won Best Internet Communication Tool at the 2005 Shareware Industry Awards ceremony. Download a trial at www.feedforall.com.

- **Feed Editor**   For Windows, this $25 software uses a tab interface to create your feed and various feed items. The application is from Extralabs at www.extralabs.net.

- **RSSEditor**   A free utility that does pretty much the same things as the fee-based applications. It's at www.rss-info.com.

Chapter 8

Record Your First Podcast

How to...

- Set up to record a podcast
- Hook up your hardware
- Set up your software
- Get help setting up to record a podcast
- Interview a guest
- Record your podcast
- Speak comfortably on your recording

You have your hardware. You have your software. You're all set to record. Of course, you need to hook your hardware up and manage the settings in your software in order to get everything to come out the way you want it. You also have to decide just *how* you want to record—all at once in a single pass, or in bits and bobs. In this chapter, we'll explore the various possible permutations of podcast recording. We'll also spend some time talking about your recording style and some techniques that can help you sound more natural at the mike.

Setting Up to Record

It would be great if you could just push a button and record, the way you do when working with an old-fashioned tape recorder or one of those digital voice recorders. Recording audio destined for an audience, though—whether it's for radio, an audio book, or a podcast—requires more attention to technical detail.

We must confess before going any further that we are not engineers, and have learned only enough to be able to produce our show (and those of clients who ask for our help producing *their* shows). We're hardly the only authors of a podcasting book to make this confession. And that's an important point to make: You don't *have* to be an audio engineer to learn enough to produce a great-sounding podcast. You can start with the basics that follow, and then experiment, tweak, and adjust to your heart's content until you find the mix and balance that works right for you.

Hardware Hookups

If your recording session involves just you speaking into a microphone, the hookup could not be easier. Just plug the microphone into the computer. Of course, the microphone connector needs to accommodate the limited number of input types built into the computer. For example, most higher-end microphones come with XLR plugs featuring the triangular three-pin configuration, but computers have no XLR inputs. If you have this kind of microphone, you will also need an adapter to get it into the microphone-in jack on the computer or laptop. USB microphones (as we noted in Chapter 6) present no problem for reasonably current computers and laptops. Microphone headsets come with both configurations, one-eighth-inch "mini" connectors designed to plug into the microphone-in and headphone-out jacks as well as USB.

Adding a second input to the podcast does not have to mean a more complicated setup than this, assuming your additional inputs are on your computer. You can play a song or an audio comment, for example, using your computer's media player software—like iTunes or Windows Media Player—and it will record right along with your own voice. If, however, your additional inputs are coming from some other source, you need to add the means by which you can get multiple inputs into a single audio file. That's where a mixer comes in.

To hook a mixer up in preparation to record your first podcast, you need to connect your microphone to the mixer, then connect the "main out" to the line-in jack on your computer. Now you can connect other devices to other open inputs on the mixer. These devices can be anything from a digital media player (like an iPod) to another microphone for a second participant in the podcast, from another computer that has sound files you want to use to a telephone. If it produces sound and can connect via a standard input jack, you can hook it up to a mixer.

You don't need to do your recording on your computer. As an alternative, you can use some kind of digital recording device (like those discussed in Chapter 6). In this case, just use a cable to connect your "main out" from your mixer to the line-in on the portable recorder.

There are, of course, more complicated ways to set up your rig, depending on what you are trying to do and what kind of additional equipment you want to add into the chain. We'll cover one particularly complex setup called a "mix-minus"— applicable when you plan to conduct a lot of interviews or work with a co-host over a Voice over IP (VoIP) connection—later in this chapter.

Software Setup

The software you install to record your audio must be configured to capture the input at the right settings. The wrong settings will produce a variety of negative results, ranging from poor sound quality to having your podcast sound like it was recorded by chipmunks whenever it's played over Flash-based streaming audio players (which allow listeners to play a podcast directly from a web page).

Each software application features different approaches to their setups; obviously, we cannot cover them all here. Ultimately, though, the actual settings themselves are the same. We'll use Audacity as the example for our walk-through of software settings.

The settings we're about to recommend are just to get you started. You should most definitely experiment until the settings produce just the sound quality you're after. However, since you have to start somewhere, you might as well begin with these recommendations.

The first settings to consider are for audio quality. Two settings are required here:

■ **Sample rate**   The word "sample" refers to any sound stored digitally on your computer's hard drive. The sample rate is the frequency at which that sound was recorded (or "sampled") and converted into digital information. Sample rates are referenced in terms of the number of samples per second, so a sample rate of 44,100 Hz was recorded at 44,100 samples per second.

■ **Set your sample rate to 44,100 Hz**

■ **Sample format**   This is your "float" or bit rate, which refers to the number of bits processed per unit of time. In audio, the bit rate refers to the number of bits stored per unit of time of a recording. The more bits stored per second, the better the audio fidelity and the larger the resulting file.

■ **Set your sample format to a 32-bit float**

You will produce a smaller file if you use a 16-bit float, but your sound quality won't be as good.

You can leave all the other settings in this tab at their default values. Figure 8-1 shows how these settings look in the Windows version of Audacity.

Next, you'll need to take care of the settings for the format to which you will export your file. Remember, you *should* export your file to the MP3 format. In the File Formats tab, you'll see several options, including an uncompressed export format, which we won't address here because this produces massive files that are not used for podcasts. You may decide to produce an OGG version of your podcast to accommodate those few listeners who prefer this format, but here we'll concern ourselves mainly with MP3.

First of all, you'll need an MP3 "library" since Audacity does not come with one. This is essentially an MP3 codec, software that compresses and decompresses (hence the "co" and "dec" in *codec*) audio files. The most commonly used is the LAME codec, which you can find at http://www.free-codecs.com/download/Lame_Encoder.htm.

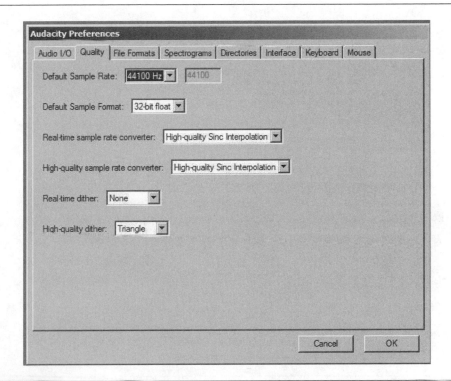

FIGURE 8-1   Recommended sample-rate settings for Audacity

Once you have downloaded the file, use the Find Library button to navigate to the location of the file and then link it to Audacity.

Now you're ready to set the bit rate for your export. The bit rate you use to export the file to MP3 means the same as it does when recording the original audio file: the number of bits stored per unit of time (usually seconds). A good export rate to start with is 48. Go ahead and see how your files sound at 48 bits. Our podcast, *For Immediate Release*, is converted at 64 bits, which produces better sound and a larger file. Other podcasters (like *Geek News Central's* Todd Cochrane), also convert to MP3 at this higher rate. Figure 8-2 shows the bit-rate settings in Audacity for Windows.

You can leave all the other settings at their defaults.

Now it's time to get down to the recording itself. Go to the main Audacity window. In the upper left-hand corner, you'll see controls that should look familiar

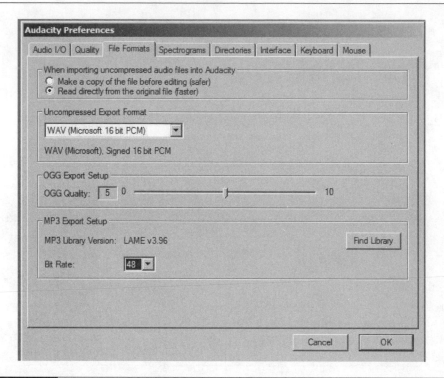

FIGURE 8-2   Recommended bit-rate settings for Audacity

to you if you've ever worked with a cassette player, a digital media player, or even a video cassette recorder.

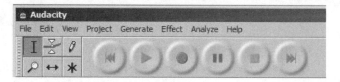

From left to right, these controls are as follows:

- Return you to the beginning of the audio file
- Play the audio file from the point where the cursor is situated
- Record

- Pause

- Stop

- Take you to the very end of the file

To begin recording, just click the button with the red circle in it. The first thing you'll see is the appearance of the waveform. The waveform is a graphic representation of the shape of a sound wave that displays amplitude variations over time.

8

The volume in this mono waveform is represented vertically; note the numbers to the left of the waveform are 1.0 at the top and −1.0 at the bottom. These represent the highest volumes, while 0 represents utter silence. As you can see, the waveform gives you a general idea of how loud your audio is. In this example, the volume is "clipped" in two places, where the waveform exceeds 1.0 and −1.0. This is more volume than the software can handle, so it dismisses the audio that exceeds its limits, so as not to create distortion that results in unpleasant sound.

While the waveform gives you a general idea of the volume of the file, it is *not* the same as a meter that tells you exactly what decibels levels your recording is reaching. Ideally, you can monitor the volume of your input with your mixer or your digital recorder, which will display the actual decibels. The ideal range for volume is between −7 and −14 dB; anything exceeding 0 will definitely be distorted.

Don't think that using a digital recorder instead of a laptop gets you out of having to set recording parameters for your session. You'll still need to make sure you're recording to the right format, at the right bit-rate, and using the correct settings for a variety of other factors (such as stereo versus mono). We'll look at the settings on three different types of digital recorders just to show the variations you will encounter as you move up the scale from small, inexpensive recorders to more sophisticated rigs. These are simply overviews, though. Be sure to refer to your equipment manuals to familiarize yourself with all the various settings you should consider.

An MP3 Player with a Recording Feature

Some MP3 players (not iPods) feature a one-eighth-inch line-in jack, allowing you to turn it into a digital recorder. Both of us have the same portable device, an iRiver iFP-890 with built-in microphone, which makes an ideal portable device. Even when we don't think we'll do any recording, this tiny device just drops in our pockets, meaning we're always prepared should the opportunity for an interview or shout-out arise.

The settings for line-in recording on the iRiver are fairly simple. You start by selecting whether the input will be captured in mono or stereo. Next, set the bit rate and sampling frequency. On the iFP-890, the bit rate can be set between 8 Kbps and 320 Kbps, while the sampling frequency can be set from 11.025 KHz to 44.1 KHz. Settings at the highest possible rates—for the best audio input—44.1 KHz and 160 Kbps—will give you about four and a half hours of recording time at a mono setting.

You can also adjust the volume. Incidentally, you can also use an external microphone connected directly into the one-eighth-inch input, which presents you with a variety of additional settings.

An Ultra-Portable Digital Recording Device

Several manufacturers offer extremely small yet powerful recording devices, about the size of a deck of cards. Two options include the Edirol R-09 and the M-Audio MicroTrack 24/96. Images of these two devices appear in Chapter 6 (Figure 6-8).

Because these devices are so small, processes have been developed to ensure good recording without specific decibel readings. For example, you can adjust the recording levels on the MicroTrack 24/96, but you'll see only a visual display of the volume without associated decibel numbers. Instead, the user's guide advises you to set the volume as high as possible without clipping, which is indicated by a red light. If your input is clipping in the recording, you'll want to reduce the volume.

A High-End Digital Recording Device

The following larger devices are still portable, but too big to fit in your pocket. These rigs are most often used by professional radio journalists who conduct interviews and cover events in the field.

To record our podcast, we use a Marantz PMD-660 like the one shown in Figure 8-3. (We also record a backup version to the iRiver iFP-890. This is connected to the line-in port from the "tape out," which provides an additional output of the main mix. In fact, *any* digital recording device can be used to produce either your primary recording or your backup as an alternative to recording directly to your computer or laptop.)

FIGURE 8-3   The Marantz PMD-660 is about the size of a paperback book and includes
built-in microphones, XLR inputs for two microphones, and 1/8-inch line-
in and line-out connections.

Notice that the front panel of the PMD-660 features two rows of numbers.
These are decibel indicators for both the left and right channels. The read-outs
begin at 60 (the lowest level) and increase to 0 (the loudest possible value). Green
lights flash to indicate the current decibel level; if clipping occurs, red lights flash
at the extreme right end of the scale. Keeping an eye on these levels can help
ensure a high-quality recording.

The best way to ensure your audio comes out right, as noted earlier, is to use
a mixer and monitor the output of the mix on the board. On many devices—the
Marantz PMD-660 among them—you can set the recording levels to automatically
accept the volume of the input device (in this case, the mixer). Most decent mixers
feature two vertical rows of lights, all of which are green except the uppermost
lights—representing clipping—which are red.

Getting Help

As we noted earlier in the chapter, neither of us are audio engineers. But audio
engineers are readily available to help if you need them. In just about any city,
you can wander into a fully equipped music store—one that carries musical
instruments and audio engineering tools like mixers—and the audio experts will
be happy to talk with you about getting the best sound. If a casual in-store chat
isn't enough, many of these experts will be equally happy to come to your house
or office and help you iron out your recording issues for a very reasonable fee.

If you can't find somebody to visit you in person, plenty of message boards and discussion forums exist on the Web where you can take your questions. The following are a few to start with:

- **Music and Technology: Resources for the Recording Musician**
  www.music-tech.com

- **ProSoundWeb**   www.prosoundweb.com/forums

- **Audio Forums**   www.audioforums.com

Interviews

Recording interviews introduces another level of complexity to recording. You need to be able to capture both your voice and the voice of your interview subject (or your co-host if he or she is not in the same room as you; this is the case with us—Shel is in California and Neville is in Europe!).

Recording Telephone Calls

The simplest way to capture both ends of an interview is to use a telephone and a piece of hardware called an "inline patch," such as the one shown in Figure 6-6. These devices can cost as little as US $30 and as much as $500. Obviously, the more you spend, the better your recording quality will be. One such device, the Telecom Audio Voice Port, costs about US $100 and is recommended by one of our favorite communications podcasters, Donna Papacosta, who hosts the *Trafcom News* podcast. The device is inserted between the telephone base and the handset, and cables connect to the computer's line-in and line-out.

Voice over IP (VoIP)

Two problems arise from telephone recordings regardless of the quality of the inline patch you use. First, telephone recordings will always *sound* like telephone recordings! The computer concept of "garbage in, garbage out" applies equally well to audio recording. If the input sounds like a phone call, the subsequent recording will clearly sound just as though you were on the phone.

The second problem is cost. If the person you are interviewing happens to be in your general vicinity, you'll only pay the cost of a local call. For the two of us, the cost of a phone call between California and UK would be exorbitant. In fact, it would preclude our ability to record a twice-weekly podcast.

You can overcome both of these issues by using one of several Voice over IP (VoIP) solutions that allow you to talk over the Internet without using a telephone. These options do *not* include some of the VoIP telephone services being sold as alternatives to Plain Old Telephone Service (POTS), such as Vonage or AT&T CallVantage, since these services connect to your existing telephone. The sound, consequently, is just like a regular phone call.

The most often-used VoIP services for podcasting include Skype (www.skype.com) and Gizmo Project (www.gizmoproject.com). In addition to free calls between users of the services, both Skype and Gizmo offer the ability to call a regular phone line for prices significantly below typical telephone company costs. You can even have a phone number assigned to your account so people who don't have Skype or Gizmo—or aren't near their computer—can use a regular phone to call you. (Keep in mind, whenever anybody uses a regular phone, the resulting recording will sound like a phone call from that end of the call. In other words, your voice will sound like you were in a studio but the person you interviewed will sound like he or she was talking into a telephone.)

While telephones are being sold that work with these services, for recording purposes you would want to avoid them. Your goal is to get the much purer, cleaner sound that comes directly over your computer.

Unfortunately, neither of these software-based services have recording features built in. This is not an oversight. In many jurisdictions, it is illegal to record a telephone conversation without the consent of both parties. Still, several alternatives are available to enable you to record both ends of a Skype or Gizmo call.

The first option is to install add-on software designed to let you record both ends of the call. HotRecorder (http://www.hotrecorder.com) is a software add-on made solely to let you record both ends of any Internet conversation, although it won't let you also capture other audio, such as music playing through another device on your computer. Skylook (www.skylook.biz) integrates Skype (not Gizmo) into Microsoft Outlook and handles recordings from there.

Another approach for recording Skype calls is a complex and cumbersome software setup we won't describe in detail here. It involves a piece of shareware called Virtual Audio Cables and two instances of Skype running on your computer simultaneously, letting you record a conference call of yourself and your interview subject. The details for this setup can be found at www.henshall.com. This approach works quite well—and was how we first started recording *For Immediate Release*. However, we soon switched to our favorite option: the use of a mixer to produce what's known as a "mix-minus."

8

The Mix-Minus Setup

The "minus" part of a mix-minus can be important when recording lengthier calls over a VoIP service like Skype or Gizmo. Because the digital signal is being processed in the computer before it is sent back over the Internet to the person on the other end of the line, your interview subject could experience "latency," a delay in the signal. Your interview subject may also hear him or herself echoing back over the phone, making it extremely difficult and uncomfortable to engage seamlessly in conversation.

The mix-minus addresses this by eliminating the sound of the person on the other end of the line from the input he or she hears. Here's how it works:

First off, make sure your mixer includes "auxiliary" capabilities. An auxiliary input can be controlled separately for each line-in port. Say you have two microphones and your digital effects processor is connected to an auxiliary input. You could increase the echo on one microphone by dialing up the auxiliary level, while the second microphone has no echo at all because you dialed the auxiliary level all the way down.

For the mix-minus, use the following configuration:

1. Set your digital recorder to record in stereo.

2. Plug your microphone into the XLR input in line-in number 1. Make sure the "pan"—the left and right stereo dial—is set all the way to the right. Also make sure the auxiliary dial is set in the middle.

3. Your headphone jack on your computer connects to line-in number 2. Make sure this is set all the way to the left. Also make sure the auxiliary dial is turned all the way down. (The auxiliary "send" is used to send the auxiliary signal to the line-in jack on your computer.)

4. If you use an iPod or some other device to play music or other audio files into the mix, make sure the auxiliary dial is in the middle and that the pan dial is all the way to the right.

Now, make your Skype call. (The same technique works on other VoIP utilities such as Gizmo Project, by the way.) The person on the line's other end won't hear his own voice coming back as part of the mix. Thus, there will be no echo.

The Double-ender

A final approach to a co-host or interview is called a "double-ender." This is the ideal approach, given that both participants have recording equipment, high-speed Internet connections, and enough time for one party to transmit a large file to the other party.

To produce a double-ender, you can talk over any device you like—the phone, a VoIP service, whatever. It doesn't matter because the only voice you'll record is your own. The person you are interviewing will record his or her voice on his or her end of the call, and then send you the audio file containing his or her end of the conversation. You simply import your end of the conversation into your audio recording software as one track, then import the other person's file as the other track. If you align the two tracks carefully, you will have two high-quality audio recordings that sound like a single recording. Now, just export that file as an MP3, and nobody will know you weren't in the same room with your co-host or the person you were interviewing.

Approaches to Recording

Now that we've covered the basics of recording from a technical standpoint, we should spend a little time on the approaches you can take to producing the file. You have a variety of options:

Live to the Hard Drive

We mentioned this approach briefly in Chapter 7. A lot of podcasters prefer to simply record and upload to the hard drive. They may engage in a little postproduction of the entire file—for example, they may opt to compress and/or normalize the file (we'll discuss this in detail in Chapter 9), but they don't edit the file at all. The way it was recorded is the way it goes out.

To accomplish this one-pass recording, podcasters need to have inputs to the main mix that allow them to introduce any additional sounds they want to add to the podcast, including prerecorded interviews, music, bumpers, and other elements. One of Shel's favorite podcasters—Dave Slusher, host of the *Evil Genius Chronicles*—even lays down a music "bed" in his show—background music that plays softly behind his voice. He does this in real time rather than adding an additional track in postproduction.

In Bits and Pieces

Some podcasters prefer greater control over their shows, even though it requires considerably more time. They will record the various segments separately and bring them together in a postproduction mix using their audio editing software. For example, you would record your own voice, then splice in the music, prerecorded interviews, and other audio elements.

This provides greater control than the one-pass, live-to-the-hard-drive option, because once everything is recorded in one pass, you're pretty much stuck with it. If the fade-out of music behind your voice didn't work the way you wanted it to, you can't do much about it. But if you add the music later and fade it out in its own track, and after listening you don't like it, you can undo the fade-out and work with it some more until you get it just the way you want.

How to Talk

There is one last aspect of recording your show that has nothing whatsoever to do with the underlying technology, but is still worth a few words. How you sound will affect the way people react to your show. If you sound stiff and uncomfortable, you'll make your audience equally uncomfortable listening to you.

It's equally important to avoid sounding like a typical, polished radio announcer. Keep in mind that one reason people listen to podcasts is that they're weary of sound-alike voices on radio stations. Your goal should be to sound like *you*. That is, you should sound natural, just the way you do when talking to your spouse, friends, or colleagues.

That's not as easy a task as it sounds. When sitting alone in front of a microphone, a lot of people find it difficult to sound natural. One technique that works for a lot of folks is to tape a photo of somebody you know to the wall or monitor and talk to that individual instead of the microphone.

You may not need a photo in order to envision yourself speaking to one person. But keep in mind that, unlike radio, the vast majority of your listeners will consume your podcast by themselves. There are not a lot of stories of podcasts being played over loudspeakers in break rooms or restaurants! People listen at their desks over the computer speakers, or they listen with headphones on or ear buds jammed in their ears. In effect, you *really are* talking to just one person! So you may as well sound like it.

Of course, the nature of your podcast will dictate who that individual is! A business podcast will sound more like a business conversation in the hall at work, while a comedy podcast will sound more the way you do when you're cracking up a friend at a bar. You need to adopt the right tone to convey the sense of your show, and then employ that tone in a conversation with each individual, one at a time. You are not at a lectern in front of an audience, after all!

Another approach, if you're uncomfortable talking by yourself, is to work with a co-host. Even if you and your co-host are not in the same room, your presentation style will sound more like a phone conversation than an unnatural monologue. (We'll talk more about co-hosts and other configurations in Chapter 13 when we address the ways in which you can refine the approach to your show.)

Chapter 9

Edit Your Podcast

How to...

- Edit out words or phrases
- Add elements to your recording
- Change the channel format of your recording
- Adjust the amplification of audio bits and equalize your frequency
- Reduce noise in your podcast
- Compress your recordings
- Add special effects to your podcast
- Save your work
- Edit your ID3 tags

With the recording behind you, more than likely you now need to edit your podcast. We say "more than likely" because there *is* a school of thought called "live to the hard drive." This approach takes whatever you recorded, glitches and gaffes included, and sends it straight to the server.

The philosophy behind "live to the hard drive" is based on the core notions of podcasting. It's *not* professional radio; it's supposed to be authentic; it's supposed to be *real*. Whatever goes on in the background, whatever flubs occur during your recording, these are all just part of what makes podcasts appealing. Listen to Adam Curry's *Daily Source Code* and you'll hear him interrupted by phone calls; his daughter sticks her head in the room and asks him a question; a lawnmower passes beneath his window. It's all just part of Curry's life, and listeners love it.

It may be fine for your podcast, too, depending on what your goal is and what type of podcasting you're producing. But while these real-life sounds may be charming on a *Daily Source Code*—and make no mistake, they *are* charming and work quite well—they would have no place in IBM's investor relations–focused podcast. If you want your podcast to be free of errors and wish to incorporate audio elements after you're done recording, then editing becomes one of the indispensable tasks you'll perform with your show.

As far as gear goes, you only need your computer and a software application that handles your editing chores. Sound editing is generally an element of the same software you use to record a podcast; thus, you would utilize the same application you settled on in Chapter 7 and perhaps used to record in Chapter 8 (if you weren't recording to a digital device separate from your computer).

For examples in this chapter, we'll use Audacity, the free recording and editing application that has become so popular among podcasters.

While we will share some techniques in this chapter, we urge you to take the time to experiment. As much as some people will tell you to use setting *x* to achieve effect *y*, we've found that fiddling with the dials until it sounds just right to you is the best approach to getting the output you desire. Also, since each software application approaches various tasks differently, you should take the time to learn how your software works and then experiment using that knowledge.

Light Editing

While you *could* go live to the hard drive if you produce a casual show meant for friends and family or some other forgiving audience, we still recommend some light editing before you finalize the file and upload it to the server. At the very least, go through and get rid of those irritating "umms."

Umm is not a word. As Tom Mucciolo—a New York–based presentation skills coach—has said many times, people in Spanish-speaking countries don't say "ummo." Professional speakers and broadcasters learn to avoid "umm," but for the rest of us, it's a natural filler when you don't know what to say or you're searching for the right word. Enough of them in a podcast, though, get to be downright annoying. Editing them out can make you sound smooth and erudite, despite your fumbles during the recording session!

To understand the process of editing a sound file, we need to start with the file you'll be editing. The sound as it appears in the editing software is known as a "waveform," which can be defined as the graphic representation of the various elements of sound. (If you're reading this book in order, you're already familiar with waveform, which we introduced in Chapter 8, along with explanations of the various elements of the waveform.) Figure 9-1 shows an example of a waveform we'll use for demonstration editing. Please note that this figure is in black and white; however, the color reference will show up on the computer screen.

This particular file happens to be an audio comment one of our listeners contributed to our show. You can see from the image that it's about eight-and-a-half minutes long (a lot longer than we usually get). The person who recorded the comment—Podcast NYC host Rob Safuto—recorded in stereo, but the waveform in both the left (top) and right (bottom) channels are nearly identical, since the same voice and words were going into both channels.

Editing a file like this one would be difficult in this particular view. It will be easier to work with precision, editing out "umms" and "aahhs," if we magnify the view. Figure 9-2 shows how the waveform looks with it magnified.

9

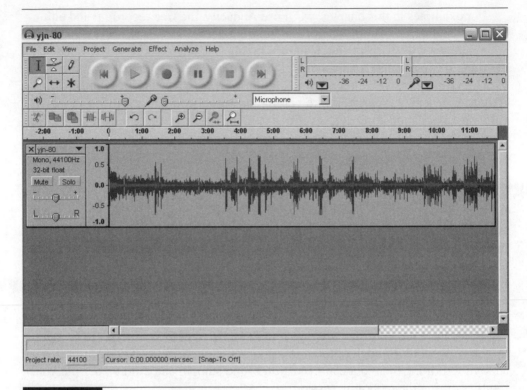

FIGURE 9-1   The waveform in Audacity

Now you can see that the same amount of space is dedicated to only about eight *seconds* of the file, and the gaps between words and where Rob stopped to take a breath are obvious. By clicking the green arrow in the toolbar at the top of the application, you can start playing the waveform; you'll see a cursor move along the waveform horizontally to indicate exactly where you are in the file. The button with two blue perpendicular vertical lines is the Pause button, while the yellow square graphic represents the Stop button. All the way to the left is a button with two purple arrows pointing left; this returns the cursor to the very beginning of the file. Its counterpart, all the way to the right, will fast-forward you to the very end of the file. The red circle is for recording; we won't be using that in this chapter.

Now, let's find a part of the file where Rob said, "Umm." It won't be easy; Rob is a very polished podcaster! But nobody's perfect, and we did find one in the first few seconds of the file. Highlighting the "umm" is no different than highlighting a word or phrase in a word processing program: Just click and drag the mouse over the part of the file in which the "umm" occurs (Figure 9-3).

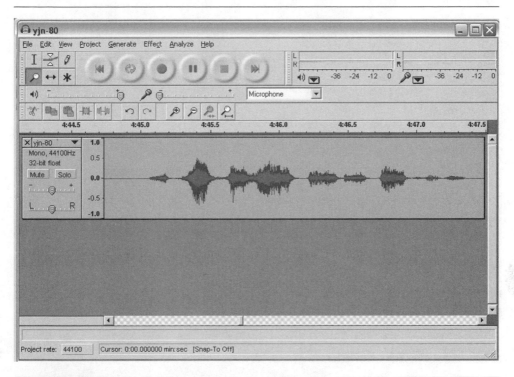

FIGURE 9-2   A magnified waveform

Now, when you click the green Play button, all you will hear is the part of the file you have highlighted. It's a great way to make sure you delete only what you want to get rid of and that you're not capturing anything Rob said that you would want to keep.

Now, all you have to do is use the Edit pull-down menu and select Delete. Alternatively, you could press your Delete key.

Now, go back a few seconds, click to put your cursor into part of the file well before the deletion, and start playing to make sure your edit sounds right. If it doesn't, you can always "undo" what you've done and try it again.

More Editing Techniques and Options

Dropping the "uhhs" and "umms" is more than enough for many podcasters who produce perfectly good podcasts. Based on your objectives (and, frankly, how serious you want to get), there's a lot more you can do in the editing stage.

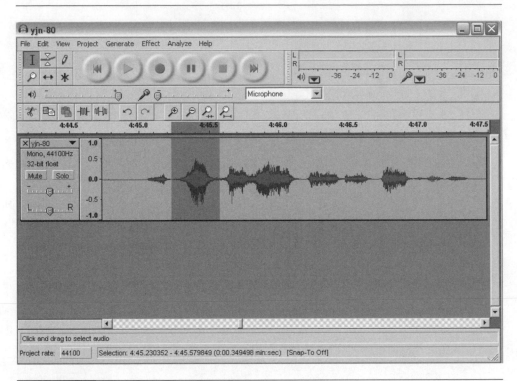

FIGURE 9-3   Highlighted vocal segment

We do want to add a word of caution. While some of the techniques we're about to discuss may, in fact, be necessary as you develop your show, others may just be cool tricks you've heard of and want to apply. While hardcore audiophiles will tell you how much better your podcast sounds, most listeners would be hard-pressed to detect a difference. We're not suggesting you avoid any of these techniques, particularly if you find learning and executing them fun. But don't feel like you *have* to perform such activities as normalizing if your podcast sounds just fine to you. The extent to which you embark on the technological activities can be equated to the extent to which you invest in hardware (which we discussed in Chapter 6). Just as there are perfectly fine podcasts recorded on microphone headsets that cost less than $50, there are plenty of podcasts that sound just fine without several rounds of audio manipulation. It's easy to get carried away, and you'll have to decide for yourself just how carried away you want to get based on the time you have available.

Adding Elements

The disadvantage to a one-pass recording is that you're stuck with the audio file you produce. When you combine the elements of a podcast in postproduction, you have far more control and can fix things that don't work out right. Of course, it also takes more time. Which approach you choose is your decision.

If you didn't do a one-pass recording—one in which all of your extra audio, like bumpers, music, and audio comments are all recorded in real time—then you need to add these items during the editing process. Even if you *do* produce a one-pass recording, you may find you need to add something later anyway. More times than we care to remember, we have neglected to record the intro to the segment by our Australian correspondent, Lee Hopkins.

Adding something to the end of a file is easy, taking advantage of a process known as a *multi-track* recording. Let's say you have a song you want to play to wrap up the show. Import the song into the file where the body of your podcast resides. It will occupy a new set of tracks, as in Figure 9-4.

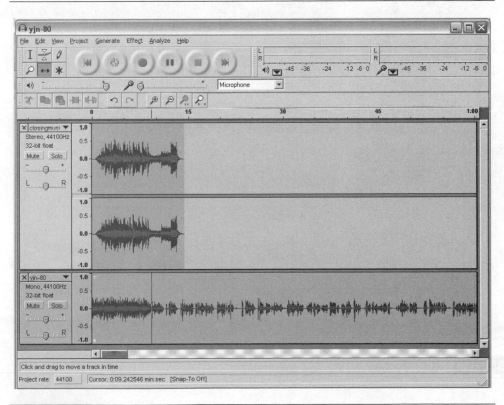

FIGURE 9-4   Adding a music track

Congratulations, you now have two tracks in your file! Unfortunately, if you played the file now, the two would overlap. You have to move the song to the end of the file. Each software application has a slightly different approach to this, but the fundamentals are the same. You have to create a starting point for the second track. In Audacity, you accomplish this by clicking at the start point to move the cursor to that spot. Then, in the Project pull-down menu, select Align Tracks and choose With Cursor. The selected track will reposition to the start point you chose, as in the example in Figure 9-5.

Adding a sound to the middle of the file is a bit trickier. The simplest approach is to open the file you want to add in a separate window, copy it, and then insert

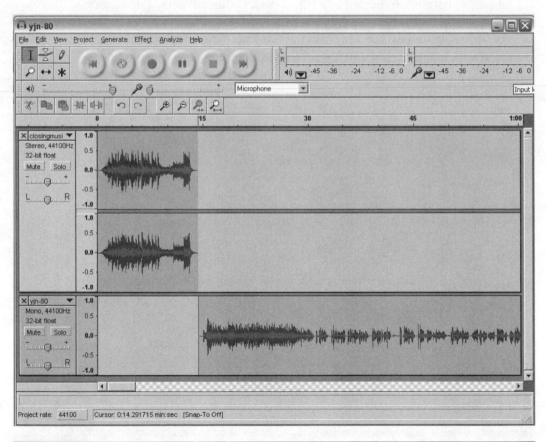

FIGURE 9-5   Repositioning a track

it at the cursor point in the main podcast file. The problem with this approach is that sometimes the added sound plays at a different speed than the rest of your file. You're better off creating separate tracks. To accomplish this, do the following:

1. Delete everything in your original file after the point where you want to insert the new sound.

2. Copy what you just deleted into a new track.

3. Import your new sound as a new track.

4. Move the new sound up one layer so your various tracks appear in the correct order.

Making Your Stereo Channels into Mono Channels

As noted in Chapter 7, the final output of your file as stereo or mono is a setting of your software, a decision you will already have made. However, there could be reasons to turn stereo tracks into mono tracks during the editing process.

Our own podcast offers an excellent example. Using the "mix-minus" setup explained in Chapter 6, Neville's voice is recorded on the left channel and Shel's on the right channel. That would result in listeners hearing each of our voices coming out of only one side of the headphones or one speaker. The music we play at the end of each show, though, can still be stereo so listeners can hear it the way the artists intended. To create a mono version of the vocal track in Audacity, use the drop-down menu near the upper left-hand part of the track and select Split Stereo Track, as in Figure 9-6.

This creates two separate tracks instead of a single stereo track. Now, for each of these separate tracks, use the drop-down menu again and choose Mono.

Amplification

As you listen to the mix of tracks, you may hear parts that are louder or softer than they should be. While it's best to record everything at the right levels, you can adjust the volume by highlighting the part you want to adjust, selecting Effects and then Amplify. You can move up the scale to make the file louder, or down the scale to make it softer.

In Audacity, if increasing the volume requires you to check the box titled Allow Clipping, you're doing so at the expense of your audio quality. Refer to what we said about clipping in the last chapter.

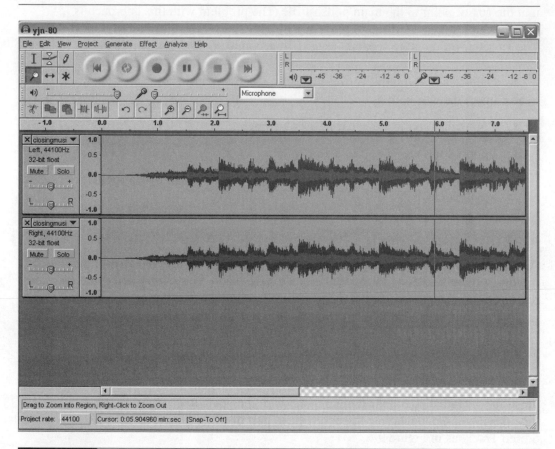

FIGURE 9-6   Splitting a stereo track in Audacity

You can also de-amplify audio to zero. Sometimes, while one of us is talking, the other coughs. It's easy to highlight the cough and de-amplify it to the point that it just doesn't exist any more!

As for increasing the amplitude of your audio, you can do this first if it's all you intend to do. You can amplify some of your file to bring all the levels to roughly the same volume, take other actions afterwards, and then come back and amplify the entire file to make it louder—or you can wait until everything else is done and amplify the whole thing. We'll cover these options as we go through the various tasks you can perform to fine-tune your audio.

Equalization

Equalization is one of those tasks you can perform either on the hardware at the time you're recording, or in the software after recording is finished—or both. (For example, say you import some audio you received from elsewhere, like a listener comment, that could stand some equalization. Even though you performed equalization tasks on your hardware when you recorded the bulk of the show, you can still equalize this segment in your software.)

Equalization allows you to adjust the high, (12 kHz), mid (2.5 kHz), and low (80 Hz) frequency bands. If you've ever modified the treble and bass levels on your stereo, you have an idea of what equalizing your audio can do. Equalization can be handled either as you record on your mixer, or afterwards using your editing software, as shown in the examples in Figure 9-7.

Equalization should be the *first* step of your audio enhancement process after you have amplified any segments of the recording that need it.

Noise Reduction

When you listen to an audio file, you might notice some noise in the background, usually a hissing sound. You probably would rather that hiss not be there, particularly if you're going to incorporate the file as an element into the podcast

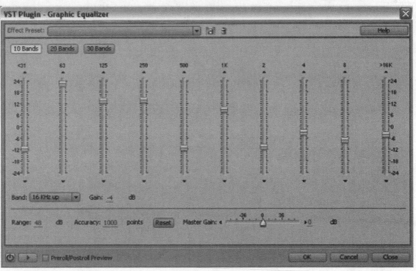

FIGURE 9-7   Left, the equalization controls on the Mackie 1202-VLZ Pro mixer. Right, the graphic equalizer built into Adobe's Audition recording and editing software.

(such as an interview you conducted in the field). Luckily, you can reduce or even remove the noise from the file in a couple of ways.

Noise reduction is achieved through a noise "gate." While noise gate techniques can be applied to live recordings, this is usually reserved for higher-end musical performance. For podcasting, we'll limit ourselves to postproduction noise reduction using editing software. The application of the word "gate" to this concept is no accident. In processing your sound file, the software will only open the "gate" to allow a sound to get through and reach the final output if it registers above a certain level. All sounds below that level are deemed noise that should be kept out. You set that level using the controls in your software.

Most recording and editing software packages include noise removal functionality. Audacity is no exception, and it's fairly easy to use. The key to reducing noise in just about any file is to have a good sample of audio that includes nothing *but* the background noise, with no talking or music running over it. We usually capture this stretch of near-silence by including 15 or 20 seconds during which nobody says anything at the beginning of any recording we undertake. Figure 9-8 shows some silence at the beginning of a file. We've highlighted the silence to use it for a noise profile.

Now, from the Effect menu, we choose Noise Removal, and then click the button that reads Get Noise Profile. The noise removal utility will analyze the noise contained in the selection (see Figure 9-9).

Now, select the part of the file that contains the background noise; the process for selecting the segment of the file is the same as for choosing the part of the

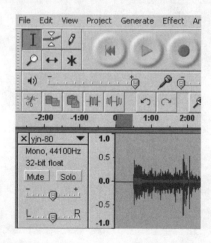

FIGURE 9-8   Silence

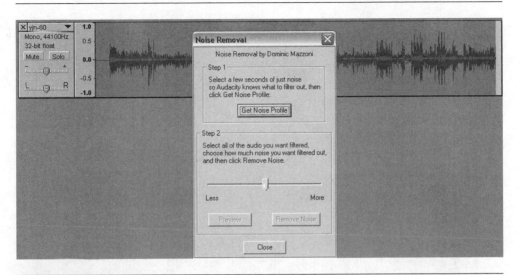

FIGURE 9-9   Analyzing noise

file that contains an "umm" you want to delete. With that part of the file selected, return to the Noise Removal utility and click the Preview button. This will let you hear how the file sounds at that particular setting. You can adjust the slider to *more* or *less* noise removal and listen to the previews to see if you can get better sound. Once you have it where you want it, click Remove Noise.

The process used by these noise removal utilities is known as "notch" filtering, which reduces the volume, or amplitude, of the frequencies that contain the hiss while leaving the other frequencies alone. Other software tools can also be used to reduce noise. For example, if you work on a Macintosh, you can use SoundSoap 2, a standalone software package from a company called BIAS (Figure 9-10). It works much the same as the built-in utility you'll find in applications like Audacity, but offers greater levels of control. As you can see, you start by having SoundSoap "learn" the noise in the file, then make selections and dial knobs to adjust the noise reduction. The software comes with detailed instructions, but we find that trial and error is the best way to employ SoundSoap.

NOTE   *You can find a list of noise reduction software applications—and other audio recording and editing software—in Chapter 7, where we introduce the range of software applications available to podcasters.*

Noise reduction should be the *second* effect you apply in your audio enhancement process.

FIGURE 9-10   SoundSoap

Compression

Compression is another one of those actions you can perform either with hardware or software. With software, compression is a simple step to take that can enhance the quality of your sound considerably. To understand what compression does, first you have to know about *dynamic range*, which describes the variances in the volume of your audio file. If, after you finish assembling your podcast, you have a lot of loud segments and some very soft segments, or the waveform shows a lot of peaks and valleys, you would be said to have large dynamic range, meaning a lot of variation.

Compression is the step you would take to level that range, lowering the loudest parts of the audio compared to the overall signal and reducing (or increasing) the dynamic range.

In this example from Audacity (Figure 9-11), the compression threshold has been set to –12 dB and the ratio is 2-to-1. This typical setting means that any sound in the original recording that exceeds –12 dB by 2 dB will be dropped to a 1-dB increase over the threshold in the finished recording. If, after compressing, you find the overall audio too quiet, you can increase the volume using the amplification settings; but the overall effect of the recording will remain more even and, as a result, more pleasing to the listener's ears. The "attack time" noted on the screen shot tells the software how quickly the effect should take effect when it's invoked. The slower it is, the more likely some sounds may get lost or muddled as a result.

Compression is the *third* step you should take in your audio processing.

There is another form of compression that might be described as compression on steroids. It's called "limiting," and it's designed to prevent the loudest segments

9

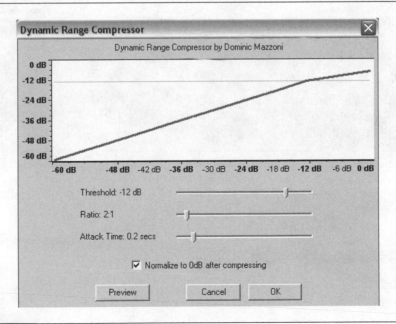

FIGURE 9-11   Compression settings in Audacity

of your recording from going over a set level. Limiting effectively "clips" the part of a signal that exceeds your threshold. Limiting capabilities are available only on a few higher-end software packages like Adobe Audition.

Finally, we would be remiss if we didn't at least mention *RMS—root mean square*. Neither of us are big math fans and RMS is not something we apply to our own efforts, but the hardest-core audio geeks do rely on RMS (also known as the "quadratic mean") to assess the overall loudness of their recordings. According to Wikipedia, RMS generally refers to "the statistical measure of the magnitude of a varying quantity." In the case of an audio recording, the varying quantity is the peaks and valleys of the waveform.

A complex mathematical formula is used to determine the RMS of an audio file that involves squaring the value for each peak level, averaging the total, and then determining the square root of that sum.

There's no reason to engage in such math, though, when some of the software applications you could use—like SoundForge, Adobe Audition, and DSP Quattro, can do it for you, as in the example from Adobe Audition in Figure 9-12. Using the

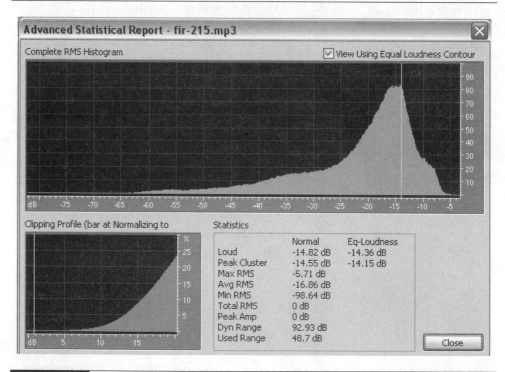

FIGURE 9-12   Adobe Audition calculates the RMS value of an audio file.

information you get from the calculation, you can increase or decrease your audio by trial and error so the RMS achieves whatever threshold you set for it.

Normalizing

Normalizing your audio adjusts the overall volume of your sample. When you normalize your audio file, the software measures the gap between the peak levels of your source recording and the level you'd like for your peaks. It then increases or decreases the overall audio to that amount. If your desired setting is louder than the current level of your peaks, the entire recording is normalized up to that level, so even the quieter parts get louder. That includes background sounds, hiss, and other distracting elements of your recording.

To understand the value of normalizing, let's say you do a podcast that includes four or five podsafe songs. Each song was recorded at a different level, so some sounds are louder than others. By applying normalization to the entire file (which includes all those songs), the volume of all of the songs will adjust so they're roughly the same and your listeners won't have to constantly turn their volume dials up and down.

In Audacity, you can set your compression to automatically normalize after the compression process is completed, a convenient feature that saves you a step.

Other Effects

In addition to sweetening the sound through the techniques just noted, there are other effects you can apply to parts of your recording. We outline them in the following sections. Many, many more exist that you can try out, but these are the ones you'll probably want to consider using most frequently.

Fade In and Fade Out

Two of the easiest effects to implement are the fade-in and fade-out, which is great because you may wind up using them a lot. For example, at the beginning of our show, we fade out the introductory music as one of us welcomes listeners to the episode. This works pretty much the same in every audio package. You just highlight the part of the file where you'd like the fade-in or fade-out to occur, and then choose the effect. In Audacity, the effect simply happens when you click Fade In or Fade Out from the effects menu. In higher-end packages, you can invoke controls, such as the curve (exponential, linear, or inverted exponential) and the length in milliseconds.

9

Echo

You can give your audio a chamber-like sound by applying an echo effect. In most software programs, you can adjust both the delay time (how soon after the original sound the repeat occurs) and the decay (how long the echo effect lingers).

Bass Boost

Once again, you can understand quickly what bass boost does if you think of adjusting the bass in your car stereo. Turn it up and the bass is more pronounced; turn it down and the bass recedes. If you have a lot of treble in your recording, you might want to boost the bass for a richer, fuller sound.

Change Pitch

Have you ever wanted to sound like a cartoon chipmunk? You can, by increasing your voice's pitch in the recording. You can also lower the pitch to sound more like Darth Vader.

Saving Your Work: File Formats

You should save your work every step or two. Audacity saves its files in the .aup format. Every recording-and-editing package has its own unique file format. At the end of the process, you need to export the file into the format your listeners will use. The software can save the file in a variety of different formats that some listeners may prefer over others for a variety of reasons. However, the absolute mandatory requirement is to produce an MP3 file. MP3 is far and away the most widely used format for podcasts.

The following lists the most common audio formats you can find on podcasts, as well as some information on the characteristics that leads some listeners to prefer one over the others.

MP3

We cannot repeat this enough: You *must* offer an MP3 file. *MP3* stands for *MPEG-1 Audio Layer 3*. MP3 files are encoded in what is known as a "lossy" format, which means data is removed from the native file without noticeable degrading of the audio quality in order to reduce the file size. We say "without noticeable degrading of the audio quality" advisedly. Serious audiophiles with good headphones will certainly notice the difference, particularly when listening to music. Podcasts are another matter. Even music podcasts sound just fine as MP3s, and the file size is markedly smaller than the alternatives, which has made it the format of choice. Due to MP3's popularity, dozens of consumer electronics companies have released MP3 players and CD players that play MP3s from a CD.

OGG

OGG is a format designed for streaming audio online while also compressing the file. The format contains a variety of other open-source codecs (the part of the program that handles the encoding and decoding) for audio, video, and text. The file format extension—*OGG*—is an abbreviation for *Ogg Vorbis*, its formal name. Some claim OGG files sound better than MP3 at equivalent bit rates.

AAC

AAC stands for *Advanced Audio Coding*. It's another "lossy" compression format. While a variety of advances of MP3 make AAC desirable, it's the ability to add "chapters" (bookmarks in the file) that makes it easy to jump from one part of the file to the next. Apple embraced the AAC format, introducing the chapter functionality in some iPod models. A copyright-protected version of AAC is the default file format for Apple's iTunes and the iPod. However, many other digital players don't recognize and won't play AAC files—and songs purchased from iTunes can only be played on the iPod, not on any other portable digital players.

A number of other file formats have their pros and cons as well, but podcasts are not distributed in these formats, mainly due to file size and player compatibility.

If your recording and editing software does not allow you to convert to the format you wish, you can acquire software (usually freeware or shareware) that will handle the conversion for you. Even Apple iTunes can convert WAV files to MP3s. Just add the WAV file to your music library, highlight it, and select the option from the context menu to convert that particular song to an MP3.

Editing Your ID3 Tags

One of the biggest mistakes many podcasters make—and one of the most irritating for podcast listeners—is the failure to edit ID3 tags. These are metadata containers built into MP3 files that contain information like the name of the podcast, the episode number, and a summary of the show's contents.

Since MP3 files were originally conceived for music, the fields within ID3 tags are aimed at the recording industry, listing album name, artist, track, and album art, among others. However, it's easy enough to put information into these fields that describe your podcast.

This information shows up on the screen of a portable media player like an iPod, as well as on the screen of a computer-based media player like Apple iTunes or Windows Media Player.

You can edit ID3 tags in several ways. Some applications, like Audacity, open an ID3 editor as soon as you start to save the file to the MP3 format. You can also acquire software applications that let you select an MP3 file and apply ID3 tags, like the AudioShell tag editor (a Windows application), shown in Figure 9-13.

You can also use some computer media software applications, like Apple's iTunes, to handle editing of MP3 tags. Finally, some of the online podcasting services, like LibSyn, let you do your ID3 tag editing online. Figure 9-14 shows an example of an ID3 tag from one of our podcasts.

FIGURE 9-13   The AudioShell tag editor for Windows

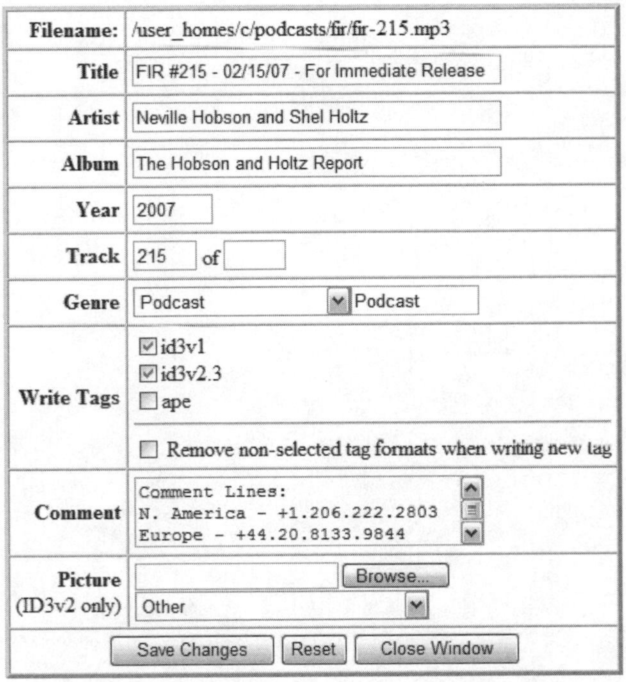

Filename:	/user_homes/c/podcasts/fir/fir-215.mp3
Title	FIR #215 - 02/15/07 - For Immediate Release
Artist	Neville Hobson and Shel Holtz
Album	The Hobson and Holtz Report
Year	2007
Track	215 of
Genre	Podcast ⌄ Podcast
Write Tags	☑ id3v1 ☑ id3v2.3 ☐ ape ☐ Remove non-selected tag formats when writing new tag
Comment	Comment Lines: N. America - +1.206.222.2803 Europe - +44.20.8133.9844
Picture (ID3v2 only)	[Browse...] Other ⌄
	[Save Changes] [Reset] [Close Window]

FIGURE 9-14   The ID3 tag editor built into the LibSyn podcast hosting service.

9

When filling in your ID3 tags, we beg you (*beg* you!!) to be consistent from show to show. The worst thing that happens when tags are completed haphazardly is that players screw up the lineup—that is, they assemble shows out of order. When tags are consistent, the chronology is always correct and your listeners who have three or four episodes backed up will be able to listen to them in order.

Chapter 10

Release Your Podcast

How to...

- Decide where to host your podcast
- Choose a domain name
- Move your podcast
- Update your RSS feed
- Promote your podcast

So you're all set. You've gone through the planning and the preparation. You've made your recording and assembled all the elements. You have an MP3 file on your disk all ready to be a podcast. Now what?

In fact, you have a *lot* of decisions to make in order to get your podcast out there for everyone to hear. In this chapter, we'll go through all those options and get you started promoting your show to the world.

Where to Host Your Podcast

The "host" is the web server that contains your podcast file. After all, the file has to be accessible over the Internet, just like any web page. It is to this server that you will upload each episode of your podcast. You can host your podcast basically in three ways: on your own server, on a shared server, or with a hosting service.

Your Own Server

You can buy a server and own the hardware and all the content it holds. A server perfectly adequate to the task can cost as little as $2000. In order to connect your server to the Net, you'll need two things:

- **Server software**   A number of different companies produce web server software, but one of the most popular is Apache (which can be found for free on the Web at www.apache.org).

- **A static IP address**   Your server has to be found by other servers. For that, you need a static IP address, one that never changes. IP stands for "Internet Protocol," and is a numeric address. An address looks something like this: 66.192.34.101.

Most home Internet connections use dynamic IP addresses, which means new numbers are generated every time you boot up your computer. You can't, therefore, use your regular home or office computer as a server. You can obtain a static IP connection through your local service provider or find a local server farm and hook your box into their network, but keep in mind: You'll pay based on the bandwidth you use. A popular podcast could end up running into some real dollars! And if your podcast gets *really* popular, you'll need to look at other alternatives that support that kind of traffic.

This approach has a distinct disadvantage. If you're on vacation and the server acts up or goes down, you're out of luck. Even if you contract with a specialist to handle server issues for you, it's not the same as the 24-hour onsite support that characterizes most shared server services.

Shared Server

The marketplace is overflowing with hosting companies that will, for a monthly fee, provide you with space on their servers. These services set their rates based on the bandwidth you use and the amount of file space you take up. If you need your own dedicated server, these services can handle that, too. One key advantage to this approach is that people are watching the server 24 hours a day. Another is that a lot of the infrastructure you need is already in place, including, for example, the database you most likely will wind up needing when you install blogging software.

Hosted Services

Your final alternative is to not waste your time with any of the technical gobbledygook previously outlined and just use a service configured to host your podcast for you. With these services, you just upload your file and update your podcast blog—usually also provided with the service. Your podcast will have a name that includes the service domain, like this one for our podcast on LibSyn: fir.libsyn.com.

You can always get a dedicated domain and redirect it to the actual location if having a unique URL is important to you.

We cover services like these in Chapter 19, where we go into considerable detail on the wide variety of services available to podcasters.

More on Domain Names

Whatever option you choose for hosting your podcast, people who want to find it will need to uncover its address. The IP address—that series of four sets of numbers—doesn't mean anything to most people. Fortunately, the Internet has a nifty

10

feature called the domain name system (DNS) that translates domain names into IP addresses. That's how you can type in "www.podcastalley.com" and the Internet finds its IP address.

These days, you have a lot of options for the type of domain you get. You're no longer limited to dot-com, dot-org, and dot-net. There's dot-biz, for example, dot-info, dot-tv, dot-name, and dot-us, among many others. Opting for dot-com is almost always going to be your best bet, because that's what most people continue to assume. You can also try to buy *all* the possible permutations, which prevents anyone from taking advantage of your hard work should your podcast become popular. That could run into money, but not a lot as the cost of domain name registration has plunged to as little as six or seven dollars per year per name…and less if you pay for more than one year at a time. In any case, these days, owning the dot-com and maybe the dot-biz is not a bad idea.

Make the name you give the URL memorable and try to keep it as short as you can. If the name can be an exact match to your podcast name, so much the better, like these:

- www.dailysourcecode.com

- www.acrossthesound.net

- www.accidenthash.com

The hosting service you select may let you register a domain name as part of the sign-up process. If not, you can use services like Network Solutions (www.netsol.com) or GoDaddy (www.godaddy.com) for your domain name registration.

If you're hosting your files on a service like LibSyn and don't plan to buy your own domain name, you still need to name the site, like those in the following:

- barbecuesecrets.libsyn.com

- dawnanddrewshow.podshow.com

Obtaining these names is just part of the registration process with your service.

Getting Your Podcast from Here to There

The means by which a file moves from your computer to the server is *FTP (file transfer protocol)*. As you might suspect, there's more than one way to use FTP to get your file to the server.

First, if you're an intrepid computer geek, you can use UNIX commands on a command-line interface. If you know what that means, you probably can do it. If not, there's no reason to mess with it. Just get FTP software that provides a Windows or Mac interface that's a lot easier to use. Most of it is shareware and there's even some freeware that'll handle this task.

With that software, the first step is to connect to your podcast host—the host will provide you with login and password details, as well as the FTP server address. Navigate to the folder that contains your audio files. In the second pane, you'll see your computer hard drive's files and folders. Navigate to the folder that contains the file you want to upload. Highlight that file, and then click the icon— usually an arrow pointing up—to transfer it from your computer to the server.

Finally, podcasting services like LibSyn automate the process. With LibSyn, for example, you simply click a button that says Upload, browse to the file on your hard drive, and then click Load File.

Updating the RSS Feed

Next, you need to update the RSS feed. Like everything else, how this gets done depends on several factors.

If you're using a service like LibSyn, there's really nothing at all you need to do. The feed is updated automatically when you use the Publish form to update your blog after you upload the MP3 file. If you use WordPress (www.wordpress.org), you can install a plug-in called PodPress (http://www.mightyseek.com/podpress) that lets you fill in a simple form to handle linking to the podcast and updating the RSS feed. PodPress even adds a utility that lets visitors play a stream of the podcast directly from the blog page.

If you need to update the RSS feed manually, you must understand *enclosures*. An enclosure is the part of each "item" entry in an RSS feed that handles multimedia files. Let's look at a typical item entry coded in XML, just the way it goes up to the server. This one is for our podcast, *For Immediate Release*:

```xml
<item>
 <title>For Immediate Release: 06/05/06</title>
 <itunes:author>Neville Hobson and Shel Holtz</itunes:author>
 <link>http://www.forimmediaterelease.biz/</link>
 <description>A summary of the contents of the show goes here.</description>
 <pubDate>Mon, 05 Jun 2006 22:15 GMT</pubDate>
 <enclosure url="http://libsyn.com/media/fir/fir-143.mp3" length="31952904"
type="audio/mpeg" />
```

```
<guid>http://libsyn.com/media/fir/fir-143.mp3</guid>
</item>
```

It's the "enclosure" part that is unique to feeds delivering multimedia content, like podcasts. You can just use the format you see here and substitute your own URL and file size (the one shown here is a 31MB file, which would have taken forever to download in the old dial-up days, but today takes only a minute or so with a high-speed connection).

If you're creating the RSS feed from scratch, you need more information than we can provide here. However, you can find some great resources on RSS online, including the following:

- mnot's Web Log at www.mnot.net/rss/tutorial/#Versions

- www.techxtra.ac.uk/rss_primer

- www.wizard-creek.com/rss/tutorial/index.htm

Apple iTunes and RSS

We'll talk about Apple iTunes in more detail a little later in this chapter, but as long as we're addressing RSS here, we should cover some of the extra steps needed to make sure Apple iTunes is able to find and deal with your RSS feed.

First, you need to add some tags to the "channel" part of your RSS feed. These include the following:

- <itunes:subtitle> A subtitle for your podcast

- <itunes:summary> A brief description of your podcast

- <itunes:owner> Tells iTunes who you are, and includes two second-level tags, <itunes:name> and <itunes:email>.

- <itunes:explicit> Lets people know whether your podcast contains adult language or other adult content

- <itunes:category> Puts your podcast into the right category and subcategory in the iTunes directory

Here's how the "channel" entry in our RSS feed looks:

```
<?xml version="1.0" encoding="UTF-8"?>
<channel>
```

```
<title>For Immediate Release Podcast</title>
<itunes:author>Neville Hobson and Shel Holtz</itunes:author>
<link>http://www.forimmediaterelease.biz/</link>
<description>The Hobson and Holtz Report is a twice-weekly podcast
covering the intersection of organizational communications and the online
world.</description>
<itunes:subtitle>At the intersection of PR/communications and the online
world.</itunes:subtitle>
<itunes:summary>For Immediate Release is co-hosted by Neville Hobson,
based in Wokingham, Berkshire, England, and Shel Holtz, based in Concord,
California, USA. Hobson and Holtz are two seasoned communications
professionals who believe they have something to say.</itunes:summary>
<language>en-us</language>
<copyright>This work is licensed under a Creative Commons License, http://
creativecommons.org/licenses/by-nc-nd/2.0/</copyright>
<itunes:owner>
  <itunes:name>Shel Holtz</itunes:name>
  <itunes:email>shel@holtz.com</itunes:email>
</itunes:owner>
<itunes:explicit>no</itunes:explicit>
<image>
  <title>For Immediate Release</title>
  <url>http://www.forimmediaterelease.biz/images/logos/fir-itunes-art.jpg</
url>
  <link>http://www.forimmediaterelease.biz/</link>
  <description>Conversations and content from the intersection of public
relations and the online world.</description>
</image>
<category>Business</category>
<category>Business</category>
<itunes:category text="Business">
          <itunes:category text="Management & Marketing"/>
</itunes:category>
```

Next you have to add some iTunes tags to each "item" entry. Among the tags
you'll need are these:

- ■ <itunes:author>   Who are the hosts of the podcast?

- ■ <itunes:summary>   What's in the show? This can be an exact duplicate of
  the <description> tag that's already a part of your RSS feed

■ <itunes:duration>   How long is the podcast? Expressed in hours, minutes, and seconds, like this: 01:12:37

■ <itunes:keywords>   Search terms your audience may use when trying to find podcasts like yours on iTunes

The following shows how a typical FIR item looks in RSS:

```
<item>
 <title>For Immediate Release: 06/08/06</title>
 <itunes:author>Neville Hobson and Shel Holtz</itunes:author>
 <link>http://www.forimmediaterelease.biz/</link>
 <description>Summary description of the show goes here.</description>
 <itunes:subtitle>The Hobson and Holtz Report</itunes:subtitle>
 <itunes:summary>Summary description of the show goes here.</itunes:
summary>
 <pubDate>Thu, 09 Jun 2006 03:15 GMT</pubDate>
 <enclosure url="http://libsyn.com/media/fir/fir-575.mp3" length="31952904"
type="audio/mpeg" />
 <guid>http://libsyn.com/media/fir/fir-575.mp3</guid>
 <category>podcasts</category>
 <itunes:explicit>no</itunes:explicit>
 <itunes:duration>1:16:04</itunes:duration>
 <itunes:keywords>public relations, PR, communications </itunes:keywords>
 </item>
```

One final word about RSS: If you must handle your feeds manually, we know they look daunting. They looked that way to us when we first started producing podcasts, too, but you'll get very accustomed to them. For our show, we simply copy the last item, paste it in as the *new* item, then change the file name, description, dates, time, file size, and length. It only takes a couple of seconds.

The Podcast Blog

We keep talking about your podcast blog, and we go into far more detail about the role of blogs as the home for your podcast in Chapter 14, where we discuss the various elements of a podcast.

No rule says your podcast *has* to be housed on a blog. Any web site will do. After all, there are only two requirements any web site can fulfill in this instance:

■   A link to the RSS feed so people can subscribe

■   A link to the podcast file so people can download it

A blog just makes sense. Your podcast is episodic, after all, and your blog posts appear in reverse chronological order, with the newest post appearing first. Feedback mechanisms are built in and archives are generated automatically. Blogging software also generates a "permalink," a permanent unique link for each episode. Many blogging platforms also produce the RSS feed with the enclosures handled by software plug-ins.

There's no reason *not* to use a blog.

Promoting Your Podcast

You are now at the point where your podcast is online and ready for people to listen. But if you build it (as the overused cliché goes), will they come? Most likely not. They need to find out you're there. You need to promote your podcast, which is the equivalent of a marketing effort any organization would use to introduce any new product or service to the marketplace.

Listing Your Podcast in Podcast Directories

Once, there was only one podcast directory, the one Adam Curry created called iPodder.org (now Indie Podder at www.indiepodder.org). Today, there is even a directory of podcast directories! The directory (at www.podcast411.com) currently lists 125 different podcast directories.

Your job is to get listed in as many directories as you can. Be sure to read the fine print for each of these directories to make sure you want your podcast listed there and that the service doesn't manipulate any of your content, notably your RSS feed. Tales exist of podcasters losing control of their feeds because of changes a directory made.

The key directories include the following:

■   Podcast Alley (www.podcastalley.com)

■   Odeo (www.odeo.com)

■   Podcast Pickle (www.podcastpickle.com)

■   Yahoo! Podcasts (http://podcasts.yahoo.com)

■   Apple iTunes Music Store (www.apple.com/itunes/podcasts)

The directory that is responsible for more subscriptions than any other is the one you cannot access over the Web. Instead, you have to download Apple's free iTunes music software and navigate to the iTunes Music Store. Select Podcasts and go from there. The reason this software is so popular is that subscribing to podcasts is drop-dead easy. Once you have found a podcast to which you'd like to subscribe, all you have to do is click the Subscribe button and the rest takes care of itself. The podcasts are automatically sorted into playlists, ready for transferring to an iPod (although it doesn't work with any other devices than Apple's proprietary product).

Media Coverage

If you are targeting a niche, particularly one the mainstream media already covers, try to get some media coverage.

Getting coverage could be as easy as putting out a press release that reaches the right publications. For example, if your podcast focuses on something to do with advertising or marketing, you could submit a press release to *Advertising Age* magazine and to the American Marketing Association, which publishes *Marketing News* for its members.

Issuing a press release also gets the information archived online and discoverable via Google. Thus, it will also come up in Google News searches.

You can use any number of press release distribution services, starting with the traditional stalwarts: PR Newswire and Business Wire. These aren't cheap, though, and are mostly used by businesses that need to send press releases with some degree of regularity to lots of media outlets. For a one-time announcement, consider services like PRWeb (www.prweb.com), which focuses more on small and medium-sized businesses. One more, PRZoom, is free, but does not offer all the functionality of the fee-based services.

Networking in the Podcasting Community

You should get yourself known in the podcasting community, particularly among other podcasts that deal with the same kind of material you do. This might seem odd, but podcasting isn't a competitive endeavor—at least, not yet. For example, on our podcast home page, we maintain a list of other public relations–focused podcasts.

As you're developing your podcast, spend time listening to related podcasts. Don't just listen, but post comments to the blogs, submit audio comments, become a part of that show's community. When you announce that you're launching your own podcast, you'll get the support of the rest of the community and some free publicity. For example, Bryan Person (a young PR practitioner from Boston) had been a regular participant in our community for several months when he launched his own podcast called *New Comm Road*. We then added Bryan's new show to our podroll and announced it on our podcast.

Creating Podcast Badges

Do you need a podcast "badge?" The simple answer is, "Why not?" They cost nothing and could net you some listeners. A badge is just a small graphic that contains your podcast logo or even just the podcast name. By placing one on your site and making it available to your fans, they can copy it and put it on their own sites, linking to your show as a form of endorsement. We cover badges more thoroughly in Chapter 14.

Recording Podcast Promos

A promo is a brief audio file that promotes your podcast. You can store your promo in places where other podcasters can find it, and in many instances podcasters actively solicit promos they can play on their shows. Adam Curry, for example, plays several promos on each of his daily podcasts, which are heard by hundreds of thousands of listeners.

The biggest mistake most people make with their promos is making them too long. Thirty seconds is plenty of time to give listeners a sense of what they'll hear when they "tune in" to your show. Add a couple effects—like your opening theme—and your promo could attract a batch of new listeners.

Some of the places where you can upload promos include the following:

- Podcast Promos (www.podcastpromos.com)

- Podcast Spots (http://podcastspots.com/Add-Podcast-Promo.aspx)

- Podshow Promos (http://promos.podshow.com)

You can also simply post your promo on your own site and make it available for download.

Getting Votes and Reviews for Ranking Services

Some of the podcast directories—notably Podcast Alley—let listeners vote for their favorite podcasts. By providing a link and even asking your listeners to support you with votes, you can elevate your ranking on these services. While this may seem just like a bit of ego gratification, the higher up your show ranks, the more likely it is to be found by people perusing podcast listings. They may scroll through the first 20 or 30 listings, but not the second hundred or so!

Some of these services also let your listeners write reviews. Podcast Alley and Apple's iTunes are two that believe listeners will pay attention to comments submitted by other listeners. Comments we have received at Podcast Alley—which anyone can read—offer opinions like…

- This is essential listening for PR people.

- Haven't missed a show since I first started "tuning in." Definitely on my shortlist of recommended podcasts.

- This is the best in the business category!

Part III

Refining Your Podcast

Chapter 11

Determine What Your Podcast Should Accomplish

How to...

- Determine your audience
- Choose your mission
- Boost your reputation
- Make money from your podcast

Some people podcast just because they want to. They have an aching desire to be heard, to be the voice behind the microphone. For most people, though, even if they do harbor fantasies of radio or Internet stardom, their desire to podcast involves more than that. They wish to accomplish something.

As longtime organizational communication professionals, the authors of this book are both well grounded in the principles of strategic planning. While you can apply many different templates to the planning process, it always begins with the same question: What outcomes are you trying to achieve?

The outcome is the desired state; the result of your effort. In podcasting, the outcomes are as varied and diverse as the number of podcasters pumping out shows. Still, it's not too hard to put many of these outcomes into logical categories, thus helping us discuss the impact that results due to the approach you take to your podcast. In this chapter, we'll explore some of the more common objectives podcasters set for their shows, starting with the simplest and moving up the ladder to some of the loftiest and most challenging goals.

Greeting Card Podcasts

In the old days, you would send your mom and dad a Hallmark card with a couple pictures of the kids tucked into it. Today, you can send them a podcast so they can listen in on family events or hear the voices of family members wishing them well.

We have no idea who Derek and Melissa are, except that, based on their web site, they seem like the all-American couple raising the all-American family. From reading posts, we learn Derek is in the Air Force.

Like many family web sites (this one uses a blog as its foundation), derekandmelissa.com contains entries about birthday parties, outings, and family activities. It shows photos and snapshots as well, which are also common to family web sites. In addition, there is a podcast. This isn't the kind of podcast to which members of the greater podcast audience would be attracted. If you don't know Derek and Melissa, you might find the whole thing rather mundane, like watching home movies of a family you don't know. But for Derek and Melissa's family, hearing a recap of a birthday party or going with the family to a special event can tug at the heartstrings and bring tears to your eyes. The couple even created an audio game in which family members have to identify sounds from Derek and Melissa's home.

There is no rule that says a podcast needs to target a large audience, accomplish anything more than a greeting card does, or develop money-making potential. But the greeting card analogy is a good one. Greeting cards are not meant to merely be signed and mailed. There is always plenty of room for the sender to write a warm personal message to the recipient. That heartfelt greeting can be all the more meaningful with the voices and sounds of people the listeners care about.

These podcasts—growing in popularity due to the ease of production and distribution—nearly always are part of a blog, used as a diary to keep family and friends up-to-date on goings-ons, and offer a place to post photos.

Little planning is required for such podcasts, although some editing should be considered. All those noises that are meaningful to you (because it's the sound of your baby cooing) don't mean second cousins and brothers-in-law want to hear 45 minutes of it!

Frequency is also a consideration for greeting card podcasts. The most devoted family probably won't get around to listening to a daily podcast; even weekly can be a bit of a strain. The best family podcasts are not produced on a schedule, but rather when something noteworthy has occurred: a birthday, an outing, a family holiday at home, a significant family event like a school graduation or a piano recital.

11

Audio Blogs

We have maintained throughout this book that podcasts are different from audio blogs in a number of ways. Still, since an audio blog can be made available for subscription via RSS, it's possible for an audio blog to be a podcast.

Blogs, in this context, are an outlet for people to record their personal thoughts; they are digital diaries. Audio blogs, then, provide the same outlet for people who would rather articulate their thoughts or recollect the events of the day, orally. There are disadvantages to audio blogging versus text blogging, however. For one thing, a reader cannot scan an audio blog to find the one bit that is interesting to him. Most people can read faster than they can listen, so audio blogs require a bigger investment of time. Still, some people are particularly good at articulating their thoughts, while others produce audio blogs that are downright entertaining.

If you just want to talk into your microphone for ten minutes and let people hear what you've recorded, your objectives are fairly simple. Still, if you hope to build an audience, you need to consider a few aspects of podcasting. After all, you're not podcasting just so you can listen to yourself!

In order to meet your simple objective of building an audience for your audio blog, you should find a focus for what you'll talk about. People select podcasts to listen to based on niche interests. If you talk about baseball today and relationship issues tomorrow, a lot of people will tune out. Sure, you may retain a few listeners who enjoy your sense of humor or the passion you bring to your topics, but many will forego listening altogether rather than hope to find an occasional installment where you actually talk about something they care about!

A great example of just such a podcast comes from Rob Safuto, who produces a suite of shows under the label *Podcast NYC*. While several of Safuto's podcasts serve other purposes, there's one installment—"The Pop Culture Rant"—that he uses to get things off his chest regarding irritating aspects of modern culture. Some of Safuto's favorite targets: Hollywood breakups, bad customer service, and thoughtless dog owners. He doesn't talk about work, which has nothing to do with pop culture. He doesn't complain about illness or marital issues. He stays squarely within the bounds of pop culture, which is what his listeners have come to expect. Should he ever start ranting about the weather, he would probably lose listeners. The rants are about matters of interest to his audience.

As a result, Safuto's listenership is large. Once, when he inadvertently gave away the season finale of a TV show, he got e-mail from several countries where the last episode hadn't yet aired. (He apologized later.)

You Want to Play Music

As we've mentioned before, it's possible to view all talk-focused podcasters as riding the coattails of music podcasts. Music podcasts are increasingly the forum listeners are turning to when they want to sample something new. (Music is one of the reasons podcasting is growing in popularity. As radio stations recycle the same 40 songs mandated by corporate playlists, music lovers hungry for new music are turning to channels that deliver it. Podcasting—with its "podsafe" music offered by unsigned bands anxious to get their music heard—is one of the leading sources of new music.)

We've already covered the licensing issues associated with playing music on podcasts (it was in Chapter 10 should you need a quick review), but there's plenty of "podsafe" music available to you, letting you host a music podcast and stay clear of any legal entanglements.

Presuming you do want listeners (if you're spinning the music just for yourself, you surely don't need to record it as a podcast), you should set a couple of objectives for yourself.

First, pick a genre and stick with it. Listeners will subscribe because of their interest in that music, but they won't stay subscribed if they find they never know whether they're going to hear the kind of music they like or another brand of music they're not so crazy about.

Two podcasters come to mind, both successful, who have been so intent upon adhering to their genres that they started second podcasts rather than mix two discrete musical styles in a single show. Michael Butler, host of the pioneering *Rock and Roll Geek Show*, launched a second podcast called *Indiecast* to showcase independent musicians. C.C. Chapman, host of the mainstream rock show *Accident Hash*, rolled out *U-Turn Café* to play mellower music.

Second, don't be afraid to put your passion for the music on display. In the old days (35 years ago), FM radio DJs in the U.S. would exclaim their enthusiasm for the songs they liked. That kind of personal approach to radio ended with the mainstreaming of radio program consultants who were behind some odd radio rules (like a prohibition against playing multiple songs by the same artist in a given time period). People miss that enthusiasm, so don't be shy. Let your listeners know you picked this music because you love it.

You're on a Mission

Some podcasts are designed to motivate you to do something. What they want you to do can be as varied as voting for a particular political candidate to changing your lifestyle habits to enjoy a longer, healthier life if you happen to suffer from a particular condition.

John Edwards is a former U.S. Senator who ran as John Kerry's running mate in the 2004 presidential election. Generally, losing candidates do not have much of a future in U.S. politics, but we suspect John Edwards may surprise a few people. He's flying under the radar, at least as far as traditional political visibility is concerned, but his efforts are establishing a strong connection between Edwards and his wife, Elizabeth, and those who listen to the couple's podcast.

The show, simply titled *John and Elizabeth Edwards' Podcast* (www .oneamericacommittee.com), features the couple seated at their kitchen table talking to each other about family, Elizabeth's battle against cancer, and—of course—politics. In one recent installment, they answered listener questions (naming the person who asked the question and noting that many of the questions were left on the podcast's associated blog), engaging in two-way communication with the audience. Sen. Edwards also discussed his recent travels.

Podcasting is not communication as usual, and politicians should not approach podcasting as politics as usual. Edwards' approach is instructive, not only for politics

11

at the national level, but for anybody seeking to influence listeners around issues of society and policy. Nothing is scripted in the Edwards podcast; the couple sits at their kitchen table and talk (except for those episodes produced on the road). Listeners not only learn about Edwards' politics, they learn about him, his wife, and his family. They get to feel as though they know Edwards personally and, should the opportunity arise to consider him for office again, it won't be his party affiliation or his position on issues that lead many to cast their votes for him. They will vote for John, whose kitchen table conversations they have been a part of for so long.

What, then, are Edwards' objectives for his podcast? You'd have to ask him to know for sure, but we can make a very educated guess. His objective is to rise above the clutter of typical political campaigning and build a base of supporters devoted to him and his family on the personal level that a podcast can create. Specifically, then, Edwards addresses policy and politics but subordinates these themes to the candor and authenticity of a conversation that includes as much commentary about his son's softball games as international relations. He lets the occasional "um" creep into his remarks and he complains about the length of his travels. He reads from no prepared document, and he allows his wife to participate in the conversation as an equal. He listens to the issues raised by his audience and answers off-the-cuff, without the comfort of documents prepared by a staff.

(Please note that we are not taking a political position by spotlighting Edwards. We're just impressed with the way he has embraced podcasting!)

Not all podcasts designed to earn a commitment from listeners are seeking votes. Jerry Cahill lives with cystic fibrosis, a hereditary disease that affects several parts of the body, characterized by frequent infections and growth problems. Most cystic fibrosis sufferers die young from lung failure.

Cahill, however, is 49 (as of this writing) and believes that lifestyle changes can keep cystic fibrosis sufferers alive and thriving. Partnering with the Boomer Esiason Foundation, Cahill produces *The Cystic Fibrosis Podcast* (www.jerrycahill.com), which usually features interviews with others with the disease who have overcome obstacles to lead full lives. Recently, for example, he interviewed the survivor of a double lung transplant who, two years later, was back on the dance floor.

Cahill's objectives are as clear as Edwards', even though the outcomes they seek are as different as night and day. Cahill believes cystic fibrosis should not be an obstacle to a complete and vibrant life, and he believes he knows how to live with the disease. His interviews, as well as his own commentaries, all reinforce this message, interspersed with support for fundraising and research efforts.

Clearly, you are not likely to listen to Cahill's podcast if you (or someone you care about) don't have cystic fibrosis. Then again, if you don't have cystic fibrosis, you're not part of the audience Cahill wants to reach! Knowing his objective, and knowing that his listeners are most likely cystic fibrosis sufferers themselves, Cahill uses a combination of inspiration, case studies, and practical advice to get his message across.

A mission does not have to be so lofty. Michael Geoghegan is on a mission. He doesn't want you to waste your time watching bad movies in your living room. Geoghegan is the host of *Reel Reviews* (among a few other podcasts), with its slogan, "Films Worth Watching." Geoghegan—who is also the author of a terrific podcasting book called *Podcast Solutions*—loves movies. His mission is simply to share with you those movies he truly believes you should watch so you'll enjoy them as much as he did. He sometimes watches a movie several times before doing a show, just so he can talk with enthusiasm and authority about the reasons the movie is so great—and that's all he does on *Reel Reviews*.

The authors' own podcast, *For Immediate Release*, is about the practice of organizational communication, which includes public relations, corporate communications, marketing communications, investor relations, media relations, and the broad range of other business activities designed to strengthen a company's relationship with its various publics. Our particular interest is the role the online world plays in communications, and our objective is to educate our listeners—most (but not all) of whom work in one of the organizational communication disciplines about the new tools of communication and the best ways to use them. We don't sell anything on our podcast other than logowear, like t-shirts that bear the podcast logo (more on this in Chapter 18) —that is, we do not overtly market our individual consulting practices. Marketing is not our objective (although we don't complain about it as a secondary outcome). Our objective is to help our profession get up to speed on changes affecting it. In that sense, we are, we suppose, evangelists of the medium.

As such, our podcast features news, analysis, commentary, case studies, and interviews that support our belief that the social computing revolution is turning communication models on their heads. The feedback we get reinforces our success. Many of our listeners tell us that as result of listening to our podcast they are getting a free education, which is enhancing their careers. That's exactly the kind of feedback we want, because that is our objective!

You Want to Boost Your Reputation

You can use a podcast to improve a company's reputation through a variety of means. It depends partly on the reputation you already have, and partly on the issues your organization faces. Since we are both veteran organizational communication professionals, we want to be clear upfront: No communication effort—not a podcast, not a multi-million-dollar ad campaign, not even a generous donation to a worthy cause—can fix a damaged reputation if you don't address the underlying problem.

What communication can do is deliver messages and engage in discussions that get the word out that the organization deserves a healthy reputation because of its positive behaviors.

Of course, reputation wouldn't be an issue if every organization delivered unparalleled customer service, sold high-value products at reasonable prices, served as a role model for corporate citizenship, was green environmentally, exercised social responsibility, took the right stand on every issue, and never fell victim to unfortunate circumstances.

In the real world, of course, it's not so black and white, and organizations must display those behaviors that can help build or repair a reputation. A podcast is not a panacea, but it certainly is a low-cost, low-risk way to make the company's affirmative behaviors tangible, as well as make the people engaged in them seem human.

Oracle provides an outstanding example. The business software company is not exactly suffering from any serious reputation issues—their growth has been impressive, and the company ranked 66th in the *Financial Times* Global 500. Recognizing that excellent customer relations will always benefit a company's image, the company launched its Oracle Technology Network podcast aimed at Oracle developers, those implementing and working with the company's massive and complex database-driven products. Check out the following description of a recent OTN Podcast:

> *Oracle Fusion Middleware product strategy director Frank Knifsend chats with Peter Lubbers, author of the Oracle Fusion Middleware and Microsoft Interoperability Developer's Guide, about the various ways developers can integrate Oracle Fusion Middleware functionality with Office functionality, and the technologies that make it possible.*

Note that nothing is being sold in this podcast. Listeners probably already have Oracle Fusion Middleware; they just don't know how to make it work with Microsoft Office. The podcast is a service instead of a pitch, providing useful information customers genuinely want.

This is the key to brand-enhancing or reputation-building podcasts. *The American Family* is another example that adheres to this principal even as it employs a different approach. Produced by the Whirlpool brand appliances, the podcast (according to the web site where it can be found — http:// www.whirlpool .com/custserv/promo.jsp?sectionId=563), "will address matters that impact families with diverse backgrounds and experiences. The podcast will feature real, everyday people and/or subject-matter experts." One recent episode, for example, featured "The Accidental Housewife" Julie Edelman, offering tips for reducing stress on Mother's Day. Like Oracle, the podcast does not sell anything. Instead, it establishes a connection between Whirlpool and a service that offers usable, useful advice aimed at its core audience.

The objective, put simply, is to use your podcast to demonstrate the kind of company you are by serving an audience's need for information. The end result will be earned appreciation. Purina's podcast features veterinarians talking about pet care. Jupiter Research, on the other hand, gives away some of its research insights.

Let's face it. It's unlikely anybody will want to download and listen to a 15-minute commercial. Unless the stories are unique and presented with flair and style, few people will listen to feature stories about how your company gave money to the Special Olympics or how employees banded together to clean up a local park. That's neither entertainment nor useful. If you use a podcast to deliver customer service, however—if you can reduce hassle in someone's life—you're bound to experience an uptick in reputation.

The final step is to bolster the community-building, collaborative side of your podcast in order to make your effort more of a conversation. To be perceived as an organization that listens and engages its customers will also serve you well.

(Note: We'll address podcasting for reputational purposes in considerably more detail—including a look at podcasting during difficult times—in Chapter 23.)

11

You Want to Make a Buck

Frankly, there aren't too many podcasts today that are designed to simply generate revenue. The British comedian Ricky Gervais most definitely makes money from his podcast. Initially released as a free podcast, it earned a place in the Guinness Book of Records as the most downloaded podcast. After its initial run, Gervais started charging. Not much, to be sure, but enough that keeping only ten percent of his original audience would make him a very rich…well…richer man.

Not everybody can simply charge for a podcast. Heck, hardly anybody can. Rush Limbaugh, the U.S. political talk show radio host charges for his, but like Gervais, he's an exception.

The best way most people and organizations make money from their podcasts involves getting their listeners to their web sites. Once a listener is on a web site, there are plenty of ways to make some money, and we'll cover them in a few upcoming chapters. (In Chapter 16, we'll talk about sponsorships and advertisers, and in Chapter 18 we'll tell you how to sell merchandise through a podcast.)

Whatever it is on your site that is potentially profitable—from a store to Google Adwords—your objective is to get the listener to go to your web site. Achieving that objective means there must be a reason to visit the site other than the audience's burning desire to give you their money. Some of the reasons listeners might be enticed to visit your site include the following:

- Useful, thorough show notes

- The opportunity to participate in the conversation by posting comments or participating in a live chat during the recoding of the podcast

- The opportunity to do something, like add oneself to the podcaster's Frappr map (www.frappr.com), a free service that allows your listeners to pinpoint themselves on a world map

- A special offer, such as access to a secure part of the site that contains special material or the download of a free whitepaper or PowerPoint presentation

Chapter 12

Define Your Audience

How to…

- Decide the way to target your content to the right audience

- Determine whether to *broad*cast or *narrow*cast

- Identify your audience's interests

In the world of terrestrial radio, the audience is usually easy to define: everybody within reach of the radio station's signal. Of course, the demographics of a radio station vary. Right-wing talk radio will attract a different audience than an album-oriented rock station. But within those broad categories, the scope of the audience is huge.

Podcasting, on the other hand, focuses on niches. An album-oriented rock radio station, for example, might play some Aerosmith followed by Bob Marley. In the world of podcasting, reggae music would most likely be offered in a reggae-themed show.

In other words, the audience for many podcasts will be far more narrowly defined than the audience for a typical radio show.

Broadcasting

You may opt to ignore the niche nature of podcasting and target your show to a broad audience, not unlike that of a radio show. This is what we mean by "broadcasting" (as opposed to the technical definition which involves transmission of a show in real-time).

Plenty of podcasts seek to reach as wide an audience as possible. For example, some of the politically charged talk podcasts are reminiscent of the same kind of shows on talk radio. Some music shows also appeal to generic audiences. *Coverville*, for example, is a podcast during which host Brian Ibbott plays cover songs—new renditions of songs by artists other than the singer or band that played the original. On one recent show, Ibbott played songs originally recorded by Queen, the Eagles, Britney Spears, and the Rolling Stones.

If that's the kind of podcast you want to produce, then mosey on over to Chapter 13—you don't need to read anything else here. However, the world of podcasting (and blogging, for that matter) is far more effective when focused on niches.

Narrowcasting

By identifying a specific audience for your podcast, you enable yourself to take advantage of any number of benefits that come with focusing on a niche through *narrowcasting*:

- **Advertising**   If you should decide to seek sponsors or advertisers to support your podcast, you'll have an easier time if you can identify the niche at which your content is aimed. For example, the fact that our podcast targets communicators and public relations practitioners led a news clipping service to seek us out as a possible venue for the company's ads. If your podcast is about, say, things to do in San Antonio, it's likely that San Antonio businesses will be more inclined to advertise on your podcast than they would on a generic left-wing political talk show.

- **Discoverability**   As people look for podcasts to listen to, it's more likely they'll find yours if your content addresses their unique interests. Take a look, for example, at the Podcast Alley directory of podcasts. If a listener is interested in knitting, a search produces 58 podcasts. That's right: There are 58 podcasts focused on knitting! But it's a lot easier to sift through 58 shows than the 200 that result from a search of "politics" or "music" (the Podcast Alley search utility tops out at 200 results). Furthermore, as your listenership begins to expand, you're bound to find that members of the existing online knitting community will recommend their favorite knitting podcasts to others in the community, building your ranks of listeners even more.

- **Categorization**   Most podcast directories ask for a category and subcategories that define your podcast. The more refined your niche, the easier it will be to slot your podcast into a specific category that, in turn, makes it easier for prospective listeners to find you.

- **Community**   We keep returning to the idea that podcasting isn't just do-it-yourself broadcasting, but rather one of the dimensions of the broader social media phenomenon. That means (among other things) it is an ideal tool for building community. As we have noted in more detail elsewhere in this book, our podcast has built an extensive community of listeners who have come to know us and each other. *For Immediate Release* is the home, then, for this growing community of communicators. Similarly, many other podcasts have become the center of communities of people who share common interests linked with the theme of the podcast. Conversely, it would be hard to build a real community with a broad category like "country music" or "technology."

■ **More community** The preceding bullet discussed building a community of listeners. Another element of community is the group of podcasters to which you can find yourself belonging. *For Immediate Release*, by way of example, has become part of a loose affiliation of podcasters whose shows deal with similar topics, the Communications and Advertising Podcasters of the World (CAPOW). CAPOW is really nothing more than a mailing list, but it's a surprisingly active one with participation from podcasts like *Six Pixels of Separation* (by Mitch Joel, who owns a marketing agency in Montreal, Quebec, Canada), *Across the Sound* (the new marketing podcast by author and speaker Joseph Jaffe), *Managing the Grey* (a marketing podcast by longtime music podcaster C.C. Chapman), *Inside PR* (a Canadian podcast addressing traditional public relations), *NewComm Road*, and a host of others. By leveraging the relationships that emerge from this community, we wind up with better content, more listeners, and greater insights. The same kind of network has emerged around a variety of other podcast niches. Whatever the subject of *your* podcast might be, you'll probably find yourself part of a community of podcasters (and bloggers, too) who address the same topic.

How Deep to Dig?

While niches are great, it is possible to establish a niche that is *too* narrow. By way of example, let's look at podcasts dealing with cars. Some general podcasts of this nature include *AutoTalk*—"devoted to cars, the auto industry, racing, and other car-related observations. Listen to the rants and raves of this automotive enthusiast," according to the description in the Podcast Alley directory.

Within this broader category, however, several podcasts look at one angle or another related to cars. For example, there are podcasts about...

■ **Automotive technology** *Podcast Auto* is "a show about automotive technology. If you are a car geek, or just want to know more about what is happening underneath the hood, this show is for you."

■ **Auto racing** *Motorsports Minute* with Dick Sisich, in which the veteran motorsports announcer and commentator "brings his unique and entertaining take on all forms of auto racing, including NASCAR,

Indycar, Champ Car, NHRA, Formula 1, IMSA, FIA sports cars, the cars, competition, and personalities."

■ **Automotive design** *CarDesign TV*, a video podcast "from car designers for car designers, showing all the latest car design news as well as extensive analyses of new car designs and new car design technology."

Get the idea? Many others exist, including shows that help you make a car buying decision and shows that help first-time drivers. Pretty good niches, eh? But the focus can get even narrower than that. Within the auto racing and motorsports niche is a podcast called *VolksCast Radio*, which is "the only show in the universe that covers the world of competitive air-cooled VW drag racing and collecting. We interview the movers, shakers, and innovators."

Now *that's* a niche! But there are probably enough people engaged in competitive air-cooled VW drag racing and collecting (along with casual fans) to generate a few hundred subscriptions to this podcast's feed—or even considerably more, depending on how well the show was promoted and how much the word spread about it among the VW drag racing community (which we didn't even know existed until we began research for this book!).

Could a show launch with an even narrower focus? "Mechanics and repairs for air-cooled VW drag racers?" Sure, there's no reason it couldn't. But you have to wonder how many people belong to the community of air-cooled VW mechanics, and among those, how many might listen to a podcast?

In order to settle on your niche, you should ask yourself these questions:

■ What am I passionate about?

■ What level of expertise do I have? Do I have a generalist's knowledge of my topic, or can I talk in greater depth on a specific aspect of the subject?

■ How big is the potential audience for the topic about which I am most passionate or knowledgeable? Are there enough prospective listeners to make it worthwhile?

■ Are there other podcasts already addressing this topic? What do I have to offer, or what approach can I take, to offer a different perspective? Is there a subniche of the topic that would be worth a podcast?

■ If I were to offer sponsorships or advertising, what businesses would benefit from reaching my niche audience?

12

Knowing Your Audience

Now that you have settled on a target audience for your podcast, you need to get to know something about them. And it wouldn't hurt if they got to know you, too!

You should learn what you can about the audience in order to produce content you know they will find interesting, compelling, and useful. Remember, the audience isn't everybody interested in your topic—at least, not yet. For now, it's everybody interested in your topic who is already engaged to some extent in the social media space. To learn more about these people, begin (if you haven't already) reading blogs on the topic (Technorati.com is a good place to start looking for these blogs). Subscribe to podcasts on related themes. Several communications podcasters have credited *For Immediate Release* as their inspiration for starting their own podcasts. Reading existing blogs and listening to existing podcasts can help you refine your content focus so that it addresses issues the audience is genuinely interested in.

You can learn more about your audience after your podcast has been up and running for a while by conducting a listener survey. We provide details on listeners' surveys in Chapter 16.

Your potential audience, meanwhile, can get to know *you* when you get engaged in the existing social media space around your topic. All you really need to do is start commenting on blog posts when you have something interesting to add to the conversation. As your name becomes more familiar, people will begin to get a sense that you're somebody who really knows what he's talking about. Then, when you announce that you've launched your podcast, you'll have a ready-made audience of potential listeners from among those who have already come to appreciate your insights and observations.

Chapter 13

Decide on Your Approach

How to...

- ■ Choose a hosting style

- ■ Introduce other voices

- ■ Maintain a consistent format

Knowing what to expect is one of the things that keeps listeners coming back—they like what they've heard and they want more. Your subject matter, the personalities involved, your attitude, and approach to the material all count. But your format is the glue that holds it together.

No rule says you have to stick to a format for every single show, but deviating from the format should be the exception, something to liven things up and keep listeners on their toes. After a deviation, you should return to the format. Format encompasses a number of characteristics, including...

- ■ The hosting configuration

- ■ Whether you have guests or interviews

- ■ Recurring features

Hosts

Personality drives a podcast. Even if you play music on your show, it's your insights, opinions, sense of humor, passion, knowledge, or any combination of these that have people listening to you instead of another podcaster playing the same kinds of music. How the show will be hosted, then, becomes a critical decision.

The decision is a numbers game. Will you have one host? Two? More? What about alternating hosts? The answer will depend on a number of factors. Consider...

- ■ The length of the show

- ■ The nature of the information

- ■ The ability of a single host to carry the show

- ■ The value added—or subtracted—by adding more voices to the show

Solo Hosts

Some of the best-known podcasts are hosted by a single person, and the podcast itself is synonymous with the host. None of the hundreds of thousands of people who listen to Adam Curry's *Daily Source Code* could imagine him with a co-host any more than the millions of Americans who used to tune in to watch Walter Cronkite anchor *The CBS Evening News* could imagine Cronkite sharing his duties with a co-anchor.

A solo host is the optimum solution for very short podcasts in which multiple hosts would prolong the show just to give both voices a chance to be heard. Charles Hodgson, for example, hosts *Podictionary*, a daily podcast that rarely exceeds two minutes, during which Hodgson discusses the etymology of a word. There is just no time for an additional host to interject any kind of meaningful commentary.

A strong sense of presence and dynamic speaking ability will also serve a single host well. If you can talk continuously and maintain enthusiasm while conveying the information you want to get across, you will be fine on your own. You don't need perfect grammar and flawless enunciation. Infectious enthusiasm and high energy can also carry a solo podcaster. (For an example of infectious enthusiasm, give a listen to any of C.C. Chapman's three podcasts, the music-focused *Accident Hash* and *U-Turn Café*, along with his marketing show, *Managing the Gray*.)

If your show is comprised of audio segments from other sources—such as podsafe music or interviews that have been conducted in the field—your job as host is largely the introduction of these segments. If you won't be talking long between each segment, you could also solo-host your show.

Of course, there's nothing wrong with solo-hosting your podcast because it's your podcast and that's just the way you want to do it! You may be doing a podcast just because you want to express your opinions. Michael Geoghegan's *Reel Reviews* gives him the opportunity to talk about the movies he loves. So why would he want to share the mike with someone who may not agree? Just be sure to read our advice in Chapter 8 on how to talk to your audience as individuals, not as a group.

13

Co-hosts

Just as there are some great podcasts with just one host, many podcasts take the co-host approach (including, obviously, ours). One of our favorites, *American Copywriter*, is co-hosted by advertising creatives John January and Tug McTighe from Kansas City. Their banter is so natural and so in synch that it's a pleasure to listen to them riff off one another.

That's one of the keys to the co-host approach: Your podcast will be more engaging to the audience because they are listening to two real people involved in a genuine conversation rather than listening to one person whose talk into a microphone sounds forced.

On *For Immediate Release*, we strive to produce each show with both of us participating in a conversation. Our work and travel schedules, however, mean that sometimes one of us isn't available at the time when the show's recorded. For the first 18 months we produced the program, one of us would host the show alone, usually playing an audio segment the other one produced and forwarded along. Our listeners complained. The show moved more slowly and was far less engaging with only one host—it didn't matter which one of us was behind the mike. So we decided to change the format for days at a stretch when one of us isn't available. We now bring one of our correspondents on as a fill-in co-host so the show can continue to be a conversation instead of a monologue. We have not received a single complaint since moving to this approach.

With co-hosts, you are not limited to a duo. Podcasts can be found with three hosts, including one hockey-focused podcast that features three rabid hockey fans talking about their favorite sport. Some podcasts even feature four or more co-equal participants, such as the most popular independent podcast, *This Week in Tech*, and another technology-focused show, *The Gillmor Gang*.

Both of these shows take on a panel discussion approach. These shows are popular because each of the participants is knowledgeable and brings unique expertise and viewpoints to the discussion. There are risks, however. Both shows have been described by some critics as exercises in listening to people try to talk over one another.

In *This Week in Tech*, lead host Leo Laporte brings together four or five technology experts, ranging from commentators like *PC Magazine*'s John Dvorak to tech innovators like Digg.com's Kevin Rose to talk about the technology news of the week. Ziff-Davis commentator Steve Gillmor, host of *The Gillmor Gang*, similarly brings together some configuration of a regular stable of co-hosts, including *Cluetrain Manifesto* co-author Doc Searls and Ziff-Davis editor Dan Farber to tackle a single issue. The conversations can be equal parts stimulating and frustrating: stimulating because the give-and-take produces insights and surprises, frustrating because it is often difficult to hear one voice over the others competing for dominance.

Time is another factor to consider in these panel discussion–like shows. Both *The Gillmor Gang* and *This Week in Tech* can last well over an hour, almost a requirement if each participant is going to be permitted enough time to share his thoughts and insights. Is your audience willing to sit for 60 to 90 minutes to hear four or five people talking?

Technology is the final factor to consider. How will four or five people join a recording if they are not going to be in the same room? One of the problems many listeners have with *The Gillmor Gang* is the varying audio quality: Gillmor is recording himself on a microphone; some of the participants are calling in via Skype, producing a high-quality sound; and others call in on telephones or even cell phones, generating a lower-quality sound. Bouncing back and forth between these is sometimes disconcerting.

There's also the issue of deciding who will talk next. When the participants of a panel discussion are all in the same room and can see each other (think of something like *The Capitol Gang* on CNN), it's easy to take a cue from one of the other speakers. Trying to figure out when to jump in when you are sitting by yourself and listening to three or four other competing voices can be harder—and produces a podcast that can be difficult to listen to.

Revolving Hosts

Some shows can succeed with a different host each episode. In these shows, the host's personality is considerably less important than the content of the show. IBM's *The Future Of…* is a terrific example, with a couple of hosts taking turns manning the microphone and conducting interviews with IBM staffers who are experts in their fields. The show does not suffer at all for lack of a consistent voice since the interviews—not the host's personality—are the draw.

Interviews

Conducting an effective interview requires some skill. Journalism schools offer entire classes on this topic. If you've ever seen a good interviewer at work, you know it's not just a matter of sitting down with a microphone and asking questions.

The first question to ask is whether interviews are appropriate to your show. You may decide they're not, and you'll never do one. P.W. Fenton's *Digital Flotsam*, which offers brilliantly produced tales of the host's youth, simply is not conducive to interviews, even if PeeDub (as he's known) could round up one of his old childhood chums for a bit of reminiscence.

You may decide an occasional interview is appropriate, particularly if somebody is available who can enhance your discussion of a particular topic. Dave Slusher, the host of *Evil Genius Chronicles*, solo-hosts most of his shows without the addition of any other voices. Every now and then, though, he rounds up an interview with a musician he admires.

You may even decide your show should be nothing *but* interviews. *Podcast 411* is such a show, featuring an interview each episode with a podcaster to discuss that

13

podcaster's show and the way it's produced. *Endurance Planet* consists entirely of interviews with endurance athletes and others involved with endurance sports, such as coaches and book authors.

If you are going to conduct interviews on your podcast, though, you may as well do it right. A good interview is based on solid upfront research. You should know everything you can learn about your interview subject, including the opinions he holds, the actions he has taken, and the influence he has had. Your questions should come from this base of knowledge.

Don't assume, though, that your audience knows everything you know about your interview subject. You can begin a question by stating the fact that drove the question, providing context for the audience. For example: "Senator, you supported legislation that would have made it illegal to sell books by writers who have been convicted of a crime. It seems to me that would keep people from reading Cervantes and Solzhenitsyn. Is that something that occurred to you, or did you have other thoughts about addressing people wrongly convicted or convicted of crimes that shouldn't be against the law?" That question provides much better context than, "How could you support a law against selling books by convicted criminals?"

Ideally, you will have your questions lined up in advance and can simply move down the list as your interview progresses. One important interviewing technique is called "probing." Too often, once a question has been answered, the interviewer simply moves on to the next question when he could have stimulated some interesting responses by following up on the last answer: "Senator, you just said that only books by Americans currently in prison would be covered under your law. Doesn't that create a double standard? An American who has gone to prison as a matter of conscience—protesting an activity he believes to be unjust, for example—can't have his book sold but a child rapist in prison in Peru can benefit from the sale of his books in American bookstores?"

Most of your podcast interviews probably won't be confrontational. In our case, we conduct interviews with people who provide insights into various aspects of online communication. Our goal is simply to use our podcast as a venue for sharing their knowledge with our audience. Every now and then, however, you may find yourself interviewing a guest with whom you disagree. Rob Walch, the host of *Podcast411*, was lucky enough to get U.S. Senator Ted Stevens to agree to an interview on the subject of Internet neutrality (which Stevens opposed and Walch supported). The pair squared off in an engaging and lively debate that garnered a lot of attention in the podosphere.

We have not heard too many interviews conducted in real-time as part of a "live to the hard drive" approach. Most interviews are conducted sometime other than the day of the podcast itself. Shel's wife, Michele, hosts a weekly podcast that is nothing but interviews. She conducts most of the interviews face-to-face, hauling her portable recorder and two microphones to a location where she can sit with her subject. Then she assembles the podcast, importing the opening music, then her intro (which usually concludes with something like, "Earlier this week, I was able to spend some time with Jane Smith, the director of the Acme Museum. Let's listen."), then the interview, followed by her outro, followed by the closing music. Thus, five separate elements are married into a 15-minute (or so) podcast. Her approach to production of *Your Jewish Neighborhood* is typical of the way most podcast interviews are handled.

We have taken a different approach altogether. Our podcast is already long enough without interviews, so we post interviews as separate podcasts outside the scope of *The Hobson & Holtz Report*. We refer to them as *For Immediate Release Interviews*, and promote them on our regular show.

Special Guests

In addition to interview subjects, you could have special guests on your show. Rather than simply ask questions for your guests to answer, these guests could participate in the give-and-take and flow of the show. For example, let's say your podcast is about movies. You're lucky enough to get the movie critic from your hometown newspaper to join you on the show. He can serve as a special one-time co-host or offer his insights and thoughts over the course of the episode.

Correspondents

Having regular correspondents submit regular segments can liven up a podcast, add variety, and introduce a new voice to keep the pace moving along briskly.

Each correspondent should bring something unique to the show in addition to a different voice. Some approaches to correspondents include the following:

- **Geography**   Reports from different parts of the country (or world, or city) could be appropriate, depending on your podcast's theme. If you're focused on sports in the UK, for example, you could have a correspondent from Wales, another from Ireland, and a third from Scotland, to provide updates on sports in those parts of the British realm.

- **Area of expertise**   The range of knowledge of each of your correspondents provides different angles or insights. On our show, Lee Hopkins is

13

an Australian communicator, so he brings a regional flavor to the show, while Dan York works in VoIP security, so his contribution focuses more on technology and is geographically agnostic.

■ **Special segments**   A correspondent can be the host of a recurring special segment, a concept we'll discuss next.

You certainly don't need to have all your correspondents reporting on each and every episode of your show. On *For Immediate Release*, Australian correspondent Lee Hopkins reports on Mondays while U.S. East Coast correspondent Dan York contributes his report on Thursdays.

Recurring Features

Recurring features, like correspondents, can add variety and spice to your podcast. In fact, as noted earlier the role of a correspondent can be as the host of a recurring feature. That's just one approach, however, and by no means a rule—even a solo-hosted podcast can include recurring features.

A recurring feature (which needn't make an appearance in every episode) can be anything from this week's recipe to the joke of the month, from a review of a new car to a rant.

Recurring features present an excellent opportunity for special musical or vocal introductions. Joseph Jaffe, the advertising/marketing guru who hosts the marketing-focused podcast *Across the Sound*, has had themes produced by musician Geoff Smith for segments titled "Rant of the Week" and "Winners and Losers" ("Oh yeah, oh no, here we go, it's Winners and Losers!").

Switching Formats

Things change, and there could be reasons you would want to—or have to—alter your format. Joseph Jaffe, mentioned earlier for the musical themes that introduce his recurring features, began *Across the Sound* as a co-hosted program with A-list public relations blogger Steve Rubel. After a handful of shows, though, Rubel opted to focus his time on blogging and left Jaffe as the solo host. Jaffe has tried several different approaches, including guest co-hosts and solo shows, all of which works well as a mix that provides the audience with some variety. But Jaffe suffered considerable angst trying to decide what to do when Rubel left him alone.

Jaffe's experience is instructive: If you're going to switch formats, think it through and even consider testing it with your listeners. Get some feedback and figure out what they'd like. Once you introduce the change, unless you determine something is fundamentally wrong with it, stick with it long enough for the new format to gel—don't be too quick to abandon it.

Of course, you can also switch formats for a single show. Adam Curry's format is already very loose on *Daily Source Code*, but it is usually Curry in his studio playing some music, talking about the state of podcasting, enthusing about his interests, catching his audience up on his family life, and reporting on Podshow goings-ons. Then suddenly he'll do a show in which he's walking around someplace with a portable rig, chatting with people on the street and making observations about what he's seeing. Curry calls these "soundseeing tours," and they are often welcome breaks from the routine of his daily show. But the next day, he goes back to his standard format, a practice worth emulating.

13

Chapter 14

Incorporate Standard Podcast Elements

How to...

- Use audio inserts effectively
- Break your podcast into segments
- Integrate your podcast with your web site

Most podcasts aren't just recordings. They are shows. They follow a progression that gets familiar to listeners over time, even if occasionally you take a detour or try something different to keep things fresh. Generally, however, there is a beginning, a middle, and an end that contain similar content from week to week.

Some shows may have simple formats. IBM's *The Future Of...* features an introduction to the episode's topic, followed by an interview. Others may be more complex. In producing *For Immediate Release*, we arrange an opening theme, an introduction, news and commentary segments, interviews, reports from field correspondents, listener comments, and an "outro."

For the short, simple shows (and the longer ones as well), you can make them more listenable and give it a sense of pacing by incorporating a mixture of audio elements. Many of these elements will be familiar from the radio. They include the following:

- Opening theme
- Sweeps
- Section introductions
- Shout-outs
- Idents

In addition, we'll look at some typical segments of a podcast to add to the main content of the show:

- Intros
- Outros
- Feedback
- Interviews

Lastly, we'll look at the core elements of your show to include on the web site that serves as your podcast's home, including the following:

- Show notes
- Contact information
- Podcast information
- Archives
- E-mail and privacy policies
- The Creative Commons license
- Advertising or sponsorship information
- Interaction resources

Audio Inserts

How dull would a program be if it started with talk followed by more talk and ended with yet more talk? Even if the content was fascinating beyond belief, the uninterrupted drone of voices would encourage the mind to wander. Your listeners' ears can use a bit of ear candy. A combination of musical and verbal themes, or some appropriate interruptions can help keep listeners focused.

Opening Themes

From business productions to music-oriented shows, most podcasts have some kind of opening theme. These usually involve music, but not always. The point of an opening theme is to kick off the show, immediately let listeners know which show they've selected, and set the tone for the material to come.

Podcasting pioneer and *Daily Source Code* host Adam Curry's theme doesn't feature music until the tail end, despite all-musical themes that introduce special sections of his show. Instead, a mix of sound effects and voice-overs occupy most of the theme. Curry's voice is interrupted by a send-up of a famous line from the movie *Treasure of the Sierra Madre*:

Curry: With 16 million pounds of airplane strapped to my ass...

Bandit: Transmitters?

Curry: ...and the next-generation radio content in my ears...

Bandit: We don't need no stinking transmitters.

Curry: ...I like to think I'm flying into the future.

After which, some music kicks in that allows Curry to start his narrative as the music fades out.

14

Other shows take a similar approach, including Todd Cochrane's *Geek News Central*, which begins with the sound of an old modem connecting as a narrator's voice kicks in.

Many shows opt to use just music for their themes. The music show, *Accident Hash*, for example, has unique music recorded just for host C.C. Chapman's podcast. Even podcasts produced for business, like IBM's *The Future Of…*, use instrumental music to introduce the show. In IBM's case, the music begins just after the ident which says, as simply as it gets, "IBM…podcast!"

For most podcasters, the thought of paying somebody to produce unique theme music is daunting at best. There is an alternative, though, in the form of podsafe music.

Podsafe music is music by artists that are not signed to contracts with record labels represented by the Recording Industry Association of America (RIAA) or one of its many counterparts in other countries. This is the organization that has been suing its customers for downloading or sharing music online. Artists in the podsafe world willingly share their music, usually in hopes of getting additional exposure and broadening their fan base.

The licenses for use of this music vary from site to site, but usually you are allowed to do what you want with it as long as you give credit to the artist. Some musicians, like David Henderson, overtly insist that you can slice their music up into bits and pieces, mix it, mash it, do what you will with it, just so long as their name is associated with it.

Some sources of podsafe music include

The Podsafe Music Network: http://music.podshow.com

PodsafeAudio: http://www.podsafeaudio.com

Garage Band[1]: http://www.garageband.com

Sweeps

Sweeps are short musical or sound-effect segues between parts of the show. National Public Radio (NPR) has made an art out of musical sweeps in its signature broadcasts, *All Things Considered and Morning Edition*. For years, listeners have wanted to know the songs from which the sweeps were extracted. To answer the question, NPR has actually started a podcast that plays these songs in their entirety!

Of course, NPR pays the appropriate fees to be able to play licensed music. (We covered the licensing issues in Chapter 10, where we addressed legal issues.)

---

[1] Not all music on Garage Band is podsafe. Check each artist to see if they allow you to use their music without requesting permission from them.

Most podcasters aren't willing to make that kind of investment. So, like the musical themes that introduce many podcasts, podsafe music is used to create these interludes.

Sound effects work nicely in this situation, too. You can order CDs filled to the brim with sound effects, and even take advantage of some web sites that let you download different kinds of sounds. Some of these include the following:

- **A1 Free Sound Effects**   http://www.a1freesoundeffects.com

- **Sound Effects Library**   http://www.sound-effects-library.com

- **Sound Dogs**   http://www.sounddogs.com

- **Partners in Rhyme**   http://www.partnersinrhyme.com

- **Sound Effects CD Libraries**   http://soundfx.com/sfxcategories.htm

In addition, FindSounds is a search engine for sounds on the Web, and is located at http://www.findsounds.com.

Section Introductions

Transitioning from your routine content to a recurring feature can be awkward. Finding a new way each week to say, "Well, now it's time to hear about our weekly trivia contest" can get old in a hurry. What's more, listeners whose attention is drifting may not even pick up on the fact that you have introduced the trivia feature.

Playing a very brief introduction that your listeners come to recognize is a logical and professional way to overcome this situation. As soon as your voice stops and this audio file begins to play, your listeners' attention is heightened: "Something's happening here," they say to themselves (subconsciously, of course). These introductions provide a bit of variety to your show and offer natural points at which to pause the show if your listener needs a break.

The nature of these introductions can take just about any audio form. *Daily Source Code* podcaster Adam Curry uses musical themes recorded for him by a musician named Geoff Smith (www.thegeoffsmith.com). Comments by two regular contributors are introduced with lyrics like these for segments by a listener named Roger Smalls:

Oooh, aren't you glad he called?

Here's another message from…Roger Smalls…Roger Smalls…

Topic-specific segments also have their own themes on Curry's show. The "metrosexual moment" includes music that continues playing so Curry can speak over it, associating the entire run of the segment with the music. The same is true for the segment on bio-diesel automobiles.

14

For those without the resources to hire someone like Geoff Smith to produce these introductions, there are alternatives. For example, Radio Daddy (at http://www.radiodaddy.com) is a web site where you can submit text for an intro, and a voice-over professional will record it for you, often with background music. For our podcast, for example, we use a section introduction for one of our regular correspondents, an Australian named Lee Hopkins. Here's what we submitted to Radio Daddy, which was recorded as an audio introduction and made available to us in a matter of days:

> *And now, direct from the southern hemisphere, here he is, taking a break from putting another shrimp on the barbie, it's Lee Hopkins!*

Hearing the professional voice makes it clear we are transitioning from whatever we were doing before to Lee's report.

Another one of our correspondents took an even simpler approach. David Phillips had his wife record a simple voice file in which she says, "You're listening to *For Immediate Release*, the Hobson and Holtz Report, with David Phillips." And that's it. No music, no banter, just a simple introduction. Because it's a different voice, though, when Phillips' wife begins talking, the fact that something different is about to begin becomes very obvious.

Shout-Outs

Shout-outs are another effect you can use to break up long tracts of talking, giving listeners a reason to perk up and pay attention. Shout-outs generally refer to some kind of celebrity acknowledging the show: "Hi, this is Mick Jagger, and you're listening to *For Immediate Release*, The Hobson and Holtz Report, the only podcast I ever listen to."

(Of course, we never got such a shout-out, but we can dream.)

Shout-outs, in most cases, are related to the theme of the show. Musicians provide shout-outs to music shows while prominent business people would offer the shout-out for a business show.

To obtain shout-outs, we carry portable digital recorders. When we encounter someone from whom we would like to get a shout-out, we ask politely and, once we get an agreement, we review the kind of thing the individual should say, then we just hold the device up to their lips and press Record.

Idents

Idents—short for "identification"—tells listeners what you're listening to. On the radio, a listener switching stations needs idents to figure out what he's tuned to.

These are usually incredibly short statements, something like, "WARP, all-news radio for the greater Tri-Cities area, 770 AM on your radio dial."

In a podcast, listeners actively select the show they're going to listen to next. On first blush, you would think idents aren't necessary for a podcast. For a couple reasons, though, it's worth adding these extremely brief clips.

First, there are listeners who are visually impaired. They cannot see the information displayed on the screen of a portable digital device and so rely on the idents to make sure they're listening to the episode they intended to. These idents appear at the very beginning of the show and simply list the name of the show, the episode number, and/or the date:

"The Lamp Hanger's Podcast, episode number 35, Wednesday, January 23, 2006."

Idents can also appear at the quarter, third, or halfway point in your podcast. At this point, of course, everybody knows what they're listening to, right? Some podcasts are now being added to the programming of Internet radio stations. Todd Cochrane's *Geek News Central*, for example, is played on multiple Internet radio stations. Since Internet radio content is streamed in real time, listeners hear whatever is playing at the time they tune in; the ident will help them figure out what they're hearing. Mid-show idents can be a bit more conversational:

"You're listening to the Lamp Hanger's podcast, episode 35, on Wednesday, January 23, 2006."

Show Segments

Some shows have only one segment, like IBM's *The Future Of…*, while other shows involve long rants or rambling narratives. For most shows, however, it's not difficult to identify discrete sections or "segments" that are clearly distinct from one another. Creative podcasters can come up with unique segments that nobody has ever dreamed of before.

Intros

The introduction is just what it sounds like. It comes at the beginning of the show and is where you take care of what is fondly known in business circles as "housekeeping." In the intro, you welcome your listeners (it's especially nice to give a special welcome to new listeners while thanking returning listeners for staying subscribed). This is also the place to introduce any program notes—for example, "Be sure to listen next week when we'll have a special guest. In a podcast exclusive, we'll be talking with Popeye the Sailor Man about those arms of his and whether steroids played a role in their development."

14

Any promotions or contests you've introduced should be dealt with here, as should any references to sponsors or advertisers.

Outros

Again, much like it sounds, the outro is the end of the show where you wrap things up. Once again, thank your listeners and invite their feedback; run down the various means by which they can send comments to you (for example, e-mail, a dedicated comment telephone line, or the comment fields on the show blog). Let your listeners know when you'll be back with another episode (if you know) and any special content you plan to present on that program.

On *For Immediate Release*, we also use the outro to remind listeners of any special content that is available—such as PowerPoint presentations or whitepapers— and to remind them of various things they can do, like add themselves to our Frappr map. Other items to mention in your outro can include:

- Reiterating who your sponsors or advertisers are

- Any upcoming live appearances you plan to make (for example, speaking engagements, attending a conference)

- Appeals to buy your products, if you're selling any (we'll cover how to monetize your podcast in the chapters in Part 4)

Feedback

When you read or play your feedback, it will most likely be in a section of the show dedicated to feedback. Not that it has to be. Adam Curry plays and reads listener comments throughout his show. Then again, *Daily Source Code* is one of those podcasts that doesn't adhere to any fixed format. (Hey, when you co-invent podcasting, you're pretty much free to do what you want with your own show!)

Interviews

A lot of podcasts—running the gamut from business to music—routinely feature interviews. You should introduce your interview segment rather than simply jump into the conversation. The introduction to the interview should explain whom you're interviewing, including any pertinent background information, and why this interview would be interesting to your listeners.

Putting all these elements together should result in a "playlist." Here's what one of these playlists looks like for a typical *For Immediate Release: The Hobson & Holtz Report* podcast:

Outline for #132

Ident (Neville)
"FIR Number 132"

Intro (Shel)

Welcome/what show's about

It's the first show of the month, so please vote for FIR at Podcast Alley

News and commentary

Survey results (Neville)

Another pay for placement scandal (Shel)

Lee Hopkins' report

PR, new media, and academia (Neville)

Includes audio comment from Richard Bailey

Kids and communication (Shel)

Brief interview with Shel's daughter about IM, SMS, and MySpace

Shout-out from Robert Scoble

David Phillips' report

Listeners comments (Neville)

Dan York on Podzinger and Podcast Legal Guide (text comment from Gmail)

Sebastien Keil (audio comment)

Sallie Goetch (text comment from show blog)

Outro (Neville)

Where to send comments

Frappr update

Please buy something from our online store (hats, shirts, mugs etc.)

Reminder to vote for us at Podcast Alley

Show notes will be up later today

Closing music (Neville)

14

In addition to keeping us on track, these outlines also help line up the audio clips we'll be playing throughout the show.

Web Site Elements

The final set of elements to address in this chapter is the one that will become an integral part of the online home for your podcast. (Remember, we strongly recommend you use a blog as the place where people can find, subscribe, download, listen to, and interact with your show.)

Show Notes

Show notes are the single most important component of your podcast's online presence—and the one most often ignored by podcasters, professional and independent alike. Show notes offer listeners—and prospective listeners—detailed information about each show. Visitors to your site can get a sense of the nature of the content, while regular listeners can see if you're addressing anything of interest to them. Also, if you do your show notes right—a time-consuming activity, to be sure—listeners can figure out exactly where to fast-forward to in a podcast to hear the bit that most interests them.

A quick journey through several popular podcast sites reveals a variety of approaches to show notes. Music-focused podcasts tend to list the songs played, in order, usually with links either to the site of the artist or a place where listeners can pay to download the song (or both). Talk-oriented podcasts list the topics they discuss and the main segments of the show. The trick to these outlines is to include time codes—the exact minute and second at which the referenced part of the podcast begins.

At *For Immediate Release*, we are proud to have been praised for the detail in our show notes. Each episode's notes include the following information:

- Content summary—A quick overview of what's in this episode. We constrain this to a single paragraph.

- Information on how to retrieve the show, including RSS subscription and direct download, such as links to Podcatching software. We also include the file size and the length of the show in this section.

- Links to people and things we've talked about on the show.

- A detailed outline with time codes

Producing good show notes means you'll need to sit and listen carefully to the entire show, pen in hand. You'll also spend a fair amount of time online, chasing down the links you don't already have. For example, if you talk about an individual in the news, you'll want to find and link to that individual's bio, blog, or web site.

It was taking several hours to produce show notes for each of our twice-weekly shows until we followed Adam Curry's lead and split our show notes into two parts. As we mention in Chapter 15 (on building community with your podcast), we have moved the "links" section of the podcast to a wiki where listeners add links. It still takes plenty of time to produce the time codes, though!

In addition to the practical aspects of show notes, listeners appreciate the effort on their behalf, increasing loyalty to the show.

Contact Information

If you're interested in building community and turning your podcast into a conversation, you need to make it easy for listeners to get in touch with you. Of course, you should cover your contact information in the content of the podcast itself. (We had one listener who was listening to *For Immediate Release* in his car. He heard something about which he wanted to comment, and when he heard us read out the number of our comment line, he used his cell phone to call in his remarks.) But your site is a static reference to your e-mail address, phone numbers, and any other channels you have to encourage feedback. After all, not everybody is in a position to jot down your e-mail address when they're listening; they could be listening on the treadmill or while gardening. Finding the exact point in your podcast where you mentioned your contact information can be a hassle. But a quick visit to your site should make it quick and easy to find that information.

Subscription Links

People can listen to a podcast any way they like (see the next item for an example), but it's the inclusion of the MP3 file in an RSS feed enclosure that defines it as a "podcast." Your must make sure listeners can subscribe to the podcast by providing a link to the RSS feed. It doesn't hurt, in these early days of podcasting, to add some information on how to use the RSS feed by linking to podcatching software, offering instructions, and providing one-click links to services like Apple's iTunes. On many podcast sites (including ours), a listener can click the Subscribe With iTunes button, launching the iTunes software (assuming he has installed iTunes on his computer) and subscribing him so that the podcast now appears in his own list of subscribed shows.

14

Streaming Audio Players

More and more podcasters are giving listeners the option of streaming the podcast directly from the show site. Using Adobe Flash–based players, the listener simply clicks the Play button on the web page and the podcast starts playing.

Streaming podcasts have their disadvantages, of course. If a listener is only halfway through the show and has to close down the browser, the podcast stops playing and the listener would need to revisit the site in order to start playing it again; it does not reside on his hard drive. The program may be interrupted with pauses and gaps if the server is slow in its delivery of the file.

But the streaming ability also lets prospective new listeners sample the show without making the commitment to download it, and sometimes even regular listeners just aren't in a position to retrieve the file. These players are easy to install and, because Flash is platform-agnostic, it will work on Windows, Macintosh, and Linux platforms.

We use a player called Dew, available from http://www.estvideo.com/dew/index/2005/02/16/370-player-flash-mp3-leger-comme-une-plume. The site from which you get the Dew player is in French. We had no trouble figuring it out, and we doubt you will either.

Wimpy is an alternative to Dew (several others exist as well). Available at www.wimpyplayer.com, the Wimpy Flash player allows you to maintain multiple files, letting listeners select what they want to listen to. It also is "skinnable," which means you can apply a look to the player that is consistent with the design theme of your site.

If you use the LibSyn podcasting service, you'll be able to use the Flash player they have created and made available to their subscribers. And for those who house their podcasts on WordPress blogs, a podcast plug-in is available that makes it easy to incorporate a variety of elements to each blog post, including a built-in streaming player. You can get the plug-in at http://www.mightyseek.com/podpress. Another one is available at http://garrickvanburen.com/wordpress-plugins/wpipodcatter.

Podcast Information

Every web usability expert who has ever graced the pages of a book or magazine has included an "about us" page as a fundamental usability requirement. Your podcast site is no exception. Let listeners know who you are. Especially if you're discussing serious topics (as opposed to performing comedy, ranting, or playing music), you should offer your credentials to help listeners make an informed decision about your credibility. Of course, subscription decisions will be based on the quality of your show, not the credentials you present.

Archives

Let people explore your previous episodes by offering an archive of your entire body of work. At *For Immediate Release*, we provide two distinct archives: One is an archive of everything posted to the show blog. (This is easy, since the blogging software we use automatically produces this listing.) The other archive lists, chronologically, links directly to the MP3 files.

E-mail and Privacy Policies

We can thank the vermin of the Net—spammers and phishers—for the need to include e-mail and privacy policies somewhere on your site's home page. These policies should articulate how e-mail is used by your show and what you will and/ or will not do with any e-mail addresses you may gather.

One reason to include these policies as a site element is to provide visitors with some level of reassurance. Another reason, though, is to ensure the vigilante community of blacklisters that your endeavor does not include spamming or phishing among its various activities.

In mid-2005, we found that our domain, forimmediaterelease.biz, had been blacklisted. This did not affect us directly, since we use the domain only for the blog; we send and receive no e-mail at this domain. However, anybody who sends an e-mail with our domain in it could find their e-mail rejected by servers employing one of those blacklists. That's what was happening to e-mails distributed by the International Association for Online Communication (IAOC) when one of its e-mail newsletters represented our show.

We have no idea how we wound up on that list, since we send no e-mail at all, least of all spam. It took several exchanges to have our domain removed from the blacklist, but the blacklister let us know that an e-mail policy on our site would make it easier to avoid these issues. (To their credit, blacklisters are trying to do something about the scourge of spam. However, it is often difficult to get non-spamming domains removed from their lists.)

Creative Commons License

We'll cover Creative Commons in more detail in Chapter 10, where we focus on legal issues, but it's worth noting here that your Creative Commons license should be displayed on the home page of your site or blog.

The Creative Commons license informs visitors to your site of the rights you are providing for your podcast and gives you legal protection against anyone who uses your copyrighted material—yes, your podcast is copyrighted—in a manner contrary to your wishes. Clicking the Creative Commons icon will link visitors

14

to the specifics of your license. The *For Immediate Release* license is a "non-commercial, attribution" license—that is, the podcast is available for anyone to play (in whole or in part) as long as they…

- Don't make money by playing the show
- Give credit to us

Be sure to read Appendix A for more details on the Creative Commons license.

Advertising or Sponsorship Information

If you want to make some money off of your site, you should provide a link to information about how someone can become a sponsor or advertiser. We'll cover this material in greater detail in Part 4 of the book, in the chapter that deals with making money from your podcast. In short, though, you should include a downloadable fact sheet that covers…

- Your advertising/sponsorship rates
- Details about what an advertiser/sponsor gets for his money
- Information about your audience, with as much detail as you can muster

Interaction Resources

In addition to your contact information, you may have various channels through which listeners can interact with the show. For example, in Chapter 15 (where we discuss building community with your podcast), we talk about Michael Butler's use of a chat room to interact with fans who are listening live to the show. We also point you to Frappr, a service that lets your listeners pinpoint their geographic location on a world map. If you provide these or other channels, make sure your listeners can see them on the home page of your site.

Badges

Early in this chapter, we referenced that oft-quoted line from *Treasure of the Sierra Madre*; Adam Curry uses an audio clip in his theme that is a send-up of the famous quote in which a bandit says, "Badges? We don't need no stinking badges…."

The fact is, you could benefit hugely from badges, a promotional technique that many organizations haven't yet figured out. Badges work not only for podcasts; they can help promote everything from a web site to a conference. Badges are small, rectangular graphics that display your podcast logo. Your biggest fans will put that badge on their own web site or blog, linking it to your show. It's free advertising! We offer several versions of our show badge along with the HTML code to add to it so it will link correctly. Some sites offer just the HTML, letting fans draw the graphic itself from the podcast site rather than requiring the fan to download the graphic and then upload it to their own server. This approach also has the virtue of ensuring any change you make to your logo is reflected on all the sites of those who have taken you up on your offer to display your badge.

Chapter 15

Connect with Listeners

How to…

- Use a blog
- Build a community
- Get listener comments
- Include commentary
- Develop user-created content
- Incorporate live chat

You can look at podcasts from many angles. One indisputable dimension of podcasts is their place in the pantheon of social computing tools. While radio's capacity for interactivity is limited to live call-ins, podcasts can build community through the same methods that build community in the blogosphere, among wiki contributors, and within social networks. Not only can podcasts tap into the same aspects of social computing as these tools, they *should*.

In earlier chapters, we explored the differences between podcasts and radio programming. None of these distinctions is more compelling and important than the podcast's social aspects. Building your social network is as vital a part of your podcasting effort as the hardware you use and the theme you choose to identify your show.

The failure to tap into the podcast's social networking potential is the biggest mistake made by most business podcasts and those radio shows repurposed into podcasts. The shows may be good and listeners may be able to subscribe through all the major directories, but there is no opportunity for listeners to interact with the show's hosts or one another. Building community increases listener loyalty, serves as a catalyst for content, and helps spread the word to increase your audience—and, by extension, the size of the community. Podcasts are part of the whole social media milieu. Don't ignore it!

The Podcast/Blog Relationship

The simplest and most sensible way to integrate your podcast into the online social fabric is by housing the podcast on a blog. After all, the podcast has to reside somewhere on the Web. You might as well use the tool that gives you the flexibility to publish all manner of content, list your shows chronologically, and engage your audience.

What Is a Blog?

When people say "blog," they're using a word that was created from the term "web log." *Web log* also refers to a server file that records interactions between the server and clients (such as hits to the web site), which initially caused some confusion, leading to the shortening of the word to blog (although many people continue to refer to them as web logs).

The word can reference either the software used to create and manage a blog or the web site itself.

The software resides on the server and is essentially a lightweight content management system (CMS). This means that the actual content of the blog resides in a database. Text is entered into a web-based form and submitted to the database. When somebody views the blog on the Web, that content is pulled into a template. How the blog looks depends on what template the blogger chose and how she customized it.

Some blogging software is so sophisticated and flexible it is being used to craft non-blog web sites and those web sites that include, but are not limited to, a blog.

The blog site is essentially a personal journal. Unlike handwritten journals, in which the first entry is the oldest, the first entry in a blog is the newest. That is, blog entries appear in reverse chronological order.

Each blog entry has a variety of features, including the following:

■ **Permalinks**   If somebody reads a blog post and wants to link just to that post—not the entire blog—he can link to the permalink. This is a URL dedicated to a single post. Every post created in a blog produces its own unique URL so readers with their own blogs or web sites can create a link to that particular entry; otherwise, readers would have to scroll and page endlessly through a chronological blog to find a given item. As bloggers and others write about an episode of your podcast, they'll want to link to that episode, making it easy for their readers to access the referenced item.

■ **Trackbacks**   Trackbacks are a way for one blogger to let another know that he's written something about an item in that blogger's blog. In addition to a permalink URL, blogs also automatically produce trackback URLs that are accessible with every item posted. If Bob reads a post that Mary wrote on her blog and writes about it, he copies the trackback URL from Mary's post and pastes it into the trackback field on his own blog. As soon as Bob publishes that item, his blog sends a "ping" to Mary's blog, which notifies Mary that Bob has written something about her post and lists it—along with anybody else's trackbacks—on her blog.

15

■ **Comments**   Considered by most people to be the cornerstone of blogging, commenting allows anyone who reads a blog post to add a comment to it. These often turn into multilayered conversations between a blogger and his or her readers.

■ **Blogrolls**   The blogroll lists other blogs the author of the blog reads. Blogrolls serve as a recommendation list, suggesting, "If you like this blog, you may also like these…"

■ **Automatic RSS**   One of the characteristics that defines a podcast, as we've already discussed, is that it is distributed (among other means) through the insertion of an "enclosure" in an RSS feed. Blogging software automatically produces RSS feeds, which precludes the need for you to generate the feed by hand. Several blogging tools include the ability to incorporate the enclosure. LibSyn.com (which we address in Chapter 10) is a hosted blogging service that lets you add a podcast to any blog post, while WordPress is a powerful and free blogging platform you install on your own server (a freely available plug-in for WordPress integrates podcasts into your WordPress posts).

Blogs have many other dimensions. If you're interested in pursuing blogging as an independent activity, plenty of books have been written on blogging that cover everything from how to set up a blog to using a blog as a marketing tool. For our purposes, though, we want to confine our discussion to the role blogs play in building community around a podcast.

Building a Podcast Community with a Blog

By enabling commenting on the blog where you host your podcast, you make it easy for listeners to contribute their comments in a conversational context. Unlike e-mail, which is a single message delivered by a listener to you, a post to the podcast blog is available to other listeners, who are then able to add their own thoughts and ideas. As a result, listeners get to know one another. The more they engage in conversation with each other, the more they coalesce into a community in the truest sense of the word.

On *For Immediate Release*, for example, several of our listeners have formed alliances to undertake their own efforts, some for fun and some for business. They have come to consider *For Immediate Release* the virtual location of the community to which they belong.

The value of the community for the podcaster is multidimensional:

■ **Communities grow**   Participants in the podcast community often encourage their like-minded friends, family, and colleagues to join in the fun. Many of our listeners learned about the podcast through coworkers who told them, "You need to be a part of this!"

■ **Communities come together**   You can call on the community to engage in group activities.

Listener Comments

One of the best ways to build community is to make it easy for your listeners to get to know one another. Reading the comments they contribute on the show is by far the simplest way to begin making those connections, even for those listeners who do not spend a lot of time engaged in conversation on the show blog.

Where Comments Come From

Comments can come from a variety of sources and in a number of formats:

■ **E-mail**   You should set up an e-mail address dedicated to listener comments. With *For Immediate Release*, listeners send comments to fircomments@gmail.com. Our audience is invited to submit comments as regular test messages or as audio files they can attach to the e-mail. Audio files are particularly compelling. They introduce more than just the words of the listener, they allow everyone to hear his or her voice, which helps define the individual as a real person and contributes to the listener's sense that they know the commenter.

One of the great tools for audio comments is a Microsoft Outlook plug-in called Waxmail (www.waxmail.biz). A listener simply opens a new message in Outlook, clicks the Waxmail button, and records a message that is then automatically attached to the message. There is a technical consideration for audio comments, however. Many e-mail systems will reject attachments that exceed a certain size, usually five megabytes (5MB). You would be well-advised to ask your listeners to keep the size of their audio files under that limit. You should also request that your listeners submit the files in a format you can work with, usually MP3 or WAV (although WAV files are considerably larger than MP3).

15

One note of caution about comments: If your podcast becomes popular or resonates with its small audience, you can attract a lot of comments. *Daily Source Code's* Adam Curry could not possibly begin to read and play all the comments he receives—his show would wind up being nothing but listener comments. Thus, you may need to restrict the number of comments you read or play on your show; you may need to summarize the contents of the comments you get; and you may need (as we do) to ask those creating audio comments to keep their messages to a minute or two.

- **Blog comments** If listeners are commenting on your blog, by all means, share those comments on your podcast. You can rest assured that most of your listeners—particularly those who subscribe to the RSS feed—are not visiting the show's site on a regular basis. That means most listeners are not reading the comments contributed to the blog.

- **Call-in line** Give your listeners a plain old telephone line they can call to record their comments. We have received several comments this way from audience members who were listening to the show in their cars and wanted to contribute a comment as soon as they heard an item about which they had something worthwhile to say. They probably wouldn't take the time to compose an e-mail when they got to their office, or record a comment, but as long as they were in their cars, it was no big deal to pick up their cell phones and call the comment line.

    One excellent—and free (we like free)—service for comment lines (assuming your show or a large part of your listener base is in the United States) is K7.net (http://www.k7.net). This service provides you with a dedicated phone number in the 206 area code in Seattle, Washington. You set up your K7.net account so any comments received are automatically saved as WAV files. K7.net notifies you of new comments via e-mail messages that include a link you click to download the file to your computer.

- **Trackbacks** We mentioned trackbacks in the preceding section on blogs. One reason trackbacks are worthwhile to podcasters is that they serve as a source of comments even if you haven't received any direct contributions. Feel free to use what others have written about your show as fodder for your listener comments.

- **Comment submission form** From years of online experience, people have grown accustomed to submitting queries and questions via web-based submission forms. It's not a big deal at all to create one of these for the site that houses your podcast, making it easy for visitors to submit a comment without having to launch an application or create a file.

Where to Include Listener Comments

As to where in your show you read or play listener comments is entirely up to you. Keep in mind that listener comments should enhance, not disrupt, the flow of your podcast. If you only get a few comments, you might consider leading off with them. This brings the community into the podcast early and allows you to engage with your audience and convey the idea that they help drive the show's content. *For Immediate Release*, on the other hand, generates a lot of listener comments, so we save most of it for the end of the show. Therefore, listeners who are only interested in our commentary can shut off the show as soon as listener comments come on, knowing that only our exit music remains after the listener contributions segment.

When a comment relates directly to an item you're addressing in the body of your show, you shouldn't feel compelled to relegate that comment to the comment portion of the show—go ahead and include it as an element of your report on that topic. This is not a rigidly structured mainstream media production, after all. It's a podcast, and flexibility is one of podcasting's hallmarks.

Soliciting Comments

A few podcast listeners may submit comments without any invitation from you, but most may not even think about it unless you overtly extend an invitation. Thus, the invitation to "join in" should be clear both on the podcast and on the web site where the podcast is housed.

The sidebar of every page of *For Immediate Release*'s web site includes a listing of all the ways listeners can contribute their content, as shown in Figure 15-1.

We also make an appeal for listener comments at the beginning and end of every show. Because we don't want to spend too much time on logistics before jumping into the content for which our listeners come to *For Immediate Release*, we keep the initial appeal nice and short. It usually goes something like this:

"We're a listener-driven show, so please send us your comments. Tell us what you think about what you've heard on the show and what you'd like to hear. The show blog lists all the ways you can get your comments to us and we'll cover them at the end of the show."

Then, at the end of the show, we go into more detail, usually recounting the topics we've covered, which serves as a useful reminder of the items about which a listener may have considered commenting when she was hearing it:

15

We want your feedback

Email comments with or without
audio attachments (5 MB/3 minute
limit) to fircomments at gmail dot
com.

North America Comment Line:
+1.206.222.2803

Europe Comment Line:
+44.20.8133.9844

Skype: fircomments

Or try this new Java-based application
to leave a comment no longer than two
minutes directly from your computer
right now:

My Voicemail

Messages
Shel Holtz

Leave me a message
MobaTalk Comment System

FIGURE 15-1   A sidebar element soliciting reader feedback about *For Immediate Release*.

"Tell us what you thought of the items in today's show. What did you think
of Neville's report on CEO blogs? How about Shel's coverage of the Conference
Board's technology conference? Do you have any thoughts on the future of press
releases? What about the use of podcasts for employee communications? Did any
of today's listener comments spark a thought? And, of course, please tell us what
you think of the show in general and let us know if there's anything you think we
ought to be talking about.

"Send your comments by e-mail to fircomments@gmail.com. Feel free to
attach an audio file of up to five megs; no more than two or three minutes, please.
You can also call our comment line at 206-222-2803; that's a U.S. number, so add
+1 for international dialing. And you can always post a comment to our show blog
at www.forimmediaterelease.biz."

Correspondents

At a certain point, hearing the same voice or two can get monotonous, particularly on shows that run more than 15 or 20 minutes. Adding another voice or two as a bridge between sections of the show can break up the monotony. It can also expand the community as listeners realize they have the potential to interact with other members of the audience or even become a regular part of the show.

Correspondents take on a variety of forms in the podosphere, but they all tend to start the same way—as listeners who submit comments. They wind up sending comments more and more regularly until the podcaster decides to make them a regular (or semi-regular) part of the show.

Podfather Adam Curry has turned several of his regular commenters into correspondents simply by adding a musical introduction to their comments. One regular commenter, Roger Smalls (a fan who began as someone Curry feared was stalking him), submits short, pithy audio files. Curry turned to a musician to create a theme for Smalls that begins with the sound of a cell phone ringing.

On *For Immediate Release*, we had no intention of introducing correspondents when we started. Within a couple of months, though, we were hearing routinely from a listener in Australia whose audio comments were professional and entertaining. At one point we were getting a weekly comment, and Shel said— strictly off the top of his head— "If we get one more comment from this guy, we're just going to make him a correspondent."

Sure enough, the next week an audio clip arrived from communicator Lee Hopkins, this one sounding more like a report than a comment. We had a professional record a segment intro for Lee, who now is an integral part of the show. (Lee has since launched his own podcast, a brief weekly look at the elements of effective organizational communication.) Since Hopkins became our first correspondent, we have added three more:

- Dan York, originally a Toronto resident who now reports from his home in Vermont on technical matters. (York has since started his own podcast dealing with Voice over IP security.)

- Eric Schwartzman, a Los Angeles–based public relations practitioner who hosts his own interview-focused podcast called *On the Record Online*. Eric edits his lengthy interviews into short contributions for *For Immediate Release*.

- David Phillips, a UK-based practitioner who takes an academic approach to commentary.

15

By drawing your most avid listeners into the fabric of the show, you give the audience a sense they are part of something rather than detached members of an unseen audience. It also gives your listeners additional fodder about which to add their own feedback.

Listener-Created Show Notes

As noted in Chapter 14, show notes are a vital element of a podcast. Show notes, remember, include time codes that help listeners skip to the content in which they are most interested, and links to web sites that either are referenced in the show or have something to do with content covered during the podcast.

One approach to getting your audience directly involved with your site is to invite them to expand on—or even create—your show notes.

The community creation of show notes was introduced by Adam Curry when he found he simply didn't have the time to produce them himself on a daily basis. (Even at twice a week, we find the show notes to be a time-consuming and labor-intensive task!) Curry moved his show notes from his blog to a wiki where his hundreds of thousands of listeners build the show notes as a way to participate more actively (and, of course, to save Curry the time required to do the work himself).

What Is a Wiki?

A wiki is a web site where invited individuals can create or edit web content directly on the site without needing to use (or knowing how to use) the typical tools of web content creation. By clicking a link that usually reads something like "Edit this page," readers open a basic text editor right on the web page that contains the contents of that page. The tags used to format the text are ridiculously simple to learn (particularly compared to the more complex HTML)—for example, on some wikis, putting an exclamation point (!) before a word or sentence turns that word or sentence into a headline. Inserting an asterisk (*) before a word or sentence makes it a bulleted point.

Some wikis are open to the general public. The best know wiki is Wikipedia (www.wikipedia.org), a community-created and edited encyclopedia. Most wikis, though, require the user to enter a password to access it. One we use extensively is TheNewPR (www.thenewpr.com), a wiki-driven site in which a community of mostly public relations–focused bloggers are creating a resource on the new-media implications for the PR profession. The wiki's owner, a Romanian-born PR practitioner named Constantin Basturea, asks those wanting to contribute to contact him directly in order to ensure they are real people before he will issue them a password. Other wikis require registration, like the WikiFido (www.wikifido.com), a wiki designed to build a community of dog lovers.

Wikis and Podcasts

As new media tools like blogs and wikis and podcasts emerged, few saw how they might work together. The relationship between a podcast and a wiki became clear when Curry set up a wiki where his listeners could create the show notes for each of his episodes.

For most podcasts, though, the listener audience is not large enough to ensure that show notes will be created on a regular basis. For our podcast, we continue to generate show notes for our show blog, featuring a summary of the show's contents, download and subscription links, a Flash player that allows visitors to listen to a stream of the podcast directly from the site and the time codes, including key links to related content. However, we also link to a wiki where our listeners can enhance the show notes, usually by adding pertinent links about which they know but that we may never have heard of. We ask contributors to our wiki to identify themselves, further spreading the names of our community members.

If nobody adds anything to the wiki, the value of the show notes are not diminished since we continue to generate the primary information (time codes, and so on) ourselves. When members of our community do add links and share other knowledge on the wiki component of the show notes, the value is increased for the rest of the listeners.

Incidentally, rather than set up a dedicated wiki just for our expanded show notes, we obtained our own section of TheNewPR wiki (Figure 15-2). By taking advantage of an existing wiki community, we keep the show notes in a logical place where prospective members of our audience already gather, potentially introducing the show to PR practitioners who may otherwise have never found us. Given the number of wikis on the Web, it's altogether possible for you to find one that already serves the audience for your podcast. Odds are the wiki's owner will be more than happy to let you set up shop on his site, since new content only further serves the information needs of his audience.

15

Going Live

The very nature of podcasting is asynchronous—that is, podcasts are not heard live. Rather, listeners download a recorded audio file and listen at their convenience. But in the online world, you can pretty much do whatever you want to do as long as it's possible. Pioneer podcaster Michael Butler, host of *The Rock and Roll Geek Show*,

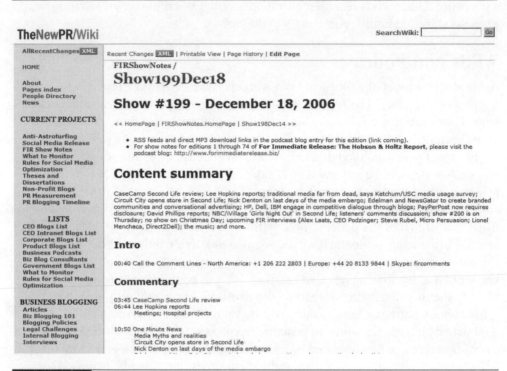

FIGURE 15-2   *For Immediate Release* on TheNewPR wiki.

records his podcast while streaming it live over the Internet. Those members of his audience who can be at their computers when he's recording can listen live and engage in a real-time conversation in a chat room Butler has set up for just that purpose.

A chat room is a utility that allows all the individuals who are logged onto the service to participate in a conversation by typing their thoughts into a text-entry field. When they submit the comments (usually by pressing the ENTER key or clicking a Submit button), the comments become instantly visible on the screen to everybody else in the chat room; the person who contributed the comment is clearly identified. Others can then reply using the same technique, creating a running text dialogue in near-real-time on the screen.

The notion of using a chat room to enhance the audio experience is not a podcasting innovation. U.S. terrestrial radio talk show host Michael Gallagher was one of the first radio personalities to open an Internet chat room where his listeners could participate in a real-time conversation about whatever political topics Gallagher had raised.

Michael Butler simply extended the concept to a podcast. As Gallagher did, Butler keeps an eye on the chat-based conversation and includes commentary about what his listeners are saying as a running part of his show. Of course, when listeners are talking to each other in real time, as shown in the example in Figure 15-3, the sense that they are all part of a community of listeners can spread quickly.

Chris Pirillo takes this concept one step further. Pirillo, host of *The Chris Pirillo Show* podcast, announces the times he'll record (every Thursday night at 6 p.m. Pacific Time), enabling him to offer the same options Butler is able to, with one addition: He has a call-in number that allows listeners to talk with him live on the show, just as in a call-in radio program. The difference, of course, is that most listeners will retrieve the file later and won't be able to call in themselves, but it does add that extra dimension of interactivity and community to the podcast.

In June 2006, we tried our hand at our own live podcast using a new service from Skype called Skypecast, which simulates the features of a conference call. Listeners joined the Skypecast and used a button on their computer screens to ask for the microphone. When we unmuted them, they were able to join us in the conversation while others on the call could talk about what they were hearing by using a chat room utility we set up on our site. By all accounts, this experiment was a rousing success!

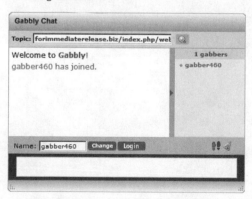

15

FIGURE 15-3   Live chat can contribute to a sense of community.

Putting Faces on Members of the Community

Most of the tools emerging from the online space that has come to be known as "Web 2.0" are collaborative or community-driven in nature. One such tool embraced by bloggers and podcasters allows readers or listeners to identify themselves using the virtual equivalent of sticking a pin in a map of the world.

Frappr (www.frappr.com) is one of a host of sites made possible by Google Maps (maps.google.com), which has released its application protocol interface (API) so anybody can create new tools from it. In this case, the forces behind Frappr have used the map to allow anybody to create a quick-loading visual image of where in the world one's listeners and readers are. Clicking one of the pins on the world map opens a window that displays the information a reader or listener has contributed (see Figure 15-4), which can include a name, company or affiliation, photo or image, and a comment.

The photos, in particular, help build the sense of community when listeners can see what other listeners look like. They can also find other listeners who happen to live nearby; face-to-face contact can further enhance the sense of community. Listeners can get together to share their common interest in the show and its theme,

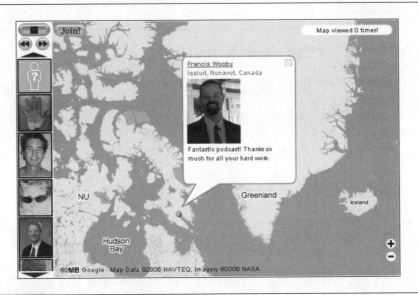

FIGURE 15-4   The Google Maps mashup Frappr lets you pinpoint the locations of listeners and their contributions.

Our listeners

| FIGURE 15-5 | The Frappr scroll lets you see what your listeners look like. |

or even find ways to work together. Since most of the *For Immediate Release* listeners work in the public relations or communications profession, there are opportunities among our listeners to collaborate on projects, form alliances (for example, a company communicator and a freelancer can strike up a relationship), and share knowledge.

One Frappr feature we particularly like is the ability to add a scrolling slide show of the listener photos submitted to Frappr to your own site, as in Figure 15-5.

Building a Community

Members of a community share common bonds that increase the sense of loyalty they feel for a show. The choice is yours though. You can incorporate features and utilities that encourage listeners to form a community or you can treat them as individual, detached members of an audience, not unlike listeners to most terrestrial radio programming. Don't wait and hope for your audience to come together as a community all by themselves. It's not likely to happen without a proactive effort on your part.

Remember, physical communities (like the neighborhood you live in) happen serendipitously; the residents of the neighborhood come together by virtue of the fact that they all happen to live in proximity to one another. Online communities, on the other hand, come together around because of a shared passion about common issues. The Internet is rife with communities, ranging from traditional message boards and e-mail lists to the newer blogs and wikis. By itself, a podcast is not a natural platform for community. Audio is a one-way channel, after all. But that doesn't mean you cannot imbue a podcast with the characteristics of community. By employing the community-building concepts outlined in this chapter, you can turn your one-way audio file into a multidirectional community that continues to grow and grow.

15

Part IV

Make Money with Your Podcast

Chapter 16

Make Money from Your Podcast Through Advertising and Other Means

How to…

- Solicit donations
- Use Google AdSense
- Acquire sponsorships
- Conduct listener surveys
- Charge for advertising
- Set up affiliate programs

Most podcasters have no illusions about getting rich from their shows. Podcasting, for the vast majority of independent podcasters, is a hobby, and like all hobbies, some investment is required. For others, though, podcasting is viewed ultimately as a new career path, a means of generating income and (as the folks at *PodShow* suggest) quitting their day jobs. Even those for whom podcasting is a hobby may find that the day will come when making a few bucks is a desirable goal, if only to cover server and bandwidth costs (along with the growing desire for more and better recording equipment, a syndrome that affects more than a few podcasters).

Podcasters have found a variety of ways to generate income from their podcasts. In this chapter, we'll cover them all with two exceptions:

- Joining a podcast advertising network (addressed in Chapter 17)
- Selling merchandise (covered in Chapter 18)

Donations

When most people think of producing income from their podcasts, their thoughts turn instantly to advertising. Based on your audience, however, there could well be a reason to resist advertising. Many listeners have made it clear that the lack of advertising is one of the things they like most about podcasting and sometimes threaten to stop listening if ads show up. (We wonder about this threat, since most podcast ads are about 10 seconds long at the beginning of the show and/or 30 seconds long at its end. Who would stop listening to content they value because of that? Incidentally, there were those who made the same predictions about blogs allowing advertising, and it just has not held up—people are still reading those blogs as long as the content continues to be worthwhile to them.)

In any case, you may decide that advertising just isn't an approach you want to take. In addition to keeping your listeners happy, you may not want to do anything that makes it seem you are biased in any way, shape, or form. If you start talking positively about your advertisers' products, your credibility could be shot. Candor and transparency apply to this situation, too. If you admit that you know the advertiser, or that you're being paid to talk about it, you can retain the credibility needed to keep your listeners—as long as you don't gush about the product or service to the point of being over the top.

One way to recover some of your costs without selling time and space to a company and its products is to solicit contributions. Several podcasts ask for a small donation in exchange for the ability to freely download and listen to the show. Among these are the extremely popular *This Week in Tech*, which asks for two dollars each month from regular listeners to the show. There is also a button that allows listeners to donate any amount, whether it's more or less than the suggested contribution. "Your donation keeps our shows on the air," the web site proclaims. It's not just wildly successful shows that solicit; many smaller shows do, too, like *Pop Culture Rant*, an entertaining podcast in which host Rob Safuto rails against whatever happens to have irked him the past week (at www.podcastnyc.net/prc/podcast.html).

What do *TWIT* and *Pop Culture Rant* have in common? Not only do they solicit donations to help underwrite the cost of their podcasts, they use the same service to take those donations. The service, PayPal, is owned by eBay, the online auction service. eBay acquired PayPal in order to provide auction bidders with a quick and easy way to pay for their purchases, and for those putting items up for bid to collect. (In the days before PayPal, you needed a merchant account to accept online payments.)

Setting up a PayPal account is simple and free. You provide PayPal with information about your bank account, which you will use to add funds to your PayPal account so you can pay others. It's also where money is transferred when people pay you.

During your podcast (generally, either at the very beginning, during your intro, or at the end when you're presenting your outro), you can direct listeners to your podcast blog or web site and the donation link. Say something like this: "We're able to continue producing this podcast due to very generous donations from listeners. If you like what you hear on this podcast and are so inclined, visit our site and click the Donate button. These donations help cover our server and bandwidth costs."

16

On the site itself, you can offer some verbiage around your request for donations, as Leo Laporte does for *TWIT* in the following illustration.

Or you can use a simple PayPal Donate button, as Safuto does on *Pop Culture Rant*. At *English for Everyone*, the English-as-a-second-language podcast features an entire page explaining the PayPal donation process (see Figure 16-1).

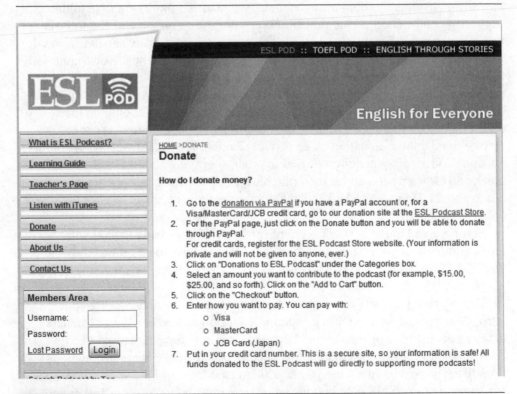

FIGURE 16-1   The PayPal donation page at *English for Everyone*

One way to inspire donations is to offer something in return. If you have stickers with your podcast logo or t-shirts, you can offer them in exchange for a donation of a certain amount (for example, $10 gets you a sticker, $25 gets you a shirt). Mainly, though, you are appealing to the kindheartedness of your listeners to help out. Their main motivation, you should make clear, is the continued production of the show whose content they find so compelling, valuable, and useful.

Google AdSense

One of the most common money-making ventures employed by podcasters and bloggers is participation in the Google AdSense program. Participating is free and easy, and usually a one-step process that doesn't need to be repeated. Unfortunately, unless you have tremendously high traffic on your site, you're not likely to make much money from AdSense. The fact that it's free and easy, though, doesn't stop a lot of people from trying!

To get involved with AdSense, visit the Google site and sign up at www.google .com/adsense. Google will make sure you have a legitimate web site. Once your site has been approved, Google will provide you with code to paste into your web page template. Once this code is embedded in your site, the space where you designated it should go will be populated with text ads every time someone visits that page—ads that are relevant to the content on your page! In other words, if your posts are about your podcast dedicated to volleyball, the ads that appear will have something to do with volleyball, or at least sports.

The way this works is through the flip-side of AdSense, Google AdWords. Here, advertisers bid for keywords. If their bid is high enough, the link to their web site will appear on the pages of AdSense users when your page has content that matches that word. Thus, the manufacturer of volleyball nets might bid on the word "volleyball," so a link to his site appears on the page of any participating site owner—including yours—that contains the appropriate key word.

Here's how Google AdSense looks on *Engadget*, a popular podcast and blog dedicated to electronic gadgets and devices (Figure 16-2).

So why won't you get rich with Google AdSense? You could, if enough people clicked the ads. That's what it takes to get paid: clicks. Just how much you'll make depends on a variety of factors, but Google won't even give a hint on its web site, explaining, "The best way to find out how much you'll earn is to sign up and start showing ads on your web pages." Most podcasters report making just a few dollars a month from their AdSense links. It also could result in your competition advertising on your site! Finally, there has been some criticism of "click fraud" that Google AdSense has enabled.

16

FIGURE 16-2   An example of Google AdSense ads in a podcast blog (in this case, *Engadget*).

Sponsorships

You can eschew advertising and still have an organization underwrite your costs by obtaining one or more sponsors. Sponsorship and advertising are different, although that difference may strike some as subtle. If you've ever watched public television or listened to public radio in the United States, you've heard about sponsors. Shows like *Morning Stories*, which also happens to be available as a podcast, are often introduced with a voiceover telling you that "*Morning Stories* is sponsored by the Edna and Horace Krumdiddle Foundation, providing grants to crumbs everywhere." (That's not a real sponsor, in case you were wondering. We made it up.)

Rather than pitch a product or service, which an advertiser would do, a sponsor just expects a mention about the organization in exchange for its sponsorship. (The whole sponsorship notion gets a little muddy thanks to television and radio introducing the phrase, "We'll be back right after this word from our sponsor." They really don't mean "sponsor," though; they mean "advertiser." But sponsor sounds a lot better.)

So who would pay to sponsor your podcast? Finding a sponsor is a matter of alignment. For instance, who would want to be associated with your show? If your show has a charitable bent to it, finding a sponsor could be remarkably easy.

For example, *The Cystic Fibrosis Podcast* is sponsored by the Boomer Esiason Foundation, which is dedicated to finding a cure for the deadly disease.

Professional associations represent another possible angle for a sponsor. If we produced a podcast dealing with human resources, we might approach the Society for Human Resources Management (SHRM) about sponsoring the show. Trade publications might represent another avenue. A podcast about the toy industry, for example, could draw the interest of *TD Monthly*, a trade magazine for the toy, hobby, game, and gift industries. Other prospective sponsors include conferences and conventions, nonprofit organizations, and publishers.

What to Charge for a Sponsorship

It's easier to set the fee for an advertisement than it is for a sponsorship. Since you're not linking the sponsorship to prospective customers and potential sales, the terms of a sponsorship can be a lot more flexible. Still, the more listeners you have, the more you can feel comfortable charging.

You can set a rate or you can invite an interested organization to make you an offer. Rather than charge on a per-show basis, it can be easier to convince a possible sponsor to part with their money in exchange for a month-long sponsorship. For example, you can offer a month's worth of audio and web promotion for $1000.

It's important to list what a sponsor gets in exchange for their sponsorship. For example, you can offer a mention at the beginning of the podcast and another at the end, along with a graphic on your blog or web page. As you'll see, these are pretty much the same offers you'll make for advertisements, but there are considerable differences between the two, both in terms of what you can charge and the pitch you'll have to make to sell an ad.

Advertising

If sponsors are less formal, advertising arrangements are the opposite: very formal. Companies advertise in the pure, unadulterated hopes of selling some of their products and services to your listeners. If you can't convince an advertiser that your audience is a perfect match for their wares, they will have no interest in talking with you.

Selling advertising, then, begins with knowing enough about your audience to be able to describe its characteristics to a company with advertising dollars to spend. This might sound like a daunting task. After all, your subscribers are mostly strangers who have found your RSS feed. You may hear from a handful who send comments and otherwise communicate with you, but most listeners are just that—

16

anonymous listeners. You can learn a few things about them from looking at your RSS statistics, but not much. The best way to gather this information is to ask, and one way to ask is to conduct a survey.

Listener Surveys

It's actually pretty easy to conduct a survey of your listeners thanks to online survey programs like Zoomerang (www.zoomerang.com) and Survey Monkey (www.survemonkey.com). Both of these services offer free levels with limited functionality, though it's probably enough to meet your needs. Zoomerang lets you develop a complete survey, but you have to wrap it up within a week. Survey Monkey's surveys last as long as you like, but you're limited to ten questions and 100 responses. A professional subscription to Survey Monkey is $19.95, which gives you one thousand responses per month and a variety of advanced features. At Zoomerang, $599 per year gets you unlimited surveys, responses, and other features. In addition, there is a wide variety of other online survey products you can explore, including:

- Infopoll (www.infopoll.net)
- Survey Crafter (www.surveycrafter.com)
- Cool Surveys (www.coolsurveys.com)
- EZ Survey (www.raosoft.com)

Once you have a survey platform selected, you need to figure out what questions to ask. This, of course, depends on what you want to know, which in turn is based on what you think potential advertisers will want to know. For example, let's say you're going to sell ads for a business-focused podcast. Advertisers may want to know the following about the audience:

- The kinds of organizations they work for (for example, for-profit or nonprofit)
- Their titles
- Whether they have budget authority
- How much experience they have in their industry

Let's look at another podcast genre. Tim Bourquin hosted *Endurance Planet*, a podcast for endurance athletes (at www.enduranceplanet.com), which he recently sold. Potential advertisers were more interested in whether Tim's audience is inclined to buy their products themselves, not with their departmental budgets. Thus, Tim listed their ages, household income, gender, education range, and—perhaps most important—how much money they spend annually on their athletic-related equipment, nutrition, and training.

Selling Ads

Once you have your audience information in order, it's time to present it to your potential advertisers. You could do worse than emulate Tim Bourquin's approach, which includes two core elements.

First, he has a page on his podcast site, linked from the home page under the simple label, "Advertise." The page is headlined, "Advertise with Audio," and subtitled, "Reach 25,000 endurance athletes monthly!" (*Endurance Planet* features about eight shows per month, so some 4000 athletes probably listen to any given episode, totaling 25,000 or so each month.)

The pitch begins, "EndurancePlanet.com offers a truly unique method of advertising to a high-affluent, tech-savvy amateur and professional athlete community. Perfect for promoting races, equipment, clothing, nutrition or any other company looking for a unique and effective way to gain repeated exposure to endurance athletes." From there, a bullet list covers all the various benefits sponsoring the show, including a mention at the beginning and end of a show, a logo and link on the home page, and a link in the podcast RSS feed.

Next, Bourquin explains how podcast advertising can help a company sell more of its product:

> EndurancePlanet.com has built that trust with its listeners by providing great content. Because only two commercials are featured in each interview, listeners are not "tuning out" like they would during a 10-minute commercial break on FM or AM radio.

> Each daily interview is listened to by an average of 3500 listeners on the first day, and on average another 5000 times after it is moved into the archives. Eighty-five percent of those listeners listen to the interview in its entirety because we limit the length of each interview to 12–15 minutes. Visitors to the site listen to an average of three interviews on each visit.

> Twenty-five thousand UNIQUE listeners tune into EndurancePlanet.com each month. Many return day in and day out to hear the new daily interview—resulting in repeated exposure for your brand to a highly targeted audience—a critical component of advertising success.

16

Recently, Arbitron did a study (click here for a free copy of the research) on the effectiveness of advertising on Internet broadcasts. In Arbitron's own words: "Internet broadcast consumers spend more, are more eager to try new products and services, and are a compelling advertising target."

The final element of Tim's advertising page is a link to a downloadable Adobe Acrobat PDF file called a "media kit." This kit goes into considerably more detail than the brief web page, based on the idea that a potential advertiser has become intrigued by the web page and now wants to know more. The two-page media kit includes the following elements:

- **General information**   Background about the podcast

- **Competitive edge**   Information about *Endurance Planet*'s unique ability to attract a target audience, along with general information about the value of Internet audio in general as an advertising platform, including a quote from an Arbitron study: "Internet broadcast consumers spend more, are more eager to try new products and services, and are a compelling advertising target…"

- **How EndurancePlanet.com attracts amateur and pro athletes**   A discussion of the techniques—such as search engine optimization—used to draw the right people to the podcast

- **Listener demographics**   The breakdown of listener ages, gender, income, education, and athletics budget

The sheet also reiterates parts of the advertising web page, such as benefits of advertising and an explanation of how the podcast can aid a company's sales effort.

Companies that have taken *Endurance Planet* up on its advertising offer include Gatorade and Fleet Sports.

How Much Should You Charge?

Podcast advertising is a new concept and no rate guidelines have emerged as they have for virtually every other medium. Some experts talk about CPM—cost per thousand (M is the Roman numeral for one thousand), but CPM really does not work in the podcast world. The notion of CPM is based on traditional advertising, as in a magazine or a newspaper, or television or radio show. Here's the idea: With mass market advertising, advertisers hope that some percentage of the entire audience is interested in their products or services. Think about a popular television series or a highly rated radio talk show. The audience may have some demographic characteristics in common, but beyond that, they are a diverse group. Still, advertisers can make certain assumptions from the demographics they have. Based on that information, they pick the shows most likely to attract their target audience. Among every thousand viewers of the show, or readers of the magazine, advertisers can hope enough belong to that target audience. Thus, the amount they pay is based on how many thousand viewers, listeners, or readers see or hear the ad.

CPM doesn't work in podcasting for a lot of reasons. First, not many podcasts have the hundreds of thousands of listeners they would need to make any money charging for each thousand. More significantly, though, if the podcast is specialized, the audience could be made up of one hundred percent of the target audience! Looking at *Endurance Planet* again, you have to wonder how many people would listen to these interviews who aren't endurance athletes. Not only is an advertisement reaching a concentrated segment of the target audience, but likely a very influential one. It's not difficult to imagine a listener telling others in her community what she learned on the podcast.

Endurance Planet charges $500 per interview (episode) with a minimum four-episode buy. That's $2000 for reaching up to 25,000 hard-core endurance athletes who could influence the buying habits of others. Who wouldn't find *that* attractive?

Until some standards emerge, you will need to assess the value of your podcast's audience to potential advertisers anxious to reach those listeners and test your rates, making adjustments until you find the right level. It is a good idea, though, to offer bundles in which advertising is offered for a month's worth of shows.

An additional alternative was used to great success by the video podcast, *Rocketboom*, which auctioned off a week's worth of ads on its daily show. The winning bid wouldn't just get the ad; *Rocketboom*'s creative team would create their entire weeklong campaign. The video blog (which has viewership in the hundreds of thousands each day) earned a high bid of $45,000.

This approach is worth considering if your show attracts a *Rocketboom* or *Daily Source Code*-sized audience. Otherwise, stick with a more basic advertising sales approach.

The Nature of the Ads

Internet service provider Earthlink was one of the first advertisers *PodShow* obtained. Podcasts in the *PodShow* fold suddenly began playing the same commercial Earthlink was running on broadcast radio, a tie-in to its television campaign. Listeners *hated* it. They perceived podcasts as different than radio and resented being made to sit through the same promotion that led them to shift from radio to podcasts in the first place.

16

Eventually, Earthlink and *PodShow* agreed to co-sponsor a contest that encouraged listeners to create their own Earthlink ads, leveraging the consumer-generated content phenomenon.

You don't need to run a contest to get advertising consistent with the podcasting ideal, but you should offer to produce the ads or help the advertiser produce ads that will work with your audience. You could just read a script, too, or talk briefly about the advertiser.

One last point about advertising: Your listeners will tolerate it even more if there's something in it for them besides a pitch. An early pioneer of podcast advertising is domain registration service GoDaddy.com, which lets podcasters customize code names listeners can use to get discounts on the company's services. *Accident Hash* host C.C. Chapman reminds listeners to enter the code "hash3" into the coupon field on GoDaddy.com's web site to take advantage of these discounts.

Affiliate Programs

One last revenue-generated opportunity warrants brief discussion. You can join affiliate programs and create a space on your podcast's web site to promote the products. Amazon.com offers the most obvious affiliate program that makes sense for a lot of podcasts. Whatever the subject of your show, you can probably find several books your audience would be interested in. Offer a bookstore on your topic and you can collect a percentage on each book sold. Your podcast could even offer a "book of the week" to highlight a particular book and encourage listeners to visit the site.

Hundreds and hundreds of commerce sites on the web offer affiliate programs—many that may be in your podcasting space, serving your market. We'll talk specifically about affiliate programs and other ways to sell merchandise on your podcast in Chapter 18.

Chapter 17

Reach Out to Podcast Networks

How to…

- Choose a podcast network to join
- Gain revenue from podcast networks
- Meet other podcasters offline

If your podcast fits into a logical category, chances are there's a network out there you can join. You could even build your own podcast network into a business. Or you could join a large network that spans topic boundaries in order to attract advertising.

So what is a podcast network? At its most basic level, it's a group of podcasts that band together based on the idea that there is strength in numbers. A network's web site serves as a kind of mini-directory of specialty podcasts. They can focus more directly on the theme than a general directory can. For example, a network of technology podcasts can offer features and bonuses unique to technology.

Networks generate linkages as each podcast touts its membership in the network. On their web sites they display badges or even more sophisticated features, like dynamic lists of items posted recently by other members of the network. Members of the network can also share their knowledge and resources with one another, using a forum or a private blog.

At another level are podcast networks whose primary goal is to generate advertising. Advertisers may not be thrilled at spending money to reach the 500 or 1000 listeners that make up one show's audience, but the 20,000 listeners that make up the audiences of 15 or 20 podcasts is another thing altogether.

Some podcast networks focus on just one theme, while others try to do it all. Let's start by looking at a basic alliance of podcasters.

Strength in Numbers

So you've started up a "podsafe" music podcast and you want people to find out about it. You've done everything we suggested in Chapter 10 (where we went into some detail about how to promote your podcast), your numbers look good, but you want more. What else can you do?

One option is to become a member of the Association of Music Podcasting (AMP), located on the Web at www.musicpodcasting.org. AMP's premise is as simple as can be. On the web site, you'll find a listing of all the member podcasts. Each of these podcasts is invited to note on their own web sites that they are proud AMP members, with a link to the AMP site (as in the example in Figure 17-1, from Audio Gumshoe at www.richpalmer.com/podcasts). Thus, anybody listening to one AMP member show is in a position to find others.

| FIGURE 17-1 | Audio Gumshoe announces its membership in the Association of Music Podcasting |

That's not where the advantage of belonging to AMP ends, however. AMP produces its own podcast, a weekly show called *AMPed* that features songs played on several of its members' shows. This showcase introduces listeners to the styles and genres covered by participating members.

In essence, AMP is a simple execution of the social computing model in which links within the community drive traffic to individual podcasts based on listener interest and reaction. The AMP site (Figure 17-2) is not perfect by any stretch of the imagination. Categories would be a good idea, for instance—it's difficult to figure out which podcasts play blues versus those that play punk. Still, the give-and-take between member podcast sites and the AMP site benefits everybody.

Everyone Profits

The next level of a network brings money into the equation. As noted earlier in the chapter, it's easier to convince an advertiser to spend money to get exposure on 20 podcasts with a combined listenership of 10,000 than one podcast with a listenership of a few hundred. A consortium of like-themed podcasts can present its advertising offer to prospective advertisers based on the cumulative reach of all member podcasts. When a deal is struck, each podcaster in the network runs the same ad and each gets a slice of the income.

An example of such a network is the brainchild of Todd Cochrane, whose *Geek News Central* podcast was an early entrant into the podosphere (you'll find it at geeknewscentral.com). *Geek News Central*—or *GNC*—is one of many podcasts dedicated to discussions of technology issues; Podcast Alley lists nearly 3000 of them. Cochrane created Tech Podcasts, a network for technology podcasters, designed primarily to generate income through common advertising. At the time this chapter was written, several ads appeared on the TechPodcasts.com web site,

17

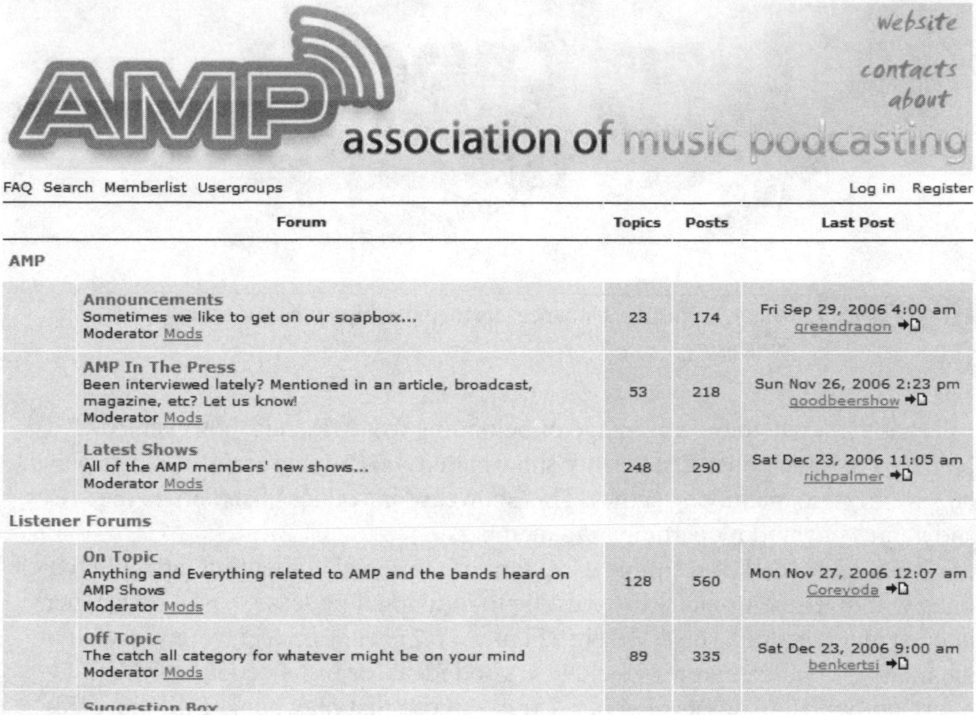

FIGURE 17-2   AMP provides a community for music podcasts

including domain registration service GoDaddy.com and online meeting provider GoToMeeting.com. In addition, the network is collecting some revenue by including Google AdWords on its site.

Some 80 podcasts have joined Cochrane's network, categorized into several logical buckets (like Apple, Digital Imaging and Video Production, Gaming, Programming, Tech Trends, and Technology News, among others).

The Tech Podcast Network (TPN) has two tiers of membership: member and affiliate. Members' shows are listed in the directory and, in return, they agree to produce family-friendly content (Cochrane, a father of young children, prides himself on shows that are free of any explicit content). Affiliates agree to include the TPN banner on their site, among other conditions. TPN affiliates also participate in advertising programs, sharing 90 percent of the revenue generated; the other 10 percent covers administrative costs.

TPN is just one of Cochrane's podcast ventures. TPN is part of Podcast Connect, which also includes the annual Podcast Awards (presented at the Portable Media and Podcasting Expo, held in 2005 and 2006 in Ontario, California), RawVoice (a second business venture), and some other properties. One of the RawVoice efforts is the Podcaster News Network (PNN), another type of network worth looking at.

On the PNN, 59 podcasts that offer the latest news on just about anything are organized by category. These very short podcasts—usually under five minutes—cover topics like sports, entertainment, lifestyle, health, business, politics, technology, and travel. Some of these podcasts are available elsewhere on the Web, like Alan Lew's *Travelography*. Allowing additional distribution through the PNN simply exposes the podcast to more prospective listeners. Other shows are recorded exclusively for the PNN, and it is through the network that these podcasters distribute their shows.

Registered users of the PNN can assemble the podcasts they'll receive through a single RSS feed. For people interested in producing short, newsy podcasts, inquiring about becoming part of the PNN network may be the way to go, with much of the ground work—like handling the online home for the show—done by the network.

The process of joining a network varies from network to network.

Big-Time Networks

Some big networks are less interested in satisfying a topic niche than they are in providing the infrastructure needed to generate advertising revenue, and lots of it. These ventures cover the waterfront in terms of the types of shows they bring into their fold, and they offer a host of services to make affiliation with the network desirable.

PodShow is the granddaddy of these mega-networks. Founded by podcasting innovator Adam Curry and his business partner, musician Ron Bloom, *PodShow* seeks to be a soup-to-nuts solution for podcasters. Curry has repeatedly expressed his desire for *PodShow* to allow podcasters to concentrate on their content and make money—some, he hopes, will even be able to "quit their day jobs," as the *PodShow* slogan goes. Signing on as a *PodShow* podcaster gets you the PodShowPDN (Podcast Delivery Network), which the company hosts in conjunction with its partner, Limelight Networks, a digital content delivery service. *PodShow* podcasters share advertising revenue and are listed on *PodShow*'s directories, they receive traffic reports, and take advantage of other services the network provides.

17

Most of the other large networks are advertising-specific in nature. The names in the space include the likes of *Podtrac*, *Kiptronic*, and *RadioTail*. Most have venture capital backing them (as does *PodShow*) based on the belief that podcasting could produce advertising revenues in the billions of dollars.

To attract podcasters, these networks offer services like tracking downloads and subscriptions. They also handle the insertion of ads into shows. Advertisers can upload pre-recorded advertisements, and can also upload scripts the podcast host can read. The services tend to offer 10-second spots to be played or read within the first minute or two of the podcast, or 30-second spots that play at the end of the show. Some services are working on a means of inserting ads into the body of the show. Some services also are able to insert local ads into shows that cover a defined geography (such as a show focused on one football team). In addition, the networks are selling ads for some of the most popular podcasts through auctions.

Social Networks for Podcasters

Not all networks are designed to produce revenue or build your audience. Some networking is done to make contacts and share knowledge. These are the goals of a new breed of podcast networks characterized by *PodShow+* (an outgrowth of PodShow, Inc.) and *Blubrry*, a venture of Todd Cochrane's RawVoice project.

These services work like most other social networking sites. They allow podcasters and listeners to build their own home pages with profiles and lists of their favorite podcasts, as shown in Figure 17-3. *PodShow* promises that you can "build your own network of people and podcasts that are fueling the podcast revolution." (At the time this book was being written, *PodShow* was accepting pre-registrations for PodShow+.) *Blubrry* promises "a place where podcasters and listeners can meet, interact, and learn from each other." *Blubrry* also plans to run advertising campaigns. According to its web site, the company wants members of the network to "build *BluBrry* by mentioning us in your podcast and giving our team the opportunity to help you find sponsors and underwriters for your show."

Blubrry provides a broad range of features to entice podcasts to its network. Listeners can "hot pick" a show, creating a social ranking of shows much the same way Digg.com lets readers rank news stories. Visitors to the site can play a live stream of any podcast without having to subscribe or download.

As the number of podcasts continues to increase and podcasters look for ways to find an audience, the number of networks like *Podshow+*, *Blubrry*, *Kiptronic*, *Podtrac*, and *RadioTail* will continue to grow and the features they offer will continue to expand.

FIGURE 17-3   The *For Immediate Release* profile on Blubrry.com

Face-to-Face Meetups

The final type of network to discuss is the kind you take advantage of *offline*. In virtually every large, and many mid-sized cities, you can find a local podcasters network of meetups that makes it easy to get together with other podcasters to share resources and knowledge.

These groups usually meet monthly in restaurants or bars. The formats of the sessions vary, from casual mixers to more formal gatherings in which each participant introduces himself and talks about what he's working on.

As shown in Table 17-1, local podcasters associations meet in the following U.S. cities, among other places.

It's easy to find podcast meetups, networks, and associations by using Google, which will help you find organizations in other U.S. cities, as well as those in Canada, Great Britain, continental Europe, Australia, and other parts of the world.

New Jersey Podcasters Association	http://www.njpodcasters.org
Hawaii Association of Podcasters	http://www.hawaiipodcasting.com
New York City Podcasting Association	http://podcasting.meetup.com/33
Utah Podcasters Association	http://www.utahpodcasters.com
Greater Houston Podcasting Association	http://www.houstonpodcasting.com
Los Angeles Podcasters	http://lapodcasters.com
Kansas City (MO) Podcasting Meetup Group	http://podcasting.meetup.com/15
New England Podcasters	http://newenglandpodcasting.com
Chicago Podcasters	http://chicagopodcasters.org
Orange County (CA) Podcasters	http:// www.ocpodcasters.com
San Diego (CA) Podcasters	http://podcasting.meetup.com/14
San Francisco Podcasters	http://podcasting.meetup.com/20
Detroit Podcasters Network	http://www.detroitpodcasters.net
Miami Podcasting Meetup Group	http://podcasting.meetup.com/59
Phoenix/Scottsdale Podcasting Meetup Group	http://podcasting.meetup.com/67
Portland (OR) Podcasting	http://www.portlandpodcasting.org
The Seattle Podcasting Network	http://www.seattlepodcasting.net
The Indianapolis Podcaster's Guild	http:// www.indypodcasters.com
The Nashville Podcasters Meetup Group	http://podcasting.meetup.com/44

TABLE 17-1   A Listing of Local Podcaster Associations

Chapter 18

Sell Merchandise Through Your Podcast

How to...

- Sell your own merchandise
- Sell third-party merchandise

While advertising may represent the future of revenue generation for podcasts, not everybody is comfortable with the idea. As we mentioned earlier, some listeners have been very clear about their plans to defect from podcast audiences if their favorite shows ever start playing commercials.

One alternative to running banner ads on your site and playing commercials on your show is to actually sell something. Of course, the sale of merchandise on your site should never become a dominant part of your show. After all, who wants to download an infomercial and listen to it? Nonetheless, a brief mention that you have t-shirts, mugs, CDs, or other stuff available on your site, the sale of which supports your server costs, won't upset anybody.

That's the approach Dave Slusher takes. Slusher, an experienced radio host and a podcasting early-adopter, sells a combination package for $35, offering up a t-shirt with his show's logo on the front and back, along with a CD from the band that provides him with his opening music, the Gentle Readers. Slusher's *Evil Genius Chronicles* site explains the offer:

> *Hey friends and neighbors, have you been yearning to let your EGC flag fly? Now you can. We're offering a special deal of one special psychedelic black EGC t-shirt (Note: now also in dazzling white!) plus the Gentle Readers CD Hihoney—the release that contains our theme song—for the price of $35 postpaid. Support EGC and the Gentle Readers, too. We get the disks straight from the band themselves so put some money in their pockets, too.*

One wouldn't expect to get rich with an offer like Dave's, but on the other hand, you might clear enough cash each month to cover your bandwidth costs. On the other hand, you may be able to align yourself with a product that is such a close fit with your audience that you wind up selling a million of the things and retiring to an island in the South Pacific.

Concerning the items you might sell on your podcast site, it's easiest to categorize them into your own merchandise and somebody else's.

Your Own Merchandise

Your own merchandise usually refers to show-related products. T-shirts with your show's logo, mugs featuring the logo, and other logo-based merchandise are the most common items sold on podcast sites. That's because there's a company called CaféPress that makes it easy. Thus, there's no need to invest upfront in inventory you need to sell off in order to recoup your investment before you ever make a nickel in profit.

CaféPress's services are remarkably easy to use. It costs nothing to open an account. Just visit the site (www.cafepress.com), complete the registration forms, and start adding product. From within your account, you can upload graphics (like your podcast logo) and decide where on each product the image appears. You also set the price (above the minimum price, which represents the amount CaféPress keeps for itself).

Categories of merchandise at CaféPress range from clothing (t-shirts, caps, and the like) to office items (like mousepads), and a variety of other items (wall clocks, buttons, magnets, and a variety of other items). (See Figure 18-1.) The store works on an on-demand basis: When somebody orders a t-shirt with your logo on it, CaféPress produces one and ships it out. There is no inventory. Whatever amount over the base price you set for each item is yours.

FIGURE 18-1   Podcast-related merchandise for sale from CaféPress

18

Though CaféPress is an easy option, it's not the only one. You could always buy some shirts with your logo and ship them yourself. If you have plenty of time, you could even make the shirts yourself, using an iron and a transfer kit. We're betting you don't have that kind of time, though!

You are by no means limited to t-shirts, caps, and mugs when you sell merchandise on your site. Some other options include the following:

- **Music**   If you are a musical artist, your blog could be a perfect outlet for your CDs. Plenty of artists have jumped into the podosphere, with podcasts ranging from conversations (like the Lascivious Biddies) to a collection of songs played at recent concerts (like Umphrey's McGee). *High Orbit with Matthew Ebel* (www.matthewebel.com/podcast) is a podcast by a musician in which he plays "podsafe" music by other artists he likes. Ebell doesn't pitch his own merchandise on the podcast itself, but on the podcast blog he lists his own site and a link to CD Baby, an online store that sells the music of independent musicians. The Lascivious Biddies (one of the first groups to make a splash with podsafe music when they were discovered by Adam Curry) are a bit more blatant in their pitch. Their podcast home (www.biddycast.com) features a prominent image of their newest CD and the pitch, "Support Biddycast. Buy the CD!"

- **Research reports and other documents**   If you work in the professional world, you could crank out documents of various kinds that are of value to your audience. For example, a market research company with a podcast could use the show and/or its blog to pitch the availability of a research whitepaper, presenting detailed results from a study of interest to your listeners.

- **Registrations**   Some podcasters have their own workshops, seminars, or other live events for which they charge, and the podcast can be an effective venue for promoting these events. A great example is "Podcast Brothers," a weekly show that addresses the business side of podcasting. The hosts, Tim and Emil Bourquin (we've mentioned Tim before; he's also the host of *Endurance Planet*) run the Podcast and Portable Media Expo, a trade show that takes place annually. As the show gets closer each year, the siblings mention it, letting listeners know that the early-bird deadline is approaching, which companies have signed on to sponsor the show, and what speakers have been lined up.

Somebody Else's Merchandise

In addition to selling your own merchandise, your podcast could be used to sell someone else's items, allowing you to collect a percentage of what you sell on their behalf.

The most common way to sell another's merchandise on your site is through an affiliate program. Thousands of companies offer affiliate programs through their web sites, usually paying a finder's fee for introducing new business or a percentage of income for actual sales. Amazon.com's Associates program is, essentially, a pay-per-sale affiliate program, while Google AdSense (addressed earlier in this book) most commonly pays whenever someone clicks a link.

Some businesses have emerged that aggregate affiliates into a single storefront. You sign up just once but can offer products on your site from any of the affiliate programs bundled into the service. Some of the bigger affiliate aggregators are Commission Junction (www.cj.com) and LinkShare (www.linkshare.com).

Let's look at Amazon.com's Affiliate program by way of example. The idea is to direct listeners to books they might be interested in, and then guide them to buy the book through Amazon.com. In essence, you offer a specialized bookstore containing items aligned with the focus of your podcast. You populate your bookstore on your blog or web site by adding code that includes your Associate ID number. That way, whenever a visitor to your site clicks a link to a book on Amazon.com, the company knows they came through your site and they can credit your account whenever one of those visits turns into a sale.

The kinds of books you offer would have to be consistent with the theme of your podcast. It wouldn't make much sense for a show dealing with a local sports team to sell books dealing with management styles. However, it makes *perfect* sense for *Manager Tools* (one of the top-rated business-focused podcasts; found at www.manager-tools.com) to offer a bookstore made up of books the hosts have read and recommend. In fact, that's just what they do through a link titled, "Our Favorite Books." Some 20 books are listed there, along with some narrative under each book explaining "Why We Like This Book." For example, their note under the book *Getting Things Done* by David Allen reads as follows:

This is the only personal productivity book you ever need to buy. If you even use this SIMPLE process half way, you will become 2 to 3 times more efficient. If you've ever felt like you have a million things to do rattling around in your head, this book is for you. Mike and Mark are both HUGE fans, and we're BARELY scratching the surface.

18

The bookstore at *Manager Tools*, by the way, is a blog, allowing members of the podcast's audience to comment on the books the co-hosts recommend.

You needn't feel limited to books. If you produce a technology-oriented podcast and discuss a particular piece of hardware or software, you could sell that item using your Amazon.com connection or one with some other affiliate.

One of the oddest bits of merchandise sold through a podcast was a coffee maker called Senseo. This machine uses "pods," premeasured amounts of grind wrapped in a filter-like paper. Podfather Adam Curry is the owner of a Senseo, which he raved about frequently on his *Daily Source Code*. After a while, he began experimenting with the idea of audio associations: Every time he belched on the show (we know, we know: uncouth!), he would say "Senseo," with the expectation that whenever listeners heard a belch, they would *think* Senseo. Still, this was Curry's own little test; he had no relationship with the company. Nevertheless, he came to be associated with Senseo in the minds of his listeners, so he eventually put an affiliate link for the coffee machine on his site, selling dozens of the machines in the process.

A Gentle Reminder

We mentioned this earlier in the chapter, but it bears repeating here. There's nothing wrong with trying to make a few bucks with your podcast, either in an effort to be profitable or just to cover the costs of your hobby. However, if your listeners ever feel that the reason you podcast is *just* to sell them something, they'll most likely shut you off; they get plenty of that through other channels. Many podcast listeners have switched to podcasts to get *away* from commercialization. So undertake any merchandise sales via your podcast with care.

Chapter 19

Tap into Podcasting Support Services

How to…

- Find peer-to-peer help
- Locate production services
- Use remote recording
- Obtain consulting services
- Choose a hosting service
- Increase bandwidth
- Enhance RSS feeds
- Search audio content
- Allow listener call-in
- Add professional voiceovers
- Book guests

As is the case with any hobby and profession, you're not alone. Other podcasting enthusiasts are ready and willing to help you. Plus, as podcasting continues to gain popularity, businesses are sprouting up to provide the various services podcasters need.

Peer-to-Peer: Podcasters Helping Podcasters

Podcasters are, by and large, already fully invested in the social media phenomenon. Unlike the hosts of radio content that is repurposed as podcasts, independent and, to some extent, business podcasters mostly learned about podcasting through their other online activities, such as blogging.

Some podcasters have simply assembled documents, web sites, and tutorials to help. Elsewhere, forums have been established to encourage podcasters to seek out one another for assistance.

As with the professional services listing, far too many resources exist to list them here, and even if we tried, there would be no guarantee that we found them all. Nonetheless, this list represents a good cross-section of some of the better and better-known peer-to-peer resources available on the Net.

- **Podcast Alley**   Besides the Podcast Alley directory, the forums on Podcast Alley are among the best you'll find anywhere, largely because they are populated by well-known, highly regarded, and very smart podcasters. When we needed to figure out how to record our podcast over Skype without the echo Skype produces for the person on the other end of the line (the one *not* doing the recording), we turned to the Podcast Alley forum and got a variety of answers, including the one we finally used—the "mix-minus" approach (see Chapter 8 for details on the "mix-minus")— from P.W. Fenton, the former cop and host of the wonderful *Digital Flotsam* podcast. You'll find the forums at www.podcastalley.com/forum/index.php. The topics include general podcaster discussions, technical discussions, software, how to make podcasts, hardware, podcast and web hosting, advertising in podcasts, the future of podcasting, and more. Forums even exist for podcast listeners.

- **Podcast 411**   Primarily a podcast in which the host, Rob, interviews podcasters about various aspects, both technical and program-related, of their podcasts, the site also features a wealth of tools and resources for podcasters. These include tutorials, software links, a list of sites about podcasting, another that lists links to information about how to podcast, and (of particular value) a directory of directories. Podcasters can use this to make sure that, when they register their podcasts, they hit all the possible directories a listener might use to find a podcast. The show is excellent, too; we highly recommend it. You'll find it all at www.podcast411.com.

- **Podcast Rigs**   If it's hardware you're interested in, Podcast Rigs (www.podcastrigs.com) is a great place to go. Sample systems are organized by complexity, starting with "entry" (as in entry-level) and moving through basic, ultra, and pro. Each sample system includes its price point (for example, $400 for the basic system) and links to additional information about each item and where to order it. There's also a section for headphones and consoles. Set up as a blog, each entry takes a look at another piece of equipment or some other bit of podcasting information.

- **Podcasting Tools**   A nice, comprehensive site offering A–Z on podcasting, including the little graphics that indicate a podcast is ready for copying and pasting.

- **Podcast Optimization**   A web site and newsletter to help podcasters make the most of their efforts, Podcasting Optimization (www.podcastoptimization.com) features a comprehensive article library, among other tools.

19

■ **Podcasting News**   Podcasting News (www.podcastingnews.com) uses a blog to provide up-to-date information about goings-ons in the world of podcasting. The sidebar column features a wealth of links to various resources. There's also a well-populated discussion forum associated with the site featuring major categories, including Creating Podcasts, Podcasting Business, and Using Podcasts.

Professional Podcasting Services

Far too many services exist to list them all in this chapter. Heck, there are far too many services podcasters can take advantage of to list in this *entire book*. The reason: Most of the services podcasters use have been around since long before podcasting. Voiceover talent, music creation, web site hosting, audio recording—there's nothing new about these offerings and you can probably find what you need thumbing through the Yellow Pages or skimming the ads in a computer magazine.

Still, a number of businesses have emerged that are geared at podcasters, while some existing businesses have begun targeting podcasters specifically with their offerings. Some have even created new services *just* for podcasters.

While the listing that follows is by no means comprehensive—after all, hundreds of new services could have emerged since this book was printed—it is designed to provide some insight into the types of services available and highlight some of the better known and more interesting examples.

An up-to-date version of this listing is available on this book's web site at http://www.everythingwithpodcasting.com.

Production Services

For most independent podcasters, recording and editing the show is part of the fun. For businesses and others who just want to get the content out there and have better things to do with their time than wrestle with Audacity or Adobe Audition, using a recording studio that has all the best equipment and professionals skilled in their use provides a welcome alternative.

The following is a list of resources:

■ **Palegroove Studios**   Established specifically to support podcasters, this turnkey shop offers everything from planning a podcast and identifying potential revenue streams to developing RSS feeds and tracking results. The bulk of the offerings, though, revolve around development and post-production. Palegroove Studios (www.palegroove.com) will handle the recording, editing, mixing, mastering, and encoding of your show.

- **Intellipodcast**   Billing itself as a specialist in corporate podcast production and training, Intellipodcast (www.intellipodcast.com) offers a range of services from production (including recording) to hosting and tracking.

- **Podcast Production Services**   Podcast Production Services (www.podcast productionservices.com) focuses on editing and production, but also offers voiceovers, royalty-free music, and RSS feed development.

Remote Recording Services

While production services will handle recording, recording services themselves are a bit different. Using a recording service, you can call a phone line and record your podcast directly from your phone, or use a Voice over IP (VoIP) connection like Skype or Gizmo Project to do so.

These services are fine for a podcast aimed at a small audience, particularly if it's short. Friends and family won't mind hearing your voice sound like it was dictated over the phone, and even a short newsy podcast would work fine with this kind of service. However, if you want to grow your subscriber base, play music, or produce any kind of show that requires somewhat higher-quality audio, this probably isn't a solution for you.

Some recording services include…

- *Gabcast* (www.gabcast.com) requires no microphone or audio editing software. The free service offers 200 megabytes of disk space and integration into a blog. Paid services at Gabcast include more disk space and other features, such as the ability to upload files recorded elsewhere.

- *PhoneBlogz* (www.phoneblogz.com) is another service that lets you call in your podcast (or audio blog) and deliver the output to your own blog and your own server.

- *GCast* (www.gcast.com) is a free podcast solution that will host your podcast, provide you with free podsafe music, distribute e-mail alerts, and mix your podcast audio directly from an online interface. The company also lets you phone in your recording by dialing a toll-free number and entering an ID and password. The service is free to users because it is advertiser-supported.

Consulting Services

Any number of public relations agencies, consulting firms, and individuals have hung out shingles proclaiming they can provide you with consulting services to

19

help you produce your podcast. Before you avail yourself of such services, you should be sure to ask yourself...

- ■ What consulting services do I need?

- ■ How qualified is the consultant to provide those services?

- ■ What kind of track record does the consultant have with other clients?

If you are developing a personal podcast, more than likely you won't need any of the services offered by consultants. There's plenty of information and support available from books like this one and the podcasting community (accessible through message boards like the one on Podcast Alley). However, if you are producing a podcast for a business, these services can help you get your podcast up and running.

Consultants can do everything from helping you strategize your podcast in order to produce the greatest business results to handling all of your production for you. Organizations like the Los Angeles Opera take advantage of these turnkey services; the L.A. Opera's podcast, *Behind the Curtain*, is produced by the Los Angeles public relations company Schwartzman & Associates. Another example for a smaller organization is Wiggly Wigglers, the popular podcast from a remote British garden supply mail order company, which is produced by a third-party consultant.

Some consultants specialize in marketing your podcast. Others focus on the recording and editing aspects of podcast production.

Finding a consultant is not a simple matter. A Google search for podcast consultants reveals nearly two million results, while a look at the Wikipedia entry for podcast consultants produces only three names. Some publications—like the trade publication *PR Week*—print display ads from podcast consultants. Your best bet is either to get a recommendation from someone else who is already using a consultant or post a query to one of the more heavily trafficked podcasting communities stating what you're looking for and asking for advice.

Once you find a consultant, be sure to ask for a list of clients so you can talk to a few to find out...

- ■ How good the consultant's work has been

- ■ How easy it is to work with the consultant

- ■ Whether the consultant has been meeting deadlines and coming in on or under budget

Hosting

A "host" (also referred to as an Internet service provider or ISP) on the Internet refers to a company that maintains Internet-connected servers with space you can rent for your web sites and other online content. Any of these services (hundreds exist) can host your podcast. Suffice to say, a full list of such providers isn't possible here, given their immense number. However, they do share one problem for podcasters: nearly all of them meter bandwidth. Bandwidth refers to the amount of data transmitted, and it isn't free. Internet service providers have to pay for the bandwidth they use, so they in turn charge for the amount of bandwidth their customers use.

Many web sites can handle a lot of traffic without consuming much bandwidth. After all, there's not a lot of data contained in simple, text-heavy web pages. Your podcast, however, could involve the transfer of a few megabytes to 30 or more megabytes for *every single download*. That can rack up a lot of bandwidth consumption!

When we began podcasting, we signed up with a service that provided 75GB of bandwidth every month as part of the base price. Exceeding 75GB resulted in additional bills. Until we paid, our web site wasn't available to anyone, and instead sported a message indicating the site was unavailable.

Successful shows with tens or hundreds of thousands of downloads can result in substantial bandwidth costs using these traditional services. Fortunately, alternatives are available just for podcasters. The following are a few:

- *LibSyn*, or Liberated Syndication (www.libsyn.com), is a podcast hosting service that charges only for file storage, not for bandwidth. The service not only automates the process of uploading podcasts and updating a podcast blog, but also provides detailed statistics and automatically generates your RSS feed.

- *SwitchPod* (www.switchpod.com) is a hosting service that, like LibSyn, offers file storage for podcasts with unmetered bandwidth. A basic plan is free but adds an advertisement to your podcast. Under various pricing plans, you can distribute ad-free podcasts for the cost of file storage without paying for bandwidth consumption.

- *PodLot* (www.podlot.com) is another hosting service that charges for file storage but foregoes any charge for bandwidth.

- *HipCast* (www.hipcast.com or www.audioblog.com) formerly called AudioBlog, was one of the earliest players in the field. It offers a wide range of services for podcasters, including one of AudioBlog's original features, the ability to record a file over a phone line. While the company

19

used to meter bandwidth, the name change was accompanied by a switch to services that charge only for file storage. HipCast also lets you create a blog or use an existing blog. HipCast's original service is still available for $4.95 per month for unlimited storage but metered bandwidth. The company was founded by podcasting pioneer Eric Rice.

- *Odeo* (www.odeo.com) hosts MP3 files, including those that don't really qualify as podcasts, and makes them available through download or RSS subscription. Odeo also features the ability to find and subscribe to podcasts, and even to play podcasts from the Odeo site.

- *OurMedia* (www.ourmedia.org) has the unique virtue of being completely free. More than just a podcast host, OurMedia is a social experiment in online media distribution. Labeled "The Global Home for Grassroots Media," the venture allows permanent, free storage of video, music, photos, audio clips, Flash animations, and all other manner of media. Restrictions exist, however. For example, any work that you post *must* have a Creative Commons license that provides you with the rights to post (or your own license).

- *Podshow Delivery Network* is a startup from podcasting pioneer Adam Curry and his partner Ron Bloom. Backed by considerable investment capital, it was partnered with bandwidth provider Limelight Networks to develop a turnkey podcasting solution available to any podcaster once it launches. The Network includes free unlimited bandwidth for delivery of podcasts, but also features tools for the creation, publishing, and uploading of podcast content. In addition, the network delivers advertising as part of the package.

Bandwidth

What if your show gets popular? We mean *really* popular. At the point where downloads of your show are consuming massive amounts of bandwidth—say, the amount that Adam Curry's *Daily Source Code* or Leo Laporte's *This Week in Tech* consume—your service provider may ask you to find another alternative. It's time to move into the realm of the big boys and look at other bandwidth solutions.

These services generally aren't required for a typical podcast and are used more frequently by networks and enterprises. But, again, a hugely successful podcast—particularly one generating revenue—could send you looking for solutions as your listeners begin complaining about slow downloads, broken downloads, and unavailable downloads.

Limelight Networks, for example, offers distributed content delivery for multimedia from audio to games. Another well-known name in this space, Akamai, offers a Content Delivery Service product that features some 18,000 servers in 1000 networks situated in 70 countries. This distributed approach allows large files to move quickly to users seeking to access the content.

These are just examples of high consumption bandwidth services; many dozens are available (too many to list here). A fairly complete listing of hosting options can be found on the StreamingMedia.com web site at www.streamingmedia.com/directory/category.asp?id=7.

RSS Services

Since podcasts are generally available for subscription via RSS, you may want to explore the options available for enhancing or augmenting your podcast's RSS feed. The following are two services worth considering:

- *Feedburner* (www.feedburner.com) is a well-known service that produces a user-friendly version of your RSS feed. Rather than the gobbledygook of XML code that visitors see when they click a typical RSS feed, a Feedburner link produces a human-readable version of the feed along with some resources the average person can take advantage of. The company boasts it is currently providing feeds for over 50,000 podcasts reaching nearly two million aggregated subscribers. The service offers tools to publicize the podcast, ensures proper formatting of a feed so it is recognizable by the major podcast directories, analyzes traffic, and provides reports to you about the podcast's distribution. For podcasters who don't work with blogs or other tools that automatically produce the required enclosure element of an RSS feed, Feedburner's service automatically produces the appropriate code.

- *Feed2Podcast* (www.feed2podcast) is an intriguing service that automatically turns a blog's RSS feed into a podcast. Using those robot-sounding voices, the service converts the text from a blog into speech so visitors to a blog have the option of listening to it and subscribing to the audio feed. While this isn't exactly a desirable way to produce a podcast, it *is* a solution that allows visually impaired visitors to "read" a text-based blog by listening to it as a podcast.

Audio Search

Several efforts are underway to make it as easy to search audio content as it is to use Google or Yahoo to search text. While the audio search field is rather limited at this point, one audio search service is worth noting to podcasters. Podzinger (www.podzinger.com) was developed by BBN Technologies, one of the primary organizations that drove the original development of the Internet. BBN's Podzinger searches both video and audio podcasts by searching the actual spoken words. Once you find the file you're looking for, you can start playing it from within the Podzinger interface right at the point where the word occurred. If you're looking for the episode of *Geek News Central* where the show's host, Todd Cochrane, talked about Bluetooth, you can search on the term "Bluetooth" and begin playing the episode you find at the point where the word occurred.

In addition to being able to search all podcasts, you can submit information to Podzinger, and in return you can add a field to your page that allows your listeners to search just *your* podcast. Figure 19-1 shows how a box like this looks on the *For Immediate Release* page.

Call-in Lines

One of the ways to get feedback is to offer a call-in phone number for your listeners. This is particularly helpful for those listeners who take their podcasts with them in their cars. We have received several audio comments from listeners who phoned our call-in line as soon as they heard something to which they wanted to respond. If they had to go to their computers and record a comment, save it, and send it, they might never get around to it; the moment of inspiration may be lost. But with the call-in comment line, they can express themselves immediately. Two services that can help you set up a call-in line are

- *K7.net* (http://www.k7.net). We're not sure how they do it, but K7.net gives you a phone number for a call-in line that automatically routes any comments left to an e-mail attachment—and they do it for free. This is the service we use for *our* call-in line. The same service lets your faxes get routed to you via e-mail, again at no cost. You can even get a vanity phone number, if the one you want is available, again at no cost. K7.net is based in the Seattle area, so all phone numbers do have a 206 area code.

- *Podomatic* (http://www.podomatic.com) is another hosting service aimed at podcasters. It doesn't seem terribly desirable, given that bandwidth *is* metered (which is why it wasn't listed with the podcast hosts earlier in this chapter). You can get 500 megabytes of storage and 15 gigabytes of monthly download for free, while for $9.95 you can get 2 gigabytes of file storage and 100 gigabytes of monthly downloads. But Podomatic does come with a listener call-in line as part of the service.

FIGURE 19-1   A Podzinger search box

Voiceovers, Bumpers, and More

Need a theme song? Signature music to play between segments? Vocal introductions to this or that? Because these services existed long before podcasting—they provided their wares to radio and other audio producers—there are far too many to list here. However, a few of them cater to podcasters, and even a couple have emerged that specifically support podcasting.

Radio Daddy (www.radiodaddy.com), established to serve the radio industry, has become a regular haunt of podcasters because the price is right: free. The premise, according to the web site, is simple: "You need a voiceover recorded, you come to RadioDaddy.com, post your request and a member records your voiceover as an MP3 file and uploads it back to Radio Daddy. You return to the site, download your free voiceover, and voilà! A new voice on your station! It's just that sim ple!" An "elite" service is also available that provides additional benefits for a few bucks each month. The following lists some other services:

- *Interactive Voices* (http://www.interactivevoices.com), another free service, allows you to submit criteria and find talent that may meet your needs, compare the prices of the same, and listen to voice samples.

- *Voice 123* (http://www.voice123.com), similar to Interactive Voices, also allows you to find just the right voice to record your voiceover. Rather than listening to demos on the web site, Voice 123 will send you the demos based on the criteria you submit.

- *Audiobag* (http://www.audiobag.com) is a service that produces intros, outros, promos, and bumpers (those short transitions between segments). Audiobag also provides voiceover talent.

19

Finding Guests

We're not sure how many podcasters sit around drumming their fingers on their desks, wondering just who in the world they could get for an interview. Generally, podcasters *know* whom they want to interview. Still, if you're desperate, you could always try Podcast Guests (www.podcastguests.com). The service works a lot like ProfNet, the PR Newswire service, except in reverse. With ProfNet, journalists put out the word that they are looking for a source with an expertise in a particular subject area; the request is distributed to paying customers who can respond and, with luck, get some positive press. Podcast Guests accepts submissions from PR agencies and the like that spotlight a client who might make for an interesting interview. One of the "mommycast" podcasts, for example, might be interested in Brent and Phelicia Hatch, authors of a book on child-raising who are ready to discuss "raising a G-rated family in an X-rated world."

Sharing Your Promo

People who listen to podcasts often find new podcasts because they heard a promo played on a show to which they already listen. Promos can be quick and easy to produce, or you can turn to a podcast studio to produce one for you. But what do you do with your promo once you've produced it? You can (and should) send it to podcasters who know and respect, especially those who solicit them (like Adam Curry and Todd Cochrane). However, podcasters *looking* for promos to play can visit sites that host promos, such as the following:

- *PromoPicker* (http://www.promopicker.com), organized in a Yahoo!-like hierarchy, lets podcasters upload promos and allows others to download those they may be interested in playing. You can play a stream of the promo before you download it to make sure it meets your needs (and your standards).

- *Podcast Spots* (http://www.podcastspots.com) is another service that lets you submit or find a promo. The site also offers free hosting, podcast news, a podcast music section, and a hodgepodge of other services. Primarily, though, the site is designed to allow podcasters to share their promos—but only for play on other shows listed with the service; you can't peruse promos and select one yourself.

- *Promos at Podshow* (promos.podshow.com) uses an open group blog to allow anyone to upload a promo. Its lack of database capability makes it tough to find just what you're looking for, but at least you're sure they're current, given a blog's method of posting the most recent item at the top of the first page.

- *Podcast Promos* (www.podcastpromos.com), in recognizing that podcasters have defined time slots to fill, instructs those podcasters who are recording promos to fit them into 30-, 60-, and 120-second slots so those looking for promos to play can select ones that fit their needs.

Validators

Validators are web sites where you can enter the URL of your RSS feed and find out if there are any problems that could keep listeners from getting your show. The following are two validation services:

- *Feedvalidator* (at http://www.feedvalidator.org) is a simple tool that displays any errors it finds in your feed and shows you where they occur. You can use the site's badge, which shows your feed has been validated.

- *Smoothouse Podcast Validator* (at http://www.smoothouse.com/podcast/validator.php) checks the URL, feed contents, feed items, and the enclosure. Smoothouse also offers a few other tools, such as a "play now" player and podcast buttons.

A List of Services

As podcasting continues to grow, the number and scope of services will undoubtedly expand. The list included in this chapter—necessarily a snapshot in time due to its print nature—will be obsolete before too long. We will, however, maintain a list of podcasting services that will be current and comprehensive at this book's web site, http://www.everythingwithpodcasting.com.

Part V

Use a Podcast As a Business Communication Tool

Chapter 20

Where Podcasting Fits in the Business World

How to…

- Enhance your existing communication and marketing efforts
- Find examples of other businesses achieving success with their podcasts
- Identify the tangible benefits of business podcasting

So far, our discussion has been about podcasting at the individual level. Sure, you can make money with your podcast or just have fun with it; but it's something you do because you want to, because you have something to say, because you've always dreamed of having your own radio show, or even because you're sure you can do a better job than that jerk down the street who brags about having 5000 listeners for his piece-of-garbage podcast.

Increasingly, however, companies and other institutions are figuring out that podcasting can serve their business goals. They can serve as marketing vehicles, supplement public relations and financial communication efforts, enhance customer relations, serve as a support delivery mechanism, and even entice people to apply for jobs.

This section of *How to Do Everything with Podcasting* explores the business potential for podcasts. We'll cover everything from strategizing your business podcast to looking at different approaches, complete with case studies. (In addition, the nature of podcasting makes it easy for you to go out and listen to any or all of the examples we write about!)

But first, it's important to look at the place podcasting occupies in the panoply of business communication strategies and tools.

Business Podcasting Today

Compared to the tens of thousands of independent podcasts, coupled with the tens of thousands of podcasts made up of repurposed content from radio and television productions, the number of business podcasts is pitifully small. Still, a review of the companies that are podcasting provides some sense that smart people in the world of business communication acknowledge podcasting's potential and are willing to give it a try.

Not that there's a lot of risk involved in business podcasting. Unlike a blog with comments, podcasts are entirely controlled; nothing you distribute is outside of your own control. As for cost, we've already addressed the fact that podcasting has exploded onto the media landscape largely in part because the economic barriers to entry have come crumbling down. Even with a mid-range recording rig, your company can begin podcasting for less than two-thousand dollars—chump change for most organizations, particularly when compared to the costs of other marketing channels like television advertising, which (on certain major broadcasts like the Academy Awards or the Super Bowl) can cost millions of dollars for a 30-second spot.

So, what companies are trying their hands at podcasts? In addition to many podcasts from small companies seeking affordable avenues for communication, podcasts are being produced by the likes of...

- General Motors
- Speedo
- Cisco Systems
- Disneyland
- IBM
- McDonalds
- Deloitte
- Purina
- Whirlpool

This isn't a comprehensive list, just a sampling of the companies that have undertaken regular podcasts aimed at specific audiences in order to reinforce their brand identity, improve customer relations, or provide a specific service.

Exactly what can podcasting do for a business?

To be frank, that's the wrong question. In fact, it's a question that is asked about virtually *every* communication tool, from print brochures to videos. In Chapter 21, we'll review a strategic communication planning process that will help you figure out how to apply podcasting to specific business goals. However, it's definitely worth noting here that podcasting should be applied—as should any communication tool—as a solution, not as a goal in and of itself. No business should ever begin the process of creating and launching a podcast with a statement that sounds like this:

"By God, we ought to be podcasting!"

Instead, podcasting ought to come up in discussions about ways to reach audiences, to convey particular messages, or to address specific situations and problems. Let's take a hypothetical situation in a fictitious company by way of example:

Megabehemoth Inc. is a manufacturer of personal computers with an image problem. The reputation of the company's customer support function has been deteriorating over the last couple of years, a problem exacerbated when a prominent blogger took them to task over his own unhappy experience. Now the blogs and message boards are full of snarky, rude comments about Megabehemoth's customer support.

Company representatives gather together to consider what to do to turn their reputation around. Bolstering the customer support staff and launching new customer service initiatives are a given. Good communication cannot improve a company's reputation when the source for that damaged reputation remains in the same state that caused the damage in the first place! However, since the company has decided to hire 200 new customer support technicians, launch new channels by which customers can obtain support, and introduce new policies to ensure support issues are dealt with more quickly, some communication to reinforce these changes are in order.

"We could do some television commercials showing just how excellent our new support is," offers one executive.

"Let's get the trade press to write about it," adds another exec.

"We should do a huge press conference," chimes in a third, "a real dog-and-pony show."

Quietly, in the back of the room, a younger, more junior employee tentatively raises her hand. "Excuse me," she says, clearing her throat. "But why not do a customer service podcast?"

"A *what?*" growls the eldest executive, who has barely heard the term before.

"A podcast," she says. "Once a week, a front-line member of the customer support staff can host a show that runs about 15 minutes long. The host, who deals every day with real-world customer service issues, can start by identifying any common problems that have emerged in the last week, and then interview the best person in the company to talk about what the company is doing to rectify the problem. Then, she could introduce a new customer service option or talk about the best way to use an option that was introduced recently. She could even interview a customer every week about how they got their problem dealt with most effectively, or even one who was frustrated to show that we're listening to customers who are less than satisfied. At the end, she could read and respond to selected comments from customers."

Silence emanates from the management table.

"Because it's a real person working in the real world of customer service—not a PR person writing a press release—it will have credibility. Because it's not scripted, but spoken in an authentic human voice by a real front-line worker, that credibility will be enhanced. Because it's dealing with the real issues that are driving our customers nuts, they'll find it worthwhile. Because it's short, they'll find the time to listen. Ultimately, because it will help them deal with their own support issues, they'll believe that Megabehemoth has delivered real value to them, and their perception of the company should improve measurably."

The young up-and-coming marketer holds her breath awaiting a response. Finally, one of the elder executives asks, "And just what will this cost us?"

"Under $1000," she answers and watches as the eyes of the senior staff light up.

"I still don't get it," one of them says, "but for a thousand dollars, we can give it a shot."

In this highly optimistic example, the conversation didn't start with ruminations about the possible uses of podcasting at Megabehemoth. The conversation started with the explanation of a problem, challenge, or opportunity, to which somebody was able to offer podcasting as a solution.

Podcasting as a Marketing Supplement

As we write this chapter, a new movie has opened in theaters everywhere (as they say in Hollywood). The film—which is getting *terrible* reviews—is inconsequential. It's a comedy targeting the African-American community. The producers invited a Los Angeles–based African-American podcaster to the film's premiere, where he interviewed stars and others associated with the movie. He released the interviews on his podcast, but the producers also distributed the podcasts through their own site, advertising heavily on well-trafficked sites like Technorati.com.

Of course, the film was promoted through all the usual channels, including a maddening flood of television commercials, billboards, in-theater trailers, and online banner advertising. The podcasts offered something prospective ticket-buyers couldn't get elsewhere: behind-the-scenes information in prolonged interviews with the movie's principles. (Prolonged, in any case, beyond what they would get from a segment on *Entertainment Tonight*, where segments rarely exceed two or three minutes.)

This treatment of podcasting has its shrewd elements that show somebody at this film company is on the ball (more so, one presumes, than the screenwriters). Using the existing podcast of a member of the target audience—whose audience is made up of the target audience—was smart. Getting permission to distribute the episodes from a short-term site dedicated to the movie podcast was even smarter. But creating a limited-life podcast for a movie is not new: Paris Hilton's podcast was a marketing effort for her film, *House of Wax*, for example.

20

The Walt Disney Company also chose a well-known podcaster for the company's series of podcasts celebrating Disneyland's 50th anniversary. Michael Geoghegan was given some general guidelines, then turned loose to produce podcasts in the Disney spirit. The original series of podcasts included content unavailable anywhere else to Disney fans, such as walking interviews with some of the people who designed and built the original Disneyland.

The results so exceeded Disney's expectations that they continued the podcast beyond the original planned seven episodes. As late as July 2006, Geoghegan was still hosting episodes. (One episode included the audio of actor Johnny Depp's reaction the first time he encountered the audioanimatronic version of his movie character, Captain Jack Sparrow, in the Disneyland ride "Pirates of the Caribbean," on which the film was based. Just imagine how many Depp and *Pirates* fans would want to hear that!)

Not all consumer marketing podcasts need to be as overt in their message as these entertainment-focused shows. Both Purina's and Whirlpool's podcasts target the consumer audience, but their intentions are more subtle. It is the goal of these shows to enhance the company's brand without coming right out and saying, "This is a great product, you gotta come *spend your money* on this!"

Purina's initial podcast, *Animal Advice*, proved so popular the company has expanded its offerings to a total of six separate shows, none of which deal directly with pet food. Among these are…

- *Animal Advice*   Submit a question and hear the answer from a veterinarian. The shows also offer information of interest to pet lovers, with hosts and guests talking about health problems, pet adoption, and animal trivia, among other things. (For example, "Why do cats purr?")

- *Snouts in Your Town*   The lighter side of pet care features quirky hosts covering quirky stories.

- *Complete Puppy Care*   A 14-month program that includes iPod-compatible video.

Purina also uses podcasts for special events, including an online-only dog show and participation in events like Chicago's annual Pug Party.

This content is as compellingly fascinating to pet lovers as the Disney Resort podcasts are to fans of Disneyana because it feeds their appetite for the arcane and the specialized; they just cannot get this stuff anywhere else. The question you may ask, based on the limited size of the audience is "So what?" Appeal to a small number of dedicated fans, and all you've done is reinforce their fandom. They're *already* customers, right?

Yes, but by virtue of their expertise, they are also influencers. People who know them know they are treasure troves of knowledge about Disney history and trivia, and they become resources when questions arise. Accommodating the desire of your fan base for this kind of content only makes them into bigger evangelists, spreading the viral message the podcast created.

As for Purina, most pet owners love their pets. Hearing advice that makes your pet healthier and helps it live longer—and hearing it presented in an entertaining manner—can only produce a positive reaction from listeners, who will associate that good feeling with the company that delivers the content: Purina.

One other example comes from the world of television—a medium that has embraced podcasting as a marketing tool perhaps more than any other. TV shows ranging from *Lost* to *Heroes* have podcasts associated with them. (While there are fan podcasts for many TV series—including long-canceled shows like *Firefly*—our focus here is on podcasts produced by the entities behind the shows themselves.) A terrific example of these efforts is the *Battlestar Galactica* podcast, hosted by series producer Ronald D. Moore. Moore develops a podcast to coincide with each episode of the science fiction series; the episode is not unlike the director's commentary that has become a popular feature on movie DVDs. The podcast provides insights and inside information for fans of the show, keeping them thoroughly engaged between episodes.

Podcasting's Advantages

Every medium has its strengths. Smart marketers and communicators weigh these strengths in terms of their objectives. Companies that eliminated print from their internal communication mix in order to save money failed to consider the advantages print offers over online content. (It's portable. People can sit and read long articles. You can write on print, underline passages, circle interesting facts, and make notes in the margin. The list goes on.) In a communication campaign, you need to select the tools based on their strengths. In a business context, podcasting comes with its own strengths, many of which we've already touched on from different standpoints:

- **Your audience members can listen while they are doing something else** People are inundated with text and video wherever they go. Despite its many other capabilities, the TiVo digital video recorder's most popular feature lets viewers fast-forward through commercials, yet there's no escaping commercials that play in the theater before the movie starts. The average consumer in North America, according to one study, sees or hears more than 3000 marketing messages every day. At the same time, though, people are hungry for content to play on their iPods and other digital media devices. Music is great, but people want some variety, particularly as they grow more and more accustomed to controlling the content they hear (versus having to listen to what the deejay plays). The fact that you can listen to a podcast while engaged in some other activity—driving, jogging, working out, waiting for a plane, doing the laundry—makes podcasts an appealing alternative to listening to your CD collection.

■ **You can deliver specialized content to niche audiences that they cannot get anywhere else**   Few podcasts try to appeal to the same broad consumer audience as terrestrial radio. One of the top-rated podcasts on independent podcast directory "Podcast Alley" is *MuggleCast*, aimed at fans of the Harry Potter books. Listeners to Oracle's podcast get insights on how to make the most out of their investment and developments in the world of database software. As people with a built-in interest in your content gravitate toward the podcast, you can feed them the kind of information not available through any other channels, cementing a relationship and enhancing the perceived value associated with your brand.

■ **You can convey information that is best conveyed through audio**   Sometimes audio can be a very powerful medium. To hear the passion or emotion in a voice is far more effective than reading the text. To hear a joke can be far funnier than reading it. And audio production can generate true emotion when the same story told visually can be overwhelming or uncomfortable. One podcaster produced a tribute to New Orleans following Hurricane Katrina that left the images to your imagination. It didn't beat you over the head by showing the devastation, yet it still choked you up and tugged at your heart.

■ **You can build a loyal community of listeners among your audiences**   Just like loyal readers of a blog, regular listeners to a podcast—particularly one that encourages interactivity with the audience—can form a bond with the show and the company that provides it. This can represent a source of support during difficult times, or a community to which your company can turn when needed. For example, a podcast that addresses company business issues could be a venue for a letter-writing campaign when the government threatens to impose onerous and unnecessary regulations on your industry.

- **You can use the podcast as a means of soliciting feedback** Ask your listeners what they think of this or that, and some will send you audio comments, others will leave posts to your blog, and many will be happy to answer a poll or survey.

- **You can use your podcast as an alternate channel to reinforce content being delivered primarily through another channel** Whatever message you are trying to deliver through media relations, advertising, or other channels can be reiterated on your podcast. Again, the podcast is an opportunity to provide greater detail and exclusive interviews around the issue that you cannot get to people through mainstream media due to time constraints and filters. If, for example, your company is acquiring a competitor, your podcast can go into detail about the benefits customers can expect as a result of the merger.

The Regulatory Argument

Companies that function in heavily regulated environments have been especially resistant to social media. While most of this resistance has been aimed at blogs because of their uncontrollable nature, many organizations fear the same consequences from podcasts: "We can't risk making a statement that will get us in trouble with regulators." At the top of this list are pharmaceutical companies and financial services companies.

It is easier to ensure a podcast doesn't run afoul of regulators than a blog, and it's not that tough to blog without breaking the rules. There should be no need to seek legal approval if company lawyers are confident you know what the rules are and you won't break them.

The easiest way to steer clear of the regulatory mire is to produce a podcast that does not intersect with any regulations. Let's take a pharmaceutical company, for example, that produces diabetes medications. Company lawyers would advise against a podcast dealing with one of the firm's medications. But that would not preclude a health-focused podcast on living with diabetes. This podcast could focus on diet, exercise, and other lifestyle topics. It could include interviews with researchers, specialists, and patients. It need never make reference at all to the company's diabetes medication. Such a podcast would never rouse the attention of regulators. Nor would one aimed at the academic community from which the company recruits its talent. A podcast to chemistry students would address research and development from a scientific, not a marketing, standpoint. Again, no regulatory violations there.

Heavily regulated companies should concentrate on the "niche" capability inherent in podcasts. You can target a show of interest to important audiences, the focus of which is perfectly harmless legally.

There is no business that *can't* podcast. Whether they do so should be based on a strategic plan that recognizes the benefits. How to strategize a podcast is the focus of Chapter 21.

Chapter 21

Your First Business Podcasts

How to…

- Know when a podcast is *not* the solution
- Plan the strategy for your business communication
- Choose an approach for your business podcast

For all the reasons raised in previous chapters, podcasting represents a unique channel for organizations to deliver their messages and influence core audiences. On another level, podcasts are just like any other communication channel. They are a tool, and their use needs to be strategized in the larger context of communication and, by extension, business objectives.

Podcasts would not be the first communication tool to be used poorly. Remember the first attempts by most companies to launch web sites? These were usually started on the orders of a senior manager who had just learned one or more of the company's competitors had launched web sites. The nervous executive, fearful he was missing out on an important trend he didn't understand, said, "Build me a web site." He did not know or consider the audience the site was designed to reach. He did not know or consider what problem it was meant to solve or the opportunity it was meant to capitalize on. He did not know or consider how to assess its effectiveness. He merely knew the competition had one, and worried that maybe they knew something he didn't.

Traditionally, organizations do not create their communication tools with the same motivation: "We need to produce a video. We don't know who we'll show it to or what it'll be about, but I just heard that one of our competitors produced a video, so we'd better do one right now."

This fire-ready-aim approach to communicating is typically reserved for new media. And there isn't much that's newer than podcasts. As podcasting's popularity continues to grow, and as more organizations launch podcasts, executives who have long since forgotten their early web disasters will inevitably want to produce a podcast for no other reason than fear of missing out on the latest, coolest trend.

The reality is that creating a successful business podcast starts with understanding just what the podcast can do for your business. It means taking a strategic approach. And it means not podcasting if podcasting isn't right for your organization.

Why Not to Podcast

While this book is about how to do everything with podcasting, there are a number of reasons not to podcast. Any good communicator will tell you that the tools you select to communicate with your audiences must be appropriate. Your strategic planning process will be the best determination of whether podcasting is appropriate for your company. We'll cover that a bit later in this chapter. First, let's outline a few circumstances that would definitely mitigate against producing a podcast.

- **Your message does not lend itself to audio.** As we have already noted, the wildly varying range of podcasts share one characteristic: Their tone is conversational. Some business issues simply should not be presented in so informal a manner.

- **Your audience is not inclined to listen.** Perhaps they don't have digital media players like an iPod. Maybe they are an older audience and have not embraced the idea of portable media or the idea of sitting at a computer and listening to audio. Whatever the reason, they are going to skip your show… and every other podcast on the Net.

- **Your messages require focus.** Using a podcast to outline the elements of a strategic initiative probably isn't the best way to get the message across. If you need to get detail to imprint with your audience, use a channel that will require them to focus more attentively than audio, which they can listen to while doing something else.

Now that we have cautioned you against podcasting for the *wrong* reasons, it's important to remember all the *right* reasons we covered in Chapter 20! The fact is, there are countless reasons for a business to consider podcasting as a communication channel. So, once your podcasting, you have to start at the usual place: the beginning.

Strategic Communication Planning

You can start your planning for a business podcast in two ways. One is to recognize the opportunity exists based on your day-to-day proximity to the organization, its products and services, and its issues and its audiences. The other is as a result of a strategic planning process.

Strategic communication sounds like an overblown concept, but in reality it's pretty simple. Communication is strategic when:

- It is planned as a means of addressing core business issues

- Its impact on the business can be measured.

Scour the literature on strategic communication planning and you will find five, seven, and ten-step plans. For our purposes, we are using a four-step plan.

Step One: Goal

"Produce a podcast" is not a goal. In this context, we are talking about a business goal, one you want your communications to support. For the sake of illustration, let's pick a business goal at random, for a generic company:

> Goal: Stem the defection of long-time customers to a competitive brand.

Step Two: Strategy

A strategy is a plan of action designed to achieve a goal. Strategies tend to be fairly broad in their approach. One strategy to apply to the goal listed in Step One might be as follows:

> Strategy: Increase customer loyalty to our brand.

Customer loyalty is certainly a good strategy. Loyal customers will be less likely to defect to a new alternative than those who are inclined to blow with the prevailing winds. But how, exactly, will we increase loyalty? That's where objectives come in.

Step Three: Objectives

Objectives are the measurable activities you will undertake as the elements of your strategy. You will most likely articulate several objectives for each strategy. In our effort to increase customer loyalty to our brand, we could, for example, set the following objectives.

> Objectives:
> - Help customers feel like they are privileged insiders by providing a unique window into the brand.
> - Create a bond between customers and the people behind the brand.
> - Give customers more of a say in the development of future brand extensions and marketing programs.

Step Four: Tactics

This is the step where tools are chosen. Based on the objectives outlined earlier, we might look at a variety of tools, including a customer advisory panel and a brand-focused blog. A podcast would also lend itself to achieving these objectives. Interviews with key brand representatives that let customers hear from these product evangelists in their own voices serve the cause of opening a window into the brand. The authentic human voices of these individuals in unscripted conversations or interviews can also create a sense of connection between customers and brand representatives. A podcast could also be used to introduce ideas for brand extensions and to solicit feedback—feedback that can be incorporated into future podcasts, showing customers that the organization is listening to their input.

Capitalizing on Opportunity

While strategic planning is the first approach to identifying the appropriateness of a podcast as a communication tool in your organization a less intensive and more serendipitous approach is the "lightning-strike" approach. You undoubtedly have some experience with this approach, though you may not know it.

It usually begins with a huge problem or a glaring opportunity. By way of example, let's look at a fictitious company with a problem. The investment analysts who cover the company have been unkind despite decent numbers. When the head of investor relations asks a sampling of analysts why their assessments are so unfavorable, a common theme emerges. "Your CEO is arrogant. The leaders of your competition are visible, while your leader barricades himself in his office and makes lofty pronouncements. Well, we're not buying it."

In fact, the CEO has plenty on his plate about which the analysts are unaware, including hyper-secret negotiations for an acquisition. He's also very nervous in front of crowds, partly due to an unsightly goiter that has afflicted his chin since childhood. An informal conversation with the CEO about issues of interest to analysts might go a long way toward reversing their unflattering impression of the boss. So the investor relations manager launches a weekly podcast in which he and the CEO have a conversation, each week about a different aspect of the business. Analysts are invited to subscribe to, or download, the podcast. Hearing the CEO speak regularly in a warm, conversational manner with candor and openness begins to melt the ice and, gradually, the analysts' reports grow less and less unfavorable.

Such an opportunity is not the only way serendipity can inspire a podcast. Consider General Motors, which saw the opportunity for a podcast based almost entirely on the success of its Fastlane blog. The company's first pass at a podcast was just a recording of a marketing announcement at an auto show, but subsequently, the Fastlane blog turned into an interview show with host Deb Ochs interviewing various GM employees, and not the usual suspects one might expect from a big company such as GM. Rather, she has spoken with the likes of Clay Dean, director of design for small and mid-sized cars, and Dave Hill, chief engineer for Corvette. Ochs carries over candor that infuses the Fastlane blog into interviews with insiders, which makes for compelling listening among consumers with a ravenous appetite for inside information about cars. Where better to get such information than from the people who design and build the cars?

Podcasting in the Corporation

Your planning process will reveal the opportunities your organization can leverage with podcasts.

You can aim a business-focused podcast at a variety of audiences depending on the issues your organization faces or the opportunities it is pursuing. Consider, for example, a podcast aimed at the investment community. Investment analysts, institutional fund managers, and other financial professionals are inundated with print material and have scant time to read it all. Yet, just like everybody else, they have to get to and from their offices and have time in their cars or on the train. Given a podcast in which they can listen to interviews with company representatives to help them connect more deeply with the organization, they may well find themselves more inclined to rate the company positively.

While a podcast could not be used to deliver material information subject to disclosure rules, it could involve interviews with people like the head of R&D who might discuss the exciting projects in which the company is engaged. Hearing his excitement and enthusiasm could have a deeper psychological effect than simply reading a typical review of projects written in standard stilted corporatese. A 15-minute weekly podcast with interviews like this would give your organization a significant leg up over competitors who rely on the standard approaches for reaching the investment community.

Other corporate podcasts to consider include the following:

- **Recruiting**   A look at the kinds of jobs available in the organization and the culture of work the company offers.

- **Company news**   A review of the week that was and a look at the week ahead as a form of media advisory for reporters and editors covering the company.

■ **Issues**   Public relations departments, at least those worth their salt, identify issues that could present obstacles to the organization's ability to achieve its goals. A podcast could focus on these issues, aimed at audiences that could be swayed one way or the other so that they throw their support to the organization. For example, a company facing a regulatory change could make its case on a podcast that regulation is unnecessary and even counterproductive.

While you could not launch a podcast just to deal with one issue (After all, who would subscribe?) an ongoing podcast that routinely addresses issues such as corporate social responsibility, environmental efforts, and other issues might attract the interest of those who could serve as goodwill ambassadors for the organization based on their perception that they are insiders with whom the company shares its values and beliefs. Companies that face ongoing issues can use the podcast as a vehicle to educate an audience. An oil company, for example, could interview an oil trader one week who might explain the spot market and its contribution to fluctuations in the price per barrel; the next week, a refinery manager could be the interviewee, addressing some other aspect of oil production; a tanker captain the next week; a service station owner the next, and so on.

Enhancing Product and Brand Recognition

Product and brand podcasts are two sides of the same coin. A product podcast addresses the company's product line at large while a brand podcast appeals to fans of a specific product line (for instance, the Ford Mustang, Coca-Cola, or Barbie).

Let's take a look at a product podcast first. There are already examples of companies with podcasts that target product lines. The best current example is the *General Motors Fastlane Podcast*, with Deb Ochs interviewing the people behind the development and production of a wide range of GM vehicles. Fastlane is aimed at car enthusiasts who have been dying to get a glimpse inside the process of designing and producing a car. The same approach could work in just about any industry. How about a pharmaceutical company? With the public increasingly aware of the high price of maintenance drugs, a podcast interviewing real research scientists about the drug discovery process could provide insights about the cost of developing drugs while serving a number of other purposes (such as recruiting and education).

Brand podcasts are no-brainers for companies whose products already enjoy a fan base. These are for people who are already passionate about the product. Wouldn't people who get the Harley Davidson logo tattooed on their bodies be eager to listen to a podcast about Harleys? It's a no-brainer! Collectors of products would subscribe to podcasts about their collecting passion, be it Barbie dolls,

Coca-Cola memorabilia, or Limoges boxes. Audiophiles would flock to a Bose, Harmon Kardon, or Bang & Olufsen podcast, as long as it provided insights into the best fidelity and didn't just pitch product. At the same time, the podcast would reinforce brand loyalty.

Enhancing a Reputation

Consider a pharmaceutical company that specializes in eye-care products. Its podcast would not address its own products, but eye-care issues in general. This notion lends itself to more than one podcast. Thus, one podcast would target consumers and explore the best way to find a good ophthalmologist, how to detect the onset of an optical problem for which you should see a doctor, and why you shouldn't rub your eyes when you're tired. (If you think people wouldn't listen to this kind of podcast, consider that a doctor in private practice has established a large, loyal following with a podcast about arthritis! You can find Dr. Joel Rutstein's "*Arthritis Central*" at http://www.arthritiscentral.com.) Meanwhile, a second podcast aimed at doctors keeps them current on developments in the medical community. These shows could even solicit questions for the company's experts.

Without overtly pitching products, these public service–like podcasts enhance the audience's perception of the organization's interest in its customers. This actually is the approach Purina is taking with its podcast, through which a veterinarian offers advice and information for pet owners.

Service

People who work with a company's products would appreciate a podcast that helped them take the greatest advantage of that product. This is the philosophy that drives Oracle's podcast, which provides the latest up-to-date information to developers about Oracle's development platform. We covered this application of a podcast in more detail in Chapter 20.

Special Interest

Each organization knows where its own opportunities reside for producing content of interest to special audiences (or, conversely, special content intended for general audiences). Virgin Atlantic's podcast offers an excellent example. The subsidiary of Richard Branson's Virgin empire, the airline shuttles passengers in luxury between Europe and the United States, many visiting for the first time. New York is one of the airline's destinations. Travelers can retrieve a podcast that introduces them to New York, including the culture, restaurants, transportation, and other features, produced in an entertaining style with a narrator speaking in a Brooklyn accent. While anybody can retrieve the podcast—Virgin Atlantic customer or not—the brand identity of the podcast will register with the listener and boost Virgin's stock in his or her mind.

If these examples haven't whetted your appetite, the following offers a few more ideas just waiting to be snatched up:

- **Publisher** Interviews with authors

- **Management consultants** Case studies featuring interviews with consultants and their clients

- **Insurance company** Practical advice emerging from research studies

- **Health-care company** A wellness program

Determining Your Approach

The process of determining your approach (covered in Chapter 13) applies to business podcasts as well. To summarize, see the following methodologies for your podcast; (refer to Chapter 13 for details):

- Single host

- Co-hosts

- Host(s)/interviewee

Providing Advice

Many of the currently popular indie podcasts feature self-proclaimed experts offering advice on everything from wine to Macintosh computers. Subject-matter experts inside organizations are far better than self-proclaimed—they are recognized experts. Companies can take advantage of such individuals to provide advice to audiences. It's easy to imagine how popular a podcast would become if consumers could send in their questions to be answered by the best authority. Let's take a sporting goods company, for instance. One week the host could read a question from a fisherman asking about flies; the next week, the question could come from a backpacker asking about how to avoid blisters. The host introduces the company's subject-matter expert, reads the question, and then interviews the expert in order to extract the best answer and make it interesting to all listeners.

Chapter 22

Podcast to Your Customers and Other Consumers

How to…

- Target the right audience for your business podcast
- Improve perceptions of your organization's social responsibility
- Provide support to existing customers through your podcast

The type of podcast most businesses think about first are those that help the company achieve its most fundamental objective: making money. When thinking about money, companies think first about sales. Sales come from customers (people who are already buying your products and services) and consumers (people you wish were buying your products and services).

A podcast targeting customers and consumers is a dicey idea. Nobody—not even your biggest fans—will want to listen to a podcast that is nothing more than a longer version of your TV or radio commercials. To want to keep listening to a podcast, the audience must derive some value from it—whether it's information that makes their lives easier, or entertainment that helps them while away some downtime.

That doesn't mean a podcast can't appeal to consumers. We've already looked at the series of podcasts Purina provides for pet owners. The excellent *Animal Advice* podcast represents one type of customer-focused podcast, one that seeks to provide information and knowledge the customer can use to his or her advantage. Since the podcast is associated with the company—even if the company is not overtly advertising its products in the podcast—the listener connects the brand to the value she gets from listening.

This is an important concept. While some readers may be shaking their heads right now and claiming, "A connection between brand and podcast, along with two dollars, gets me a cup of coffee!" *Au contraire*. Marketers know that they do not own their brands, nor can they control them. Too often, the idea of "brand" is confused with the "mark," the logo or graphic that appears on every box, every brochure, every billboard and commercial and vehicle used to convey content about the product. The brand, on the other hand, is more nebulous. The brand, in a nutshell, is the total perception people have about a product or service. When you hear a product's name or see its mark, how do you react? What do you think of? Wrapped up in the notion of brand are not only the visual identifiers like the logo, but the expectations you have, the stories you've read or heard, and the reputation the product or service has earned. To be blunt, the customers own your brand! Therefore, it becomes of paramount importance that you do everything you can to ensure the brand is a strong, positive one.

So what do customers and potential customers of Purina dog food think and feel when they hear Purina? If they are listeners to the *Animal Advice* podcast, odds are they perceive the brand a bit more positively than those who don't.

The American Family offers an example that adheres to this principal even as it employs a different approach. Produced by Whirlpool brand appliances, the podcast, according to the web site where it can be found "will address matters that impact families with diverse backgrounds and experiences. The podcast will feature real, everyday people, and/or subject-matter experts." One recent episode, for example, featured "The Accidental Housewife" Julie Edelman, offering tips for reducing stress on Mother's Day. Like Oracle, the podcast does not sell anything. Instead, it establishes a connection between Whirlpool and a service that offers usable, useful advice aimed at its core audience. Again, listeners who see references to Whirlpool are likely to have a better reaction—they perceive the brand more positively—than those who simply see television commercials and billboards.

Let's look at some categories of customer or consumer podcasts and various companies producing podcasts that fit within those categories.

Appealing to Fans and Enthusiasts

Your biggest fans can sell a lot of products. Think about the people who wear branded clothing such as Coca-Cola apparel or Budweiser t-shirts. These are walking billboards who at any opportunity will extol the virtues of their favorite product. Need another example? Think about most Apple Macintosh owners, whose zealotry is legendary. The Macintosh is as much a community as it is a computer operating platform. No advertisement can convince someone to switch from Windows to Mac more than a devoted, hard-core Mac fanatic.

Podcasting to these fans can fuel the fires of their enthusiasm. Since this army of devotees is already helping your organization beyond measure, doesn't it make sense to invest in them?

General Motors invests in people who love cars with its *Fastlane* podcast. Associated with the "Fastlane" blog, the podcast provides a peek under the curtains of vehicle production and other aspects of the business, including sponsorship of auto races. For instance, recent shows covered the Corvette's appearance at LeMans (we'll talk more about this in the next chapter when we talk about reputation).

Speedo is another company with a product to sell (see Figure 22-1). But a podcast about swim trunks? Neville produced Speedo's first podcast, an interview with Olympic swimming medalist Michael Phelps. In the podcast, Neville interviewed Phelps about his hometown, his early thoughts about the next Summer Olympics in China, the emerging crop of swimmers on the USA team, and what

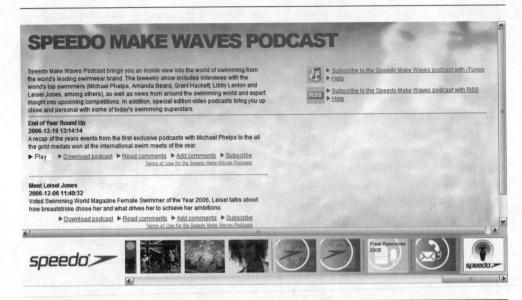

FIGURE 22-1   *Speedo Makes Waves* features interviews with swimmers.

Phelps is listening to these days on his MP3 player. Swimmers and water athletes could well clamor for this kind of content, an in-depth interview with one of their heroes (he won eight Olympic medals, after all) that is not available anywhere else. The fact that the interview is sponsored by Speedo can only result in positive views of the company, the brand, and the products.

Earlier, we pointed you to podcasts about television series, like the excellent *Battlestar Galactica* podcast that serves as a sort of producer's commentary. This is another approach to reaching out to existing customers and fans. For television and radio show producers, in fact, podcasting can extend your reach. In addition to producing podcasts *about* your show, you can podcast the show itself—a practice that has become increasingly common among radio shows. In fact, a review of the most downloaded shows reveals that most are repurposed radio content, such as NPR's *This American Life*.

Podcasting to Boost an Image of Corporate Social Responsibility

McDonald's new podcast deals only peripherally with product, instead seeking to bolster the public's view of how socially responsible the company is. Corporate social responsibility (CSR for short) is a big deal in business. Investment corporations offer funds made up of companies deemed to be socially responsible. Individuals increasingly choose to do business only with socially responsible companies, even if it means paying a little more. The dimensions of CSR include the way the company treats its employees, its involvement in the community in terms of financial contributions and volunteer efforts, and how the company's leadership is viewed. For a highly visible company that makes its money from people in the community, displaying a strong commitment to CSR is important.

The company's first podcast helped reinforce this message by talking about how it works with chicken farmers to ensure its sandwiches meet the highest quality standards and that product safety standards are met. Another episode dealt with quality assurance, while others looked at the company's involvement in communities, its employment practices, and a search among its employees for the new "voice" of McDonald's.

Podcasting to Provide a Service

One last example—and a fun one—is provided courtesy of Virgin Atlantic, which produces a series of podcasts introducing travelers to various cities to which the airline flies. Subscribing to the podcast feed means you get introduced to another city every time a new installment is released. Alternatively, you can just download the one relevant to the city you're traveling to when you're ready to leave on your trip. So far, the airline has released podcasts on New York, Las Vegas, Cuba, London, Cape Town, Dubai, Johannesburg, Shanghai, and Sydney.

These do not conform to many of the guidelines we have outlined in this book, but given the theme, the highly produced podcasts work just fine. A narrator with the appropriate accent introduces listeners to the city and then runs down some of the finer attractions, including hotels and dining spots. The City of Philadelphia, meanwhile, is producing a series of podcasts in which a real local tour guide offers insights and interviews along city routes. Listeners can assemble their own tours based on the paths they want to take and what they want to focus on (for example, history or culture).

Offering Support for Users of the Product

We can imagine one particular type of podcast (so far undeveloped) getting a lot of listenership and attention. (At least, we're not aware of one. If you know differently, please let us know!) This would be a podcast devoted to customer support of certain products of a company.

Talk to people who own products that are inclined to require customer support. We'd be willing to bet the vast majority of reactions would be negative. Companies do a terrible job of supporting their products once customers have bought them. This is a regrettable oversight since bad customer support can damage a company's reputation, particularly in this day of blogs and podcasts and other consumer-generated media!

Obviously, a podcast cannot take the place of the kind of customer support people expect and deserve. However, it can certainly supplement the effort. Consider a podcast, for example, in which customer support reps discuss the most common problems they have encountered in the last week. "We've had an inordinate number of calls about the left wrapper flange on the circuit belt, Chet," one announcer could explain. "We think this is because people are tightening the U-bolt just a little too much. So we're advising everyone to take it easy with those wrenches. It could save you a lot of problems down the road. In the meantime, our engineers have looked at the problem, and we're now shipping our X-27 model with a gasket that will let you tighten that puppy as much as you like. If you want one of these gaskets, just give us a call or fill in the form on our web site and we'll ship one off to you."

Why would people listen to such a podcast? Because their X-27 is important to them, as important as, say, a Dell Computer or a Microsoft operating system. But people don't have the time to repeatedly visit a web site to check on support issues. They can, however, spare five minutes for a weekly update they listen to between *Accident Hash* and *Nobody Likes Onions*.

Academic Podcasting

Universities and colleges have customers, too—they're called students. Many centers of education have figured out podcasting in a big way. Stanford University is one that maintains its own podcast site (see Figure 22-2) as a subset of Apple iTunes. Here, you can find faculty lectures, interviews, music, and sports content, some of which also appeals to other important audiences, like alumni.

The notion of posting lectures as podcasts has some educators and critics worried. Why would students bother to come to class if they can just download the lecture and listen to it while lounging in their dorm rooms or flipping burgers? After all, classroom interaction is part of the education.

Other educators say, exactly! If the one-way lecture can be absorbed outside the classroom, then all the classroom time can be used for interaction. Besides, not every student can understand everything communicated in a lecture the first time they hear it. The podcast allows students to go back and listen again, which is also handy for students who are studying their notes.

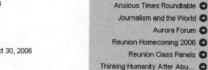

Stanford on iTunes U

Stanford University and Apple® are pleased to offer university-related audio content via iTunes®.

Heard on Campus
Last Modified: Dec 19, 2006
Total Tracks: 251

Faculty Lectures
Last Modified: Dec 11, 2006
Total Tracks: 134

What's New
Anxious Times Roundtable
Journalism and the World
Aurora Forum
Reunion Homecoming 2006
Reunion Class Panels
Thinking Humanity After Abu...

Global Issues -- Stanford Initiatives
Last Modified: Nov 15, 2006
Total Tracks: 102

Sports
Last Modified: Oct 30, 2006
Total Tracks: 79

Music
Last Modified: Oct 30, 2006
Total Tracks: 125

Books & Authors
Last Modified: Dec 19, 2006
Total Tracks: 48

Courses

IHUM 55: The Literature of Crisis
Last Modified: Dec 12, 2006
Total Tracks: 17

PHY 24 - Modern Theoretical Ph...
Last Modified: Dec 19, 2006
Total Tracks: 1

FIGURE 22-2   Stanford University's podcast site on iTunes

Duke University actually gives every incoming student an iPod that is already loaded with orientation materials. The school understands that students will load the iPod with music, which is fine. But it's also ready and available for lectures and other audio content the school makes available, such as Duke University School of Law events, the podcasts of which are also available on Apple's iTunes.

Contests and Promotions

Podcasts have become an increasingly popular way to promote something over the short term. In the previous chapter, we took a look at a couple of limited series podcasts for new movies, for example.

This short-term approach can also work for other products that have broad consumer appeal. Plus, there's nothing like a contest to draw people to products that may not have quite the same cachet as the big name brands. Cell phone lovers might have been inspired to subscribe to the podcast of the trade publication *Mobility Today* because of the chance to win a Motorola Q cell phone.

Marketers who understand the podcasting space should have no problem innovating a variety of ways to adopt podcasting into their customer-focused efforts, especially given the low cost of entry.

Chapter 23

Podcast to Build Your Company's Reputation

SUBSCRIBE

UPDATE

Podcasts

Track : 12

How to…

- Understand the importance of reputation
- Manage a reputation
- Build relationships
- Respond to crises

There's a very apt oft-repeated line about reputation: You don't pay it much mind until you lose it, then you find out just how hard it is to get it back. No podcast—not even a series of podcasts—can fix a reputation that a company has damaged through unethical or irresponsible behavior. But a podcast *can* build upon a good reputation or help turn around a bad one, assuming the company is also making changes to the underlying causes of that bad reputation.

To understand the way a podcast can help with an organization's reputation, it's important to start with a brief look at what reputation is and what contributes to it.

What Is Reputation and Why Is It Important?

Reputation can be defined as the degree to which an organization measures up to the expectations that key audiences have of it. Those audiences are the ones who can make for smooth sailing or present an impediment to achieving business goals. In one study of the general public, media, government officials, and financial institutions, the factors that comprised a company's reputation included employment practices, community investment, governance practices, the organization's mission and value statements, financial strength, the ability to work with the government (notably regulators), and product quality. Another study, looking just at investment analysts' view of reputation, found the key factors to be the perceived quality of management, market position, strategy, past performance, and governance.

Charles Fombrun, professor emeritus at New York University's Stern School of Business and founder and executive director of the Reputation Institute, along with research firm Harris Interactive has assessed companies' reputations using a mathematical formula that assigns a value to a unit of reputation; Fombrun is able to correlate the drop of a point in reputation to a related dip in financial performance. In the Harris-Fombrun Reputation Quotient, 20 attributes of a company are grouped into six categories:

Emotional Appeal

- Good feeling about the company
- Admire and respect the company
- Trust the company

Products and Services

- Stands behind products and services
- Offers high-quality products and services
- Develops innovative products and services
- Offers products and services that are a good value

Vision and Leadership

- Has excellent leadership
- Has a clear vision for the future
- Recognizes and takes advantage of market opportunities

Workplace Environment

- Is well managed
- Looks like a good company to work for
- Looks like it has good employees

Financial Performance

- Record of profitability
- Looks like a low-risk investment
- Strong prospects for future growth
- Tends to outperform its competitors

Social Responsibility

- Supports good causes
- Environmentally responsible
- Treats people well

If Dr. Fombrun's evidence that a damaged reputation results in reduced earnings isn't enough to get companies to focus on doing the things that drive reputation, consider what happens to a company when its reputation suffers publicly. Enron is the poster child for a damaged reputation, but few companies suffer so catastrophic a reputational meltdown. In the 2005 index (ranking companies from 2004), Johnson & Johnson topped the list without having done anything that made news or a splash in the blogosphere. J&J simply has values that are more than just words on the wall. The company lives their credo to the extent that it drove the firm to pull its Tylenol product from store shelves in the wake of product tampering even though there was no government mandate to do so. J&J's credo puts customers first, so they did what they had to in order to protect their customers. This kind of behavior, day in and day out, puts them at the top of the list. Near the bottom of the list are companies perceived to have cavalier attitudes toward the environment, employees who snarl at customers, lousy service, unethical leaders, a lack of concern for their customers' well-being, and unfair pricing practices. The bottom of the list is populated by the likes of Halliburton, United Air Lines, Exxon Mobil, Sprint, Comcast, and Merck. (Can you match the company with the reputation?)

Managing a Reputation with Podcasting

As we mentioned earlier, rebuilding a reputation that has taken a hit requires a lot of hard work, patience, and time. As a result, companies are best served by ensuring their reputation remains unsullied. They also need a solid crisis plan when something happens that threatens to damage a company's reputation.

Part of the challenge of reputation management is that most members of your constituent audiences never hear about the routine good behavior and attributes your company exhibits, but when something bad happens, *everyone* hears about it. That's why companies that measure up to the standards for good reputation take advantage of public relations efforts to make sure the word gets out.

23

Of course, nobody wants to take time out of their busy schedules to listen to companies praise themselves for being great companies. And nobody is going to want to listen to a podcast that simply runs down your company's good deeds. You need to take an approach that generates content your audiences will actually want to listen to.

We are certainly not advocating any trickery or deception. At the academic level, this kind of PR is known as "two-way symmetrical communication," which means it's a win-win for the company *and* the audience. Members of the audience get what they want—useful information, for example—and the company builds its reputation with people it considers important. Everybody wins.

The first step in achieving this goal is to pick the audience. Again, the key audiences to look at include the media, the financial and investment community, local communities, customers and consumers, and the occasional short-term specialty audience, such as voters.

Before we run down some ideas for podcasts aimed at building reputation, let's look at a podcast that does an outstanding job of providing useful information to a target audience. The podcast is IBM's *The Future Of...* The audience is the investment community; in fact, the podcast is hosted as part of the company's investor relations web site.

Usually hosted by IBM's blogger-in-chief, Christopher Barger, the podcast runs about 15 minutes and features an interview, generally with a couple of IBM experts. These experts are not from the marketing department, or PR, or corporate communications. They are engineers, product managers, people who are in the trenches working on real issues.

Each episode focuses on some aspect of society and the thinking going on at IBM about how technology will affect it. So far, IBM's *The Future Of...* has focused on the future of television, work, privacy, sports, video games, crime, banking, shopping, the home, and driving, among others. For the episode on the future of TV, for example, host Ethan McCarty interviewed Saul Berman, IBM Business Consulting Service's strategy and change leader for Media and Entertainment, and Steve Canepa, IBM's vice president for the Global Media and Entertainment Industry. "As technology evolves," the promotion on the podcast's web site says, "consumers are getting more and more choices for media content, when to receive it, and how to experience it. This is leading to increasing market fragmentation, which is challenging established media, programmers, and advertisers—and creating vast new opportunities for the expanding media and entertainment industry."

Why would an investment analyst or fund manager listen to such a podcast? People handling large sums of money need to keep abreast of a company's activities and its plans. They also are buried in text. They receive narrative reports, financial statements, news releases, media reports, and a flood of other material. IBM's podcast, however, doesn't require them to read a thing and they can listen while commuting to the office. (Remember, each show runs only about 15 minutes.)

Because the interviews are interesting and engaging, listeners are willing to stick with it for the duration of the show. Because it provides insight into the kind of thinking going on at IBM that will lead to innovations and thus new products and services that fill emerging market needs, they will keep listening.

Of course, anyone else from outside the investment community who's listening will only spread the word to other circles.

Another case in point comes courtesy of General Motors. Affiliated with its excellent blog, Fastlane (http://fastlane.gmblogs.com), *Fastlane* podcasts appeal to the hardest-core automotive enthusiasts. To host these podcasts, GM turned to employees who sound natural and human, not polished and practiced. These hosts then engaged in conversations with fellow employees instead of interviewing experts, a far more appealing approach in the world of podcasting. For example, in one episode, host Deb Ochs spoke with GM's Executive Director of Vehicle Structure and Safety Integration about a new rollover testing facility. The average car-buyer would find the topic so tedious they wouldn't even listen. Serious car lovers, though, eat this stuff up, because it's information about the automotive process they simply can't get anywhere else. Plus, they get to hear it from the horse's mouth.

As the legendary auto race in LeMans drew near in 2006, interviews with members of GM's Corvette team were the focus of several *Fastlane* podcasts, another peek behind the curtain for people who find it all fascinating.

Feeling like insiders, they can offer information to their less car-knowledgeable friends and wield influence. They can also line up on the company's side when it faces adversity. In GM's case, the blogs and podcasts have created a bond between the venerable carmaker and the most fanatical consumers. When the company came under attack by a *New York Times* columnist, these readers rallied to the company's defense, even though they themselves could be highly critical of GM decisions. In other words, they helped protect the company's fragile reputation.

Approaches to Audiences

Not too many companies have launched podcasts designed to build relationships and support reputations, so there aren't a lot of case studies like those from GM and IBM. However, you don't need to be one of the biggest companies in the world to produce a podcast that can help keep your reputation sparkling.

Media Relations

PRWeb, an online news release distribution service, has introduced an intriguing enhancement of its offerings, the press release podcasting service. The company conducts interviews related to the press releases it issues and makes them available as podcasts, adding an audio dimension to the tired old press release, which had been solely a text vehicle up until now.

PRWeb's service is just one example of podcasts to support an organization's media relations efforts. You could also produce a weekly summary of news coming from the company in the next week (such as upcoming executive speeches, product announcements, and earnings statements). You could offer brief interviews with executives that could spark a story idea for reporters covering your company or industry. You can summarize whitepapers, offer insight about news released the week before, or introduce new company research results. Keeping the podcast short, sweet, and informative could elevate it above the incredible clutter most reporters and editors must wade through to get at useful and usable information.

Community Relations

Community relations may seem like the least likely candidate for a podcast, but remember, podcasts in general—not just in business—serve niches. There's no reason that niche couldn't be geographic rather than subject-based. Of course, your company does not need to produce a podcast for every community with which it does business—for some organizations, that would mean *thousands* of individual shows! Instead, you can focus on communities in which you have the *largest* presence or where controversy is most likely to erupt.

For example, a community in which your company plans to build a plant that processes hazardous materials would be ripe for a special communications plan. During the critical planning stages, a regular podcast could offer questions and answers from community members, interviews with company planners, local officials talking about the benefits of the facility to the community, and other topics surrounding the facility.

An additional challenge is letting members of the community know the podcast is available. After all, listing the podcast in a directory like iTunes or Podcast Alley isn't likely to attract residents and local businesses the way a comedy podcast will attract listeners looking for a laugh. You'll have to get the word out through more traditional means.

One approach is to consider the podcast an extension of live, face-to-face meetings. "We've had some good questions here tonight, but we're sure there will be more in the days ahead. Here's a phone number you can dial to leave a question, and you can hear answers on an ongoing basis by subscribing to our podcast."

You can also build awareness through distribution of a news release to local newspapers, and even through a door-to-door flyer, doorknob hanger, or bulk mailing.

Other community-oriented topics can be covered in a podcast targeting your largest or most influential communities. A regular podcast in a city where you have a manufacturing plant can solicit grant requests, prepare residents for upcoming construction and traffic delays, cover community activities in which the company has been involved or shine the spotlight on organizations that have been on the receiving end of company gifts.

The Financial and Investment Community

IBM's *The Future Of…* has given us one look at an approach to podcasting for investment analysts and others in the financial community. Surely you realize that more than a single approach would work with this most important of audiences.

The most obvious podcast you could create is one your company most likely is already producing: Quarterly earnings conference calls. In these sessions, analysts and fund managers call in to hear company leaders (usually the president and/or CEO and the Chief Financial Officer) discuss earnings and take questions. The call usually happens the same day earnings are released (or the next morning). The calls are often recorded and made available by telephone for invitees who were unable to attend in real-time. But there's no reason you can't capture that recording, convert it to MP3, and make it available to anybody who wants to hear it. Investors would be among those who would want to subscribe so they wouldn't risk missing a conference call.

A more comprehensive podcast series would include the conference call along with other recordings, such as additional nonquarterly calls and executive speeches at investor road shows.

IBM's model is also easily adapted, featuring interviews with employees who are involved in activities investors are interested in, such as research and development.

Podcasting in a Crisis

While we have yet to learn of a business podcast that has tackled a crisis, there's no reason it couldn't. The principles of podcasting in a crisis would mirror those of a blog, and could, in fact, supplement a blog when a company encounters a crisis.

Crises represent the greatest risk to a company's reputation. Consider what happened to Exxon in the wake of the tanker spill in the Prince William Sound, Dow Corning when it was revealed that leaking silicon breast implants could be linked to serious and painful consequences for customers, or Union Carbide when its Bhopal plant in India leaked a chemical that killed hundreds of local residents.

Among people who deal with them routinely, crises are defined as an unexpected event or revelation that threatens the company's reputation. The benefits of a blog during a crisis should be obvious, including the ability to provide timely updates and for the company to address the situation in an authentic, human voice. That human voice can take on deeper meaning and be even more personal through a podcast, with the CEO providing updates and expressing his concern.

There aren't many ideas worse than launching a blog at the time of a crisis. Without established goodwill among readers, the blog could quickly deteriorate into a venue for critics to assail the organization. A new blog doesn't even have to be focused on a crisis to have this deleterious effect. A blog started by Paul Purdue, CEO of iFulfill (an e-commerce order fulfillment business), focused on lighter issues, but Purdue started the blog as the company was in the stages of failing. The comment tool allowed unhappy customers to vent their frustrations.

However, a short-term, crisis-focused podcast served up as a supplement to the blog *is* a good idea. In fact, it's a better idea than using an existing podcast that was established to serve other purposes. You could, though, let existing podcast listeners know about the availability of a crisis podcast and direct them to the page where they can listen to it, download it, or subscribe to it.

Chapter 24

Produce a Business-to-Business Podcast

How to...

- Understand the B2B podcast audience
- Assess the need for a corporate podcast
- Follow B2B podcasting guidelines

In the world of organizational communication, audience identification is one of the most important of the fundamentals. What one audience cares about is dramatically different from what interests another audience. Think about the differences between customers and consumers. While these terms are often used interchangeably, they couldn't be more different. Customers already buy your product or service; consumers represent potential future customers, although most of them probably aren't already part of your customer base. Customers look for information on how to make the most out of whatever you sold them and, from time to time, they need your help with problems or issues that arise. Consumers, on the other hand, want to know why your product or service is relevant to them in the first place. They could also have issues with your organization should you make the news in a less-than-flattering way. Consumers organize boycotts far more frequently than customers do!

One audience that will have distinct information needs is your business-to-business audience. Business-to-business (B2B) identifies a realm of commerce and relationships that is distinct and separate from business-to-consumer (B2C). Simply stated, B2B means your customer is another company instead of an individual. B2B refers to companies doing business with one another.

Companies are, of course, made up of people, so it's not as though you have to aim your communications at a bunch of buildings, bank accounts, and contracts. But the interests of the people who represent the business are different from those of individual consumers who represent only themselves.

What B2B Audiences Want

So just what would B2B listeners want from a podcast? It starts with understanding what they want from your business, and that can vary from one business to another. Ultimately, if your podcast is strategized as a tool to improve business relations, you'll talk to the right people in your organization to figure out what your key B2B relationships are and what issues are common to your most important B2B audiences. However, we can get a better handle on how a podcast can affect your B2B relationships by looking at a few examples.

24

Let's start with a high-tech company like an IBM or an Oracle. These organizations sell their equipment primarily to businesses in need of large quantities of computers and computer-related gear. Few orders come into IBM from companies looking for a single box, and Oracle sells expensive business software that requires a plan and a team to implement. These are not small decisions on behalf of the customer, nor is it like a simple purchase by an individual at an office supply store. After the purchase is complete, a relationship needs to exist between the organizations as implementation proceeds, and even after the software is up and running or the hardware is humming along, ongoing support is required, upgrades need to be implemented, and sometimes expansion is required.

Next, we'll look at a producer of consumer goods. While the end customer is the individual who buys these products—whether it is soap, toys, or shoes—the customer is the retail outlet that sells these products to the customer. For the personal care company, the toy company, or the shoe company, the actual customer is a retail outlet, whether it's a deep discount store like Wal-Mart or a high-end shopping destination like Harrods or Bergdorf Goodman. These customers depend on timely delivery of undamaged products their customers are going to want to buy. They want the lowest possible prices and they need activities like returns handled quickly and efficiently.

Finally, let's examine a consulting firm, like those that work in public relations, architecture, or business management. Here, the firms have been hired to provide their expertise to help their clients be more successful. These consultants do not work with individuals, as financial planning consultants might, but rather with organizations that need expertise that comes at a premium. While a company may have an in-house public relations staff, for example, the services of an agency that specializes in a specific PR niche may be necessary to promote a given product line. The clients want to make sure they are getting their money's worth; high invoices don't matter too much if the consultant is delivering even higher business results.

These are fairly standard B2B relationships, but others exist. In fact, each type of company listed is somebody else's customer. For example, the toy company may outsource its manufacturing to a company in Mexico or China or the Philippines. Thus, the toy company is the customer in that relationship.

In fact, some types of B2B relationships don't necessarily involve a buyer-seller model. For instance, companies form alliances and strategic partnerships. A pharmaceutical company might form an alliance with a biotech company to work together in hopes of identifying a medicine targeting a specific condition.

All of this background should help us figure out how a podcast could serve the business by enhancing relationships with our B2B partners.

Does a Podcast Make Sense?

The first question to ask is whether a podcast even makes sense. If you have one or two B2B customers, and you are in constant communication with them anyway, a podcast probably won't enhance the relationship; they're getting all the information you need. A podcast makes more sense if…

■ You have a lot of different B2B customers who share common traits. SAP, the German business software company, is a good example. SAP sells its software to thousands of companies, all of whom have to maintain it, enhance it, and upgrade it. Within each company are employees who deal with the software and could benefit from useful information. A podcast that offers advice and updates could be a worthwhile addition to the mix of channels used to communicate with these workers since they are probably overwhelmed with the amount of text-based communication they receive.

■ Your customer companies employ a number of different individuals who deal with your products or services. For example, a health insurance company sells its group policies to companies that provide them to employees in the form of medical coverage. In each company, the employees are the end users of the product. Even if a Health Maintenance Organization (HMO) had only a few hundred customers in its geographical region, each of those customers could have thousands or even tens of thousands of employees for whom more information from the insurance company could prove valuable.

Of course, in a B2B world you need to market to prospective new customers as well as offer enhanced value to your existing customers. Podcasts and blogs, given their two-way nature, provide an opportunity to do far more targeted marketing than the traditional approach of generating any viable sales lead and passing thousands of such leads to sales people who will follow up on them in the most traditional of ways.

Next, you need to ask if the individuals to whom the podcast is directed would be inclined to listen to the information you want to share. Are they likely to have computers at work? Portable media devices? Are you imparting the kind of information they can retain by listening, or would they be better off getting the information in print so they wouldn't have to take notes?

An Example: BMC Software

BMC Software makes applications that are used by Information Technology departments at businesses around the world. The company's podcast, *TalkBMC*, is part of a related blog that has kept nine writers busy since mid-2005, writing somewhere between one and three weekly posts. By covering topics the company's B2B customers are interested in (content that would not make it into any marketing or advertising copy), the company not only improves relationships with readers and listeners, but it also improves its search engine results.

According to a December 2005 article about BMC's blog and podcast from IT Manager's Journal, the traditional marketing employed by the company was not aiding its effort to be seen as an advocate of Business Service Management, "a term which means ensuring that everything IT does is prioritized according to business impact, enabling an organization to proactively address business requirements, with the goal of lower costs."

Getting the target audience of Chief Information Officers and Chief Technology Officers to pay attention to banner ads and magazine campaigns was tough, to say the least. BMC turned to RSS feeds, blogs, and podcasts to fill the gap.

While BMC's marketing department was skeptical, the low cost and low risk led them to give the blog and podcast project a thumbs up. Quoted in the IT Manager's Journal article, Tom Parish (a consultant to BMC and part of the blog and podcast team) said, "Blogging and podcasting help put a real face and real visibility to the company and its products. It made BMC Software more credible to the technical community, which tends to not be very attracted to a shiny web site with lots of marketing spin. They want real grit. So across the board we're getting feedback from developers and the public about knowing who the company is and what it does.

"Once the podcasts got into iTunes, it raised the level of visibility with the web traffic and the BMC management. That was real proof we were on the leading edge [of this kind of marketing]. And [once BMC management] saw the number of downloads of whitepapers rise from the podcasts going in all the RSS channels ... the excitement rose."

In a podcast interview Parish conducted with BMC's Online Publishing Managing Director Mike Smith (available at http://www.talkingportraits.com/About%20Tom%20Parish), Smith noted that he was inspired after listening to an episode of *Fastlane Radio*, the podcast that accompanies General Motors' Fastlane blog. The subject of the interview on Fastlane Radio was an automotive designer talking about his pride in the design of a car on which he had worked; he also explained what goes into the design of a car. Never did the engineer do anything that could be construed as "selling" the car to listeners.

24

Smith said BMC Software has software development and technology experts who can talk about the products they've worked on, what went into the development, and where the company's development efforts were headed. Listeners could hear directly from the people who create the products, not marketers, thus giving a company that makes an abstract product a tangible human face.

Smith also remarked on the importance of integrating podcasts and blogs. If, for example, an employee is interviewed on a podcast, a listener might want to hear more from this individual. If the employee had a blog on the company's web site, listeners would have a natural place to go to learn more from her. In fact, many of the individuals interviewed on the podcast do have blogs, including Chief Technology Officer Tom Bishop, who has appeared on several BMC Software podcasts (including one with a fascinating discussion about how coding a computer dating program opened up a world of programming possibilities).

Of course, working in a high-tech company does not, by itself, ensure a receptive audience when pitching something new like blogs and podcasts. Smith employs a technique he learned in previous jobs. He begins by finding early adopters who think the notion of a podcast interesting. He then produces a pilot to show that the podcast can generate results worth something to the company.

Typical podcasts from BMC discuss issues of direct interest to the target audience, such as one titled, "The Real Impact of Change on Your Data Center," which is introduced on the Talk BMC blog this way:

"Andi Mann, Senior Analyst at Enterprise Management Associates and Kia Behnia, Chief Architect at BMC Software, explore how data center managers can derive significant benefits by becoming better at planning and predicting change. The key is to implement best practices from ITIL (the IT Infrastructure Library) and important related technologies like the CMDB to help your organization thrive in a rapidly changing IT-supported business environment."

Nothing about this podcast suggests that listeners are being pitched or sold something. Instead, BMC Software is providing value to an audience in a format that overcomes the shortcomings of text (like whitepapers, for example—How many white papers can any one person read?). As Smith notes, hearing from these in-the-trenches employees puts a human face on the company, making it more real—and more desirable to do business with.

Some Guidelines for B2B Podcasting

We've already made the point that B2B customers are different from individual consumers. When reaching out with a podcast to B2B customers (and other B2B audiences), there's no point in pretending to be "Dawn and Drew" (the popular husband-and-wife podcasting team who have built a huge audience by being provocative) when your audience has come for useful business content. There are podcasting practices you should learn and adhere to which, so far, too many business podcasts are ignoring. Most business podcasts, unlike BMC Software, don't have associated blogs. (We'll talk more about that in the section "Integrate Your Podcast into the Blogosphere".)

While there are not many B2B podcasts yet, podcasting is exploding and businesses are going to figure out sooner rather than later that a podcast could be a useful B2B communication channel. Your business could, conceivably, be one of the pioneers!

With that in mind, we've assembled ten guidelines for B2B podcasting:

Being Relevant

If you're considering a B2B podcast, it's likely you've given some consideration to a theme and an audience, already. A podcast no company we're aware of has introduced is one targeting customers' sales forces. For instance, IBM's *The Future Of…* podcast targets investment analysts and others in the financial community. (We've mentioned *The Future Of…* before. We like it. A lot.)

A podcast for this audience helps elevate your content above the dozens, or even hundreds, of other companies sending content through traditional channels. But it's not enough to just focus on this audience; you have to add some value. You don't need to disclose material information for this podcast to be relevant, but you should offer insights into why your organization is a worthy investment. You might, for instance, pick a focus of your R&D efforts and give it a bit more attention than usual, talk about customer satisfaction metrics, or conduct an interview with one of your thought leaders.

Sticking to the Point

Under some circumstances, you might be tempted to use your podcast to address problems or issues that have reared their ugly heads. It's easy to view the podcast as a broad business communication tool. It's not. Podcasting is all about narrowcasting, particularly when you're dealing with a business audience. Resist the temptation to digress, you risk losing an audience that listens because of the highly focused content you deliver. Consider General Motors' *Fastlane Radio*. Like the related blog, *Fastlane Radio* is a behind-the-scenes look at how cars are designed and built. How many people would unsubscribe if GM used an episode to explain its labor issues or its earnings? That's not why people subscribed.

Avoiding Fluff

Some critics of podcasting suggested that business podcasts should be more entertaining. We don't disagree. No matter how valuable the information is, if it's so achingly boring that it would put the most curious listener to sleep, the podcast won't succeed. However, one pundit went so far as to suggest that business podcasts should play songs. Don't you believe it. Someone who listens to the IBM podcast wants to know what the future holds and they want to hear it from experts working on real-world applications.

Listeners to our podcast may argue, "But you play music." That's true; we play a podsafe tune at the end of every show. But we're not a B2B podcast; there is no business behind our show. (We're just two guys who do not work together doing a podcast.) We also save the music for the end of the show, so those who don't want to hear music can stop listening when the music starts. (Incidentally, we play music to support the independent artists whose efforts are one of the biggest drivers of podcasting and because it's our show and we want to.)

Be Infotaining

While you don't want to turn your B2B podcast into a top 40 music show, you do want to employ enough entertainment elements to make it interesting to listen to. Solid content is not compelling if it is delivered by a lone monotonous voice. Find a host who is engaging and, if your podcast includes interviews, make sure she is a good interviewer.

Use musical intros, outros, and bumpers, introduce new features, and generally take advantage of the medium. Adopt a format for your show. *For Immediate Release* is a co-hosted discussion with audio commentary from other sources. You could do an interview show, a panel discussion, or commentary by company thought leaders. Listeners get to like a format. They also like it if you shake it up from time to time.

Building and Engaging Community

There's a podcasting myth that suggests one of podcasting's great limitations is its one-way, top-down nature. We hope we dispensed with that myth in Chapter 15, where we discussed how to connect your listeners and build a community. But in case you took the nonlinear path and started reading here instead of at the beginning, we can sum up our view of this belief in one word: Hogwash. (We could have been harsher, but this is a family-friendly book!)

Podcasts routinely build communities of listeners that interact with the podcaster. Adam Curry's *Daily Source Code* offers a great example. Curry expressed an interest in biodiesel and asked for input. Listeners sent what they knew by e-mail and audio comment. Other listeners commented on what the first round of listeners said. Curry responded and asked more questions. The biodiesel discussion went on for weeks.

Our podcast, *For Immediate Release*, was the first podcast to focus on public relations and organizational communications, but we do not see the growing number of PR-focused podcasts as competition. We even link to them in what we call our "podroll," a list of other communication-themed podcasts on our show blog. Just because your audience is made up of customers doesn't mean you shouldn't recognize the interconnectedness of the medium and feed your listeners' hunger for useful and interesting content.

Not that we believe for a minute that Boston Consulting Group would ever welcome a new podcast by McKinsey & Company into the podosphere. Short of that, though, it pays dividends to be part of a bigger podcasting community.

Don't Advertise or Sell

Nobody wants to subscribe to or download a 20-minute commercial. You can brand your product, service, or company by being the provider of useful information. (Look to the BMC Software podcast as an example, putting sounds and voices to a company that produces an abstract product.) You should avoid turning your corporate podcast into an advertisement at all costs, regardless of what your throwback marketing VP wants.

Being Authentic

Businesses often are inclined to overproduce their media, striving to be as good as—or better than—mainstream public media. We remember talking to the manager of one company's video production operation who said his baseline was a local newscast; his work could never, no matter what, be worse than a typical local newscast. While podcast listeners do want to be entertained, their primary interest is in content, not polish. A podcast hosted by voice talent reading a script will be dismissed, while listening to a real engineer or designer or brand manager — replete with all his "ums" and "uhs" — will be compelling, as long as he's talking about something the listener cares about. Remember that you can edit out the worst mistakes in postproduction, as we described in Chapter 9.

Being Mindful of Your Listeners' Time

Depending on whom you talk to, B2B podcasts shouldn't exceed 20 minutes. You might argue that plenty of podcasts run longer; ours is one of them, as are some incredibly popular shows like *This Week in Tech* and *The Gillmor Gang*. The key difference is that these shows are not sponsored by a business with an underlying motive. No matter how good the content is, in a podcast or any other communication, your listener intuitively knows that, at the end of the day, your goal is to get or keep his business.

With a business podcast, you're asking your customer (or prospective customer) to give her attention to an audio program about your business when they could be listening to new rock and roll on *Accident Hash*. It's an exchange. Don't ask for too much of your listeners' time. Make sure you fill the time you do have with something useful enough to make the exchange worthwhile.

Integrating Your Podcast into the Blogosphere

Outside the pseudo podcasts from the mainstream media (repackaged pre-broadcast radio content), you'll be hard-pressed to find a podcast that doesn't have an associated blog. So far, most of the business podcasts haven't emulated this practice, with the exception of GM (where the *Fastlane* podcast is just part of the Fastlane blog) and BMC Software.

Your podcast blog page contains your show notes, another tactic common among indie podcasters but missing from businesses.) Show notes detail just what's in each show, offer links to related content, and even provide time codes so listeners know at what point of the show each topic is discussed. Listeners appreciate the heck out of good show notes because it makes listening easier.

Blogs also make it possible for listeners to comment on each show, which is tremendously important. By inviting comments on each program, you effectively build that community of listeners' that naysayers insist you can't build with a podcast.

Chapter 25

Use Internal Podcasts in Your Business

How to…

- Deliver podcasts internally
- Categorize your internal podcasts

Podcasting is already starting to make inroads in the field of employee communications, from high-tech companies (such as IBM) to more traditional firms (like pharmaceutical and insurance companies) finding that podcasts open a new avenue for reaching employees with important messages and content that improves the work experience.

Internal podcasts should be considered for a host of reasons. To understand the rationale, it's important to take a step back and look at the state of employee communications in general, which, due to computer technology, isn't very good.

Employee communications experienced a brief renaissance beginning in the mid-1970s and continuing through the mid-1990s. Before the 1970s, employee communications was the province of "house organs," cheesy publications that companies produced when times were good and funds were available, but these were tossed aside when things grew tough and budgets tightened. Most employees didn't miss them when they were gone, however. These magazines and newsletters were produced by secretaries in their free time and covered birthdays, babies, brides, and bowling scores (the dreaded "four Bs" of internal communication). Strategic internal communication just wasn't on management's radar because employees performed well without it, driven by loyalty born of guaranteed lifetime employment.

A variety of forces put an end to the idea of job security, however, and the built-in emotional bond employees had with their companies evaporated. Rather than buying loyalty, companies had to earn commitment. Communicating effectively with employees became a requirement. Strategic communication—that which is designed to achieve specific objectives—became a management function in more enlightened organizations. These companies recognized the need to provide employees with "line of sight," a connection between the topline messages from senior management and the day-to-day realities of their frontline jobs. Communication needed to become two-way, allowing employees to get directly involved in decisions that affected them. It needed to explain the business and the forces that drove management decisions so employees wouldn't be surprised when such decisions were announced.

There is, as you might expect, a lot more to employee communications than this, and ample books and other resources are available if you're interested. The point we need to make here is that professional employee communicators used a variety of tools—mainly face-to-face (such as town hall meetings) and print—to reach employees and engage them.

In the mid-1990s, though, companies discovered intranets and employee communications went to hell. Rather than view the intranet and its various components (like e-mail and a web interface) based on their strengths, companies fell all over themselves in their rush to migrate *everything* to the intranet. Why? Because the intranet cost a heck of a lot less than print. Companies couldn't *wait* to dispense with print and put everything online. Face-to-face communication actually gave way to e-mails and web copy sometimes, *even if this wasn't the best way to communicate some messages* and *even if some employees had no access to computer terminals!*

Messages formerly crafted based on careful strategic planning were suddenly dumped into e-mails or shoveled onto a web page. Employees overwhelmed by e-mail started ignoring messages somebody else had considered important. And no employee ever said to a spouse, "No breakfast for me today, honey. The communications department has new stories up on the intranet and I gotta get to work early and read them!" Employees use the intranet to do their jobs. Few employees consider staying current with company news integral to their jobs.

The intranet is good for a lot of communication activities, of course. For delivering current information, it beats the heck out of print, which can take days to produce and distribute. For analytical content, though, print rocks. To build trust, nothing beats face-to-face.

What worked best, though, didn't matter. The intranet was expedient, and communicators who previously focused on strategy now dedicated their efforts to page design and underlying technologies like content management systems. Employees found themselves buried in online text with not nearly enough time available to absorb it. To make matters worse, they couldn't take the intranet home. Fears (often unfounded) of security breaches led company IT departments to resist letting employees access the intranet from outside company offices, so the only time available to read company communications was while they were at work, when their bosses expected them to be working!

The intranet also made a lot of communicators lazy. In the days of print communication, communicators had to carefully consider what messages were truly important because there were space limitations. The publication budget only allowed for, say, a monthly 16-page publication, which forced communicators to cover only what was genuinely important. The unrestricted ability to publish *anything* on the intranet has created even more content through which employees have to wade in order to identify the nuggets. And all of this has been happening while employees continue to be loaded with more work that requires longer hours, leaving them less time to read the communications department's output.

Just in the nick of time, along comes podcasting.

25

Podcasting's Role in the Internal Communication Mix

The uses to which podcasting can be put are vast and (sorry for the cliché) limited only by the imagination. Where it fits into the mix is simple to explain. The following attributes of podcasting lend themselves extraordinarily well to the internal environment:

- **It's audio**   While this may seem like a blinding flash of the obvious, audio provides employees with welcome relief from the flood of online text. Further, audio input registers on a different part of the brain than text. Hearing a message reinforces any reading of the message you may have done. Lastly, audio means you can *hear* the actual voice of (for example) the CEO, with his sincerity, passion, and commitment, little of which comes through when you simply quote the executive's words in text.

- **It's detachable**   Employees can detach the MP3 file from the computer and offload it to a digital media device, letting them listen while they're out jogging at lunchtime, commuting to or from the office, waiting for a plane on either end of a business trip (or sitting on one of those interminable flights), or driving to the next sales call.

- **It's entertaining**   At least, it *can* be entertaining, which makes it more compelling to listen to than reading a cold article on a glowing, glaring computer screen.

- **It's cheap**   The reduced barriers to entry that drove the spread of podcasting on the Internet make it attractive internally, too.

Put more succinctly, an employee who is not inclined to sit at her desk and read endless screens of test may take ten minutes to close her eyes, settle back in her chair, and *listen* to the weekly company news show. An employee who has no time to read anything at work that isn't directly related to his job may be happy to jack his iPod into his cassette deck and listen to the news on his drive home.

Delivering Podcasts Internally

The fact that podcasts are a natural internal communication vehicle doesn't mean you won't run into opposition when you try to introduce the idea of starting one.

The most vociferous opposition is likely to emanate from the IT department. Their concerns come in two basic flavors:

- We don't have the bandwidth to distribute great big audio files.

- We're not prepared to support RSS.

These issues explain why most current intranet podcasts are not delivered via RSS. Instead, e-mail is distributed with a link to the podcast, allowing employees to download the MP3 file at their convenience. This balances the distribution load, easing the strain on bandwidth since the file isn't retrieved by most employees' podcatchers almost simultaneously.

There are alternatives to this approach to distribution. For example, you could host your file externally (using a service like LibSyn) and ask employees to subscribe from home. (This is the approach taken by one company we'll look at in just a few pages whose podcast is aimed at the field sales force, a group of employees who are *never* in the office.) You could release the file in the evening, when employees aren't using the network and a rash of downloads won't affect anybody. Most practically—and least likely—is increasing available bandwidth to accommodate the inevitable expansion of audio and video offerings over the intranet. The need for greater bandwidth will only continue to grow, but it's also an expensive proposition. A solid business case is required to secure management agreement to make this kind of investment.

Internal Podcast Content Categories

As noted in the beginning of the chapter, employee communications is valuable when it's strategic—that is, it's planned in order to achieve measurable objectives. Consequently, the approach to intranet podcast generally shouldn't be, "Podcasting rocks. Let's do an intranet podcast!" Instead, you need to consider the kind of information you want to get into employees' hands and what portion of that information can best be delivered in the audio format.

The following subsections offer some suggestions for the more basic types of podcasts you can use as part of your internal communication mix.

News Summary

Not every employee has access to the intranet. Not every employee opens every e-mail or reads every news item with careful attention. A news podcast can summarize the most important news of interest to most employees. Even for those employees who *do* pay attention to the company's text-based news coverage, a recap of the key items can reinforce and prioritize the messages they've already heard.

Internal communicators can draw inspiration from plenty of examples of news podcasts. The Denver Post's podcast, for example, is a pretty effective rehash of the headlines in each day's paper. PRWeek, the weekly trade publication of the public relations industry, has recently launched a weekly recap of its articles.

For employees, you should keep a couple factors in mind that aren't as significant in external podcasts where the audience has a built-in interest in the content and is willing to forgive lower quality in exchange for information they care about. To keep employees' interest, consider using real employees—not representatives of the communication department—to co-host the podcast. A talent search could not only uncover some great voices but also whip up interest in the launch of the news show. You also don't have to use the same voices for every show; you could opt instead to alternate between two or three sets of co-hosts.

Sprinkling a few brief interviews into the show can also liven it up. We're not talking about in-depth conversations, but rather a 30 or 60-second clip of an executive making a key point about an initiative or announcement.

Finally, keep it short. Ten minutes should be your goal for the longest news summary. Regardless of how engaging the show may be, employees already are dedicating a considerable amount of their lives to the company and won't tolerate long, drawn-out podcasts that simply suck up even more of their time.

Feature Magazine

There's more to internal communication than simply keeping employees informed. Among other communication goals, consider the following:

- Helping employees understand the connection between their jobs and top-level pronouncements

- Profiling the marketplace, including competitors and customers

- Recognizing employees who exemplify company values and achieve significant goals

- Establishing lines of communication among employees through which knowledge can be transferred

All of these objectives can be supported through internal podcasts. One approach that lets you try to accomplish all of these goals is an audio magazine, a program that contains three or four brief features rolled up into a package under 15 minutes. Presented weekly or biweekly, such a show could support and enhance your company's communication strategy.

The segments that make up the show could be repeated each week. The following are some examples.

Questions for the President

In one business unit of a major food products company, the head of employee communications found herself with a handful of questions leftover from an all-hands town hall meeting. The CEO had run out of time before he could answer every question that had been written by employees on note cards. The communications director took the questions and some recording equipment to the CEO's office, where she read him the questions, which he answered naturally and conversationally. She distributed the Q&A as an internal podcast. Employees responded enthusiastically to the format.

Now, the "Ask the CEO" segment is being woven into a three-segment podcast; currently, the communications team is working on finalizing the other two segments. For "Ask the CEO," she will keep on soliciting questions from employees.

Meeting Your Colleagues

At Sedgewick Claims Management Services, a Memphis, Tennessee–based worker's compensation third-party administrator, communications specialist Jonathan Mast and administrative assistant Aidan Hagood have been producing *QuickCast*, a short (not surprisingly) podcast for nearly a year. In each episode, the pair interview one or more employees who are doing interesting work with interesting clients. Through this podcast, which usually runs about five minutes, employees hear about colleagues they would never otherwise meet.

"What excited our senior management [was that], as we hire new people into the workforce we know many people in that age group are getting their information in different ways, more portable and on-the-go," Mast explains. Thirty-seven percent of Sedgewick's employees already owned portable digital device, and 55 percent of them said they had downloaded a podcast, according to the results of a survey the communicators conducted. In addition, employees had the ability to listen to the podcasts at their desks, as well.

"Everybody is in the human aspect of company news," Hagood says. Each show contains an interview, some directly related to work and others just offering insight into colleagues, creating connections that would never otherwise materialize. For example, during Breast Cancer Awareness Month, Hagood and Mast interviewed two employees who were breast cancer survivors.

Customer Voices

An interview with a customer provides most employees with something they never get: direct contact with the customer. Generally, only sales and marketing representatives get to meet the customer face-to-face. For most employees, knowledge of the customer comes third- or fourth-hand, if at all. Yet customers drive the business, so now knowing their issues, their preferences, what they like about doing business with the company and what they dislike, employees are often confused about the reason management makes some of the decisions it makes.

Many customers are happy to talk about what the company is doing well and what they wish the company could do better. You could record an in-depth conversation with a customer each episode, editing it down after the interview to a length more conducive to that of your podcast, ensuring employees hear the most important points. You could make the complete recording available for those interested in hearing everything the customer had to say.

Advertising and Marketing Updates

Much of the advertising and marketing introduced by a company has an audio component. A podcast lets employees hear the ads that will make their way onto television and radio before they reach the public.

Speeches

Executives make speeches everywhere, at trade shows, annual meetings, investor road shows, internal town hall meetings, and any number of other venues. Key passages from these talks can make up a brief segment, with a host or narrator providing context for the segments.

No rule says each installment's segments are the same every time. You could mix them up. Or, as the folks from Sedgewick CMS do, you could make any of these a regular short podcast that stands on its own.

Divisional or Departmental Podcasts

Most of the 250 or so Canadian employees of ALTANA Pharmaceuticals, a German company, worked in sales or marketing. Access to the intranet was difficult for the sales staff until they returned home from sales calls and could get online.

A new sales vice president named Ron Clark joined the company. This personable new executive needed a way to reach the sales staff and opted for a podcast aimed specifically at the sales team. The podcast, originally intended only to last a few episodes, grew so popular among the audience that the VP now uses the channel to conduct interviews with other executives, helping sales representatives understand things that could affect their work, such as new products or new marketing initiatives.

Other executives—even the president—have been clamoring for the opportunity to host their own podcasts, according to David Bradfield, senior vice president of iStudio, the Canadian communications company that pitched the idea and produced the podcasts for ALTANA.

Employees and Portable Digital Devices

One concern managers may have about podcasts is the perception that portable digital players are required. Sedgewick CMS launched its podcast knowing that fewer than half of their employees had such devices. In fact, most employees are perfectly content to listen at their desks.

Still, it's nice to be able to take the company show on the road. Providing inexpensive portable players to all employees is not something most companies would consider, however. National Semiconductor didn't consider it either. Instead, the company bought each of its employees *expensive* MP3 players, video iPods to be precise. The iPods were gifts from the company to celebrate the firm's most successful year in its history. "We're looking for new and more effective ways to communicate with our employees—and the iPods will help us do both," according to Brian L. Halla, National's chairman and CEO. "Our employees were vital contributors to our most successful year in National's 47-year history, and we wanted to equip them with the tools to help us create more value for our customers. The Apple iPod exemplifies the next stage of the consumer electronics revolution as content such as downloadable music, movies, and digital photos—as well as a compelling user experience—takes center stage."

In its statement announcing the gift, the company said the iPods would let employees download company podcasts and other communications.

Equipping employees with the ability to listen to podcasts could make as much sense as giving them cell phones or laptops. (In fact, as cell phones continue to integrate the ability to listen to MP3 files, a cell phone could be all employees need to listen to podcasts!) And inexpensive MP3 players bought in bulk could wind up costing less than $25 per employee. (Note that in some countries, MP3 players distributed as gifts could result in taxes accruing to the employees.)

Chapter 26

Use a Podcast to Help Your Small Business Compete

How to…

- Separate podcast marketing from other marketing
- Use the advantages of narrowcasting
- Be competitive with your podcast

Of *course*, big businesses are starting to podcast. With multimillion-dollar budgets for advertising, marketing, and public relations, it's no big deal to toss a little podcast into the mix. Why not? The investment is pocket change to most organizations and if podcasting as a communication channel doesn't work out, not much is lost. Of course, this doesn't mitigate the need to do it right if you're going to do it at all—organizations that blunder through the introduction of any new communication channel risk damage to their reputations.

For owners of smaller businesses, podcasting is an opportunity to level that playing field that so favors your larger competition. Without those millions of dollars the big boys can bring to bear, you can focus more on your social media (blogs and podcasts) to build rapport with customers and earn their loyalty. These new tools help by building strong relationships with customers, which is, let's face it, a lot better than introducing a catchy new jingle.

Blogs, podcasts, wikis, and the other tools of social computing share many virtues, not the least of which is frugality. It's possible to produce a podcast for less money each week than you spend on dinner and a movie. Getting a commercial onto the radio for broadcast to markets that include your audience can cost some small businesses their entire year's marketing and advertising budget, if they even have a budget.

On a flight during a business trip, Shel sat next to the marketing director for a growing national business. The company mowed lawns. It had been started by an enterprising youth who mowed lawns to make pocket change, then recruited others to mow, expanding his territory. The business now has regional managers and white-collar staff managing various aspects of the operations. The kid who mowed lawns is now an adult and doing quite well.

The marketing executive lamented that the company was struggling to find new channels since it was getting harder and harder to employ their most successful tool: telemarketing. The company did not have the advertising budget to go head-to-head against some of the large, franchise-supported gardening services, a number of which are even larger these days, having been acquired by pest control companies.

Shel's advice was that the company create a blog and a podcast. The blog would let the company's founder offer lawn care tips in the form of stories involving representatives from his company: "Larry was cutting a lawn in Burbank when he came across a particularly brown spot that looked like it was getting plenty of water." The podcast, though, was where the company could build huge brand equity.

Ten minutes, Shel told him. That's how much time you'd need once a week to build an audience that not only would identify strongly with the company but invest an emotional stake in it. Consider the following format:

- **Opener**   "Welcome to *Lawn Secrets*, the podcast for all those of us who know it sounds lame so we never tell anyone, but: we *love our lawns*. This is episode number seven of the show for lawn lovers to learn the secrets of lawn care from the experts…and from each other."

- **Contents**   "This is your host, Eric Watson, the founder of Happy Lawns, and today on Lawn Secrets, we'll talk to Willie Thomas, the groundskeeper at Dodger Stadium, who'll share a secret about restoring a lawn after it's been trampled. We have questions from two listeners, and then the listener secret of the week."

- **Interview**   A five-minute interview, very conversational, with groundskeeper Willie. Willie stays on the line for…

- **Listener Questions**   Listener e-mail or audio questions, which the host *and* the guest answer.

- **Listener Secret of the Week**   Either an audio or e-mail contribution from a listener, who gets something (a t-shirt?) for having his secret read on the show.

- **Wrap-up**   Thanks to Willie Thomas for that great advice about green spray paint, and also for that terrific answer to our listener's question about dog droppings. And thanks again to Melinda Snow for her secret about lawnmower rotor adjustments. Next week on Lawn Secrets, another guest expert and more of your questions and secrets. Don't forget, if at Happy Lawns, we love your lawn as much as you do, and that's just how we'll cut it. I share more tips from the field on my blog, which is also where you'll find the show notes for today's show, and where you can post your comments. Until next week, this is Eric Watson reminding you to take time to stop and smell the grass cuttings.

The company and individual names are completely made up. But the idea is that, with enough entertainment value and content that satisfies the needs of a target audience, in a format that doesn't require an unreasonable time commitment,

26

your target audience will find out and tell others about the company. They will also be most likely to influence other potential customers, including those who aren't likely to listen to a podcast (or even know what one is).

Narrowcasting Content Directly to Your Audience

For the small business, this "narrowcasting" concept is at the heart of that leveling of the playing field. Your much larger competitors spend a considerable amount of money to attract the right audience and are billed by traditional media outlets like magazines and television stations based on a model called CPM, which, as mentioned earlier, means "cost per thousand impressions." In other words, you pay for your advertising based on the number of people who will see it, regardless of whether they buy anything or are even part of your target market. If you pay someone $20,000 for, say, a banner ad on a web site, and that site guarantees that your banner ad will be seen by 2500 people, then your CPM was $8—that is, you paid $8 for every 1000 people who saw your ad.

There's a problem inherent with this approach to advertising or marketing. Think about sitting at home one evening watching television. The commercial break begins and you see a commercial for a video game. You don't play video games and even if you did, it wouldn't be a violent one like *this*. There are probably many, many others watching the same commercial and having the same reaction. Yet, out of every thousand people who see the commercial, it's likely there are *some* who *will* want that game. This is the idea of advertising and the origin of the CPM model. Your target customer is intermingled with the larger audience. That's why it's so important to pick the *right* TV shows to advertise on—companies conduct research to determine which shows are most likely to have the largest percentage of their target customers in the audience. Then, out of every thousand viewers for which they are paying, they hope to reach an adequate number of the right people to buy their products.

In podcasting, CPM makes about as much sense as buying an antenna for your podcast! That's because you are not pushing your content out to an audience. Individuals who are *already* interested are coming to your podcast and *retrieving* it. That means *everybody* who listens to your podcast is part of your target market. *Everybody!*

By way of example, let's return to our friend Ron Shewchuk, creator and host of the *Barbecue Secrets* podcast. Rockin' Ronnie has about 4000 listeners. Each of them found out, through any of a number of sources, that a barbecue podcast was available.

The only people who would sit up and say, "A barbecue *podcast?!* By God, I've got to go subscribe to that!" would be those who are already barbecue enthusiasts. Somebody who cares about barbecue only when he's able to eat what somebody else has grilled isn't going to listen, nor is the woman who thinks barbecuing is too much like camping. *Real* cooking takes place in the kitchen.

Thus, Ron Shewchuk isn't hoping that 40 or 50 of his 4000 listeners might actually want to buy his barbecue cookbook. They're *all* targets; every one of them.

A large publisher selling a competing cookbook might take out space in the cooking section of select newspapers and display ads in related magazines. That larger organization will spend more money in the hopes that a few hardcore barbecuers will see the ad and buy the book—just a handful of the total number of those skimming the newspaper or flipping through the magazine. Ron has all 4000 of his listeners getting to know him, learning to respect his expertise and his sense of humor, and desiring more and more to own a copy of Ron's *Barbecue Secrets*.

Podcast Marketing Is Affordable

We covered how to promote your podcast in Chapter 10. One of the things that should have jumped out at you in that chapter is that all of these promotional activities are virtually *free* other than the investment of your time.

Podcasts, as an element of the new media/social media/social computing/Web 2.0 world, are particularly well suited for word-of-mouth marketing. Word-of-mouth marketing is an old concept, but thanks to the Internet, it has gained new meaning and a lot of organizations, from companies to PR, marketing, and advertising agencies, are paying attention to it, trying to figure out how to make it work for them. There's even an association that has sprung up so people can work together to identify effective, ethical means of developing and deploying word-of-mouth marketing efforts. (It's called, not surprisingly, the Word of Mouth Marketing Association [WOMMA] and you can find it on the Web at www.womma.org.)

Remember, you're dealing with a targeted market—that is, you're *narrowcasting* your content to your people who are already inclined to pay attention to the contents of your podcast. If they are enthusiastic about whatever it is that engages them, then they probably also like talking about it with others, and they *especially* like talking about it with others who share the same passion. In other words, they're already predisposed to tell a bunch of other people about your podcast.

That's not to say you can't give them a nudge, though. Using some of the techniques we talked about in Chapter 15, you can encourage your listeners to let others know about the podcast. They can put one of your web badges on their own site, they can add your podcast as a link to their blogs, they can drink their coffee from a mug with your podcast's logo on it (as we noted in Chapter 18), and you can even offer listeners some kind of premium if they refer a new subscriber to the show (such as a button, a t-shirt, or some other bit of show-related merchandise). Whatever you do, remember two rules:

- Soft-pedal your pitch. Remember, you're a business and at the end of the day your listeners, no matter how much they like your show, know your ultimate goal is to get them to spend their money on your products or services. The harder you pitch, the more you risk turning off your listener.

- Promote the podcast, not the product. If you read Chapter 20, you know your podcast needs to be about what matters to the listener. Nobody will voluntarily download or subscribe to a 10- or 15-minute infomercial! (If you haven't read Chapter 20 and the other chapters in Part 5, go back and read them!)

Ultimately, though, you don't need to pitch anybody at all in order to start spreading the word about your podcast. Instead (assuming your content is compelling, relevant, and makes for good listening) your listeners will spread the word for you. Word of mouth also spreads through other channels. For example, the more people who listen and link to your podcast, the higher your podcast will appear in Google rankings. Our friend Rockin' Ronnie Shewchuk, for example, notes that you can always find *Barbecue Secrets* in Google by typing "barbecue podcast." His show will be first on the list! (Coincidentally, if you query Google with "PR podcast," Neville and Shel's podcast will appear first on the list returned.)

Another means of spreading the word is to get your listeners to vote for your podcast on directories where rankings are managed through votes. On *For Immediate Release*, for example, we have a text entry field that listeners can use to submit their votes at Podcast Alley (www.podcastalley.com). It doesn't take many votes for us to wind up in the top 10 of the business category. Hence, anybody looking for a business category is likely to find us. And while our loyal listeners may not be enthusiastic about the idea of overtly pitching their colleagues on the show, it's easy to submit a vote to support their favorite podcasters.

Being Truly Competitive

Podcasting lets you reach those coveted members of your target market for a lot less money than your competitors have at their disposal. Using the principles outlined in all the preceding chapters will help you produce a podcast that interests them, keeps them listening, engages them, features good audio quality, and helps create a connection between your organization or brand and the listeners you want to reach.

Being truly competitive, though, means adding another layer to your podcast. Wikipedia defines competitiveness as "the act of striving against another force for the purpose of achieving dominance or attaining a reward or goal, or out of a biological imperative such as survival." In other words, you're not just seeking to get people to pay attention to you even though you do not have the advertising or marketing resources of your larger competitors. After all, what's the point of getting all those people to pay attention if you can't lure customers away from the big boys?

Getting people to listen is step one. Providing content that people will listen to because it is interesting, valuable, or entertaining is step two. Step three, though, is making sure the way you present the content reflects the value you would bring to your listeners should they shift their business from a bigger business to *your* business.

To take the leap from producing a popular podcast to producing a podcast that generates business requires you to think about how you will position your organization and—if you're the host—how to position yourself.

Consider, for example, the language you will use. You may feel liberated by the fact you are not constrained from using expressive words in your podcast. (By "expressive," we mean "four-letter.") However, while some members of your target audience may chuckle at your use of colorful language, they may also reject the notion of doing business with someone who talks that way. If you talk negatively about a customer, you may turn business away because your listeners wouldn't want you talking about *them* that way. If you insult a competitor, some businesses may opt not to do business with you because they like working with people who are more civil in their business dealings.

Of course, if you need to avoid the negatives in order to be competitive, you should also accentuate the positive (as the saying goes). You already do much of this simply by embracing some of the interactive elements of a podcast, such as…

- **Listener comments**   By accepting and reading or playing listener comments, you send the message that you *listen*. Think about your biggest competitors. What does it take for a customer to be heard by one of *them*?

- **Blog comments**   The blog that houses your podcast is one of the places listeners can submit comments. Because it's on a blog, however, other listeners can use that comment to launch a conversation with one another, building a community of people who have a connection with your podcast (and, by extension, your business). Plus, since you can jump into the conversation, it reinforces the notion that you're paying attention to what customers say and think.

You also need to make sure you come off as a subject-matter expert—a thought leader for your field. Your larger competitors rely on copy written by advertising companies and press releases written by PR account representatives. On your podcast, they get to hear *your* voice and, if you're authoritative and knowledgeable, your listeners will be more likely to believe that your grasp of the issues in your industry is woven into the fabric of your entire company and that they, as customers, would be likely to benefit.

Case Study: Bearing Point

There's a fine line between being an authoritative thought leader and an arrogant blowhard. Podcasts are conversational; if you are perceived as preachy, it's likely a lot of listeners will drift away. Outside of church, not many people like being preached to!

Just how does a podcast produce these kinds of results? Take a look at Bearing Point. You may have never heard of this company, but it competes with some larger organizations you probably *have* heard of, like EDS and Accenture. The company produced a whitepaper, a fairly routine marketing tactic for knowledge-based companies. The question was: How could the company get that whitepaper in the hands of its target audience? One answer was to discuss the whitepaper in its company podcasts. As a result, the company saw a huge increase in sign-ups for the whitepaper over the numbers they had previously experienced. The company hoped that 10 percent of those who downloaded the podcast would request the whitepaper. Instead, 30 percent did, representing a 200 percent improvement over the marketing methods to which the company was accustomed.

The company used some traditional but low-cost methods to promote the podcast. For example, Bearing Point issued a press release that began…

Bearing Point Inc., one of the world's largest management consulting and systems integration firms, today announced the first in a series of new podcasts targeted to financial services executives are available on the company's web site, as well as on popular podcasting sites such as Apples iTunes.com. A podcast is the increasingly popular form of audio broadcast downloaded to be heard via digital audio players.

Each request for a whitepaper results in a sales lead. One measure Bearing Point used to assess the effectiveness of the effort was to rate the quality of the leads generated. As it turned out, the company was delighted with the quality of the leads, many of whom were converted into customers. (At the time this book was written, you could see the press release, listen to a sample Bearing Point podcast, and see other materials at www.marketingsherpa.com/bearp2/study.html.)

Personally, we feel this podcast could have been even more effective if it had adopted one of the more informal styles we addressed in earlier chapters—for example, perhaps a knowledgeable employee could have been interviewed by a host instead of having professional voice talent read a script. However, given the fact that the financial services executives could listen to the information-rich podcast on their way to work—that is, it rose above the clutter—it still produced better results than the company's management dreamed were possible.

Appendix A Legal Considerations

This chapter will be necessarily brief. First of all, we are not lawyers, so everything we say here, even though it is well-researched, should be checked with a lawyer before you take any action or make any decisions. Second, there are more arcane and detailed laws that govern nuanced aspects of copyright, trademark, defamation, and the other legal issues we cover in this chapter than we could possibly cram into it. Finally, the laws are different in every country and podcasters come from *everywhere*. We confine ourselves to the United States for this chapter, but if you're from somewhere else, don't even waste your time reading this chapter—you need to find out what the laws are in *your* country that apply to podcasting.

That said, it is important to be aware of the most important laws that can cause you untold grief if you break them. In most legal systems, ignorance is not a defense; just because you didn't *know* it was against the law to do something with your podcast does not mean the courts cannot make you suffer the consequences. And there are laws—plenty of them—that apply to podcasts. This actually comes as a surprise to some podcasters who insist that freedom from laws was one of the enticements to begin podcasting in the first place. But there is only one instance in which this so-called "freedom" exists: You can use words that would get you fined by the Federal Communications Commission (FCC) in just about any other vehicle. The FCC governs public airwaves, primarily telephones, television, and radio. The Internet is not considered a public airwave, though, making it easy for anybody creating content for the medium to express themselves with as many expletives and seamy descriptions as they like. But that's where the ability to thumb your nose at a regulatory agency—or the courts—comes to an abrupt halt. Virtually every other law that applies to the rest of the world applies equally to the Net, including podcasts.

In this chapter, we'll briefly cover the following legal issues every podcaster should be aware of:

- Copyright
- Publicity rights
- Trademark
- Defamation

Copyright

Copyright is the single most important legal issue to consider when producing a podcast. Copyright can be seen in two different ways in podcasting:

1. Most audio elements you may include in a podcast are copyrighted.

2. Your podcast itself is copyrighted.

Let's review the implications of these two dimensions.

Elements of Your Podcast

If you obtain content from somewhere else and put it into your podcast, odds are it's protected by copyright and you could wind up dealing with the copyright holder if you do not obtain the appropriate permissions and rights. This ranges from obvious content, like a song from a CD, to material you might have sworn was fine to use, such as the audio of an interview you conducted with somebody.

Once a work of any kind, good or bad, has been committed to print or a recording, copyright law applies to it (at least, in the U.S.). While there are some exceptions (which we'll cover later), you should assume that *anything* you want to put into your podcast—whether you're reading a paragraph from a newspaper or playing a sound effect you downloaded from a web site—is protected by copyright.

Whoever holds a copyright actually has several different rights. These include…

- The right to allow the work to be copied and used in other places

- The right to let somebody make changes to the work, such as turning a song into a mashup or extracting just a few seconds of a it

- The right to allow the work to be broadcast to the public

- The right to let members of the public make additional copies of the work they have received by broadcast for their own use

Copyright applies to both text and audio, so reading something aloud that was copyrighted by the author is as much a violation of copyright as playing a song. And these works are copyrighted whether the creator of the works submitted them to the U.S. Copyright Office or not. While you can *obtain* a copyright for your work, the work is copyrighted under law as soon as it is "fixed" (that is, written down or recorded).

Also, copyrights apply even if you make minor changes. For example, if you take the words somebody else wrote and read them aloud in your podcast, but make a few revisions, you haven't eliminated the need to obtain permission to use that text.

A

Thinking about the Elements of Your Podcast

Let's take a look at some of the more common kinds of often protected work you might want to include in your podcast.

Voice Recordings

Voice recordings are another area where the idea of copyright gets confusing. *Two* copyrights are actually involved, and you need to consider them both. First, there's the "underlying work." If the audio clip you're playing features somebody reading a script, the script is protected by copyright whether it was written by the performer or a third party. The second copyright is the actual performance, the recorded sound you want to use. To protect yourself, you need to get permission for *both* those rights.

Interviews

Many podcasts (including ours) feature interviews. You find someone who can offer some words of wisdom or value for your audience that relates to your podcast's theme. You make arrangements for an interview, and using the advice we provide in this book for recording, you capture the interview and incorporate it into one of your podcasts. Believe it or not, the interviewee's answers to your questions—and anything else he says—are owned by the interviewee.

It's not likely that someone you interviewed will exercise those rights, since they agreed to be interviewed in the first place. (Unless, of course, the interview winds up making him look like an idiot, in which case he may also come after you for defamation!) You can assume that the interviewee gave you an "implied license" to use the interview when he granted the request, but why take the chance? Get it in writing or record the interviewee agreeing to the interview.

Music

Music is probably the diciest copyright issue most podcasters face. An outstanding early podcast, P.W. Fenton's *Digital Flotsam*, provides an excellent example. In each episode of *Digital Flotsam*, Fenton recounted a tale from his past (and most often from his youth). At just the right moment in the story, Fenton would play a song that perfectly reflected the mood. Eventually, though, he had to stop, because the songs were protected. Fenton still produces *Digital Flotsam*, and it is still excellent, but it has lost some of its power because the songs he now plays are "podsafe." Rather than just play the song that leaps into his mind while telling the story, he has to hunt for a song that matches the tale. For the listener, the instant understanding of the association Fenton has made is lost as well.

Nobody maintains as tight a grip on their intellectual property as the major recording labels that hold the rights to the music they produce and sell. And nobody will be as inclined to come after you if you violate their rights. So, it makes good sense to know exactly what you're getting yourself into if you want to play copyrighted music on your podcast.

This is not to suggest that podcasters simply cannot play copyrighted music. There are several podcasts—*Coverville* leaps to mind—for which the podcaster has ponied up the dollars to acquire the rights. You'll just have to decide for yourself whether it's worth it to you to make that investment for *your* podcast.

As with spoken word recordings, two kinds of copyrights apply to music:

■ *The musical composition*   This refers to the lyrics and music that would appear in sheet music, although no sheet music is required. In fact, a composition could have been scribbled on a cocktail napkin; that's all a composer needs to have fixed the music in a tangible form. Most composers assign the rights for their musical compositions to publishing companies. These companies contract with organizations that collect fees and distribute them back to the rights holder. You might think these organizations are collection agencies, but in the music business they're called "collective rights management agencies." A company called The Harry Fox Agency is the most often-used organization to grant "mechanical licenses" for the reproduction and/or distribution of the composition. For example, all those sheet-music books you see in music stores? The Harry Fox Agency most likely was involved in issuing the license that allowed the publisher to publish those books. The right to play a song on the radio (or in any other "public performance") is granted by a performing rights organization, most commonly the American Society of Composers, Authors, and Publishers (ASCAP), Broadcast Music Incorporated (BMI), or the Society of European Stage Authors and Composers (SESAC).

■ *The sound recording*   The performance and recording of a composition is protected as well. Artists generally assign these rights to the record label that produced their CD. This is where things get truly confusing (as if they weren't confusing enough already). The kind of license you need to use a sound recording depends on *how* you plan to use it. It should come as no surprise that podcasts are so new they haven't even been categorized yet.

Practically speaking, this means that playing one song could lead you to have to obtain the rights from several rights holders. And to make matters worse,

A

you have to address two distinct types of rights held under copyright: one to reproduce and distribute copies of a work, and the other to perform the work publicly. Again, different entities may hold these different rights for a single song.

So just what *do* you need to be able to play a protected song on a podcast? Here's the quick rundown:

- *Reproduction and distribution rights*   Get this license from The Harry Fox Agency. This covers the composition of the song written by Bruce Springsteen, not the performance of it by Southside Johnny and the Asbury Jukes. Currently, a license from The Harry Fox Agency costs 9.1 centers for each download of a song of up to five minutes in length. There's a formula for calculating the fee for longer songs, and you need to negotiate with the agency if you plan for more than 2500 copies to be downloaded.

- *Public performance of musical works*   This license—from ASCAP, BMI, or SESAC—lets *you* perform the song yourself, but not to play a recording by an artist who recorded the song. For example, if you obtained the public performance rights for *Bad to the Bone*, *you* could sing it on your podcast—but you couldn't play George Thorogood singing it.

- *Reproduction, distribution, and public performance*   These rights let you play the song that was recorded for a record or CD. Remember, this particular license is difficult to obtain, since you'll have to negotiate separately with each record company.

Exceptions

Copyright rules have some exceptions—five, to be exact. These exceptions are very narrow and a bit confusing, so you should err on the side of caution. These exceptions include the following:

- *Stuff that can't be copyrighted*   If you wrote a book tomorrow and called it *The Tipping Point*, there's nothing Malcolm Gladwell could do about it. You could even call it *Gone with the Wind*, if you wanted. Not that these are good ideas, but the simple fact is that nobody can copyright a title. Other things that cannot be copyrighted include ideas, facts, theories, slogans, or short phrases. (Just because slogans and phrases cannot be copyrighted does not mean they cannot be protected. Slogans *can* be trademarked, for example. We'll deal with trademarks later in this chapter.) Generally speaking, though, you can talk about something another podcaster writes about all day long.

- *The public domain*   Copyrights don't last forever (no matter how much the copyright holders may wish they did). In fact, the reason copyright was embraced by the framers of the United States Constitution was *not* to protect the creators of the material, but rather to ensure that the general public would eventually be able to use it however they liked. Once a copyright expires, the material moves into what is known as the "public domain." Once a work has passed into the public domain, you're free to do with it whatever you like.

- *Government works*   Any work produced by the U.S. government, or by a government worker as part of their job duties, is not protected by copyright. This exception does *not* include materials from states, counties, cities, towns, or other governmental entities—only works by U.S. federal officials and employees.

- *"Podsafe" content*   A number of content creators may opt to allow their works to be used in podcasts. That's the idea behind the Podsafe Music Network (PMN), which allows musicians to upload their music so podcasters can retrieve it and play it. The license clearly allows podcasters to use this music, assuming they meet certain conditions (for example, they must link to the artist in their show notes and they must submit notification when they have played the song). One of the best ways to determine the rights a content creator is handing over to podcasters is through their use of a Creative Commons license. We'll cover the Creative Commons license later in this chapter.

- *Fair use*   One of the most misunderstood copyright rules is the notion of "fair use." More often than not, people citing fair use as the justification for adding copyrighted content to their materials are mistaken and they could find themselves in a world of trouble. Fair use lets you incorporate copyrighted material for limited and "transformative" uses. Some examples include critiques, reviews, reporting, and parodying of the original work. Still, even if you can show that you cited the work in question as part of a review, a court could look at other factors, like the amount of the protected work that you used and whether your use of the work significantly affected the creator's ability to sell it.

A

We should note that violating copyright does not necessarily mean you *will* find yourself in trouble over it; only that you *could*. For example, in the blogosphere people routinely cite long tracts from newspaper articles without the newspapers filing suits. That's usually because the newspaper chooses to ignore the copyright law in exchange for the links back to the newspaper site—they would rather a blogger drive traffic than try to squeeze a few dollars out of them for violating their copyright. Nevertheless, it's better to be safe than sorry!

Publicity Rights

A few years ago, California Governor and *Terminator* star Arnold Schwarzenegger sued to stop a company from selling bobble-head dolls bearing his likeness. It was under the laws governing publicity rights that he filed the suit. Publicity rights give individuals the ability to control how anybody uses their voice or likeness in public.

Not every use of a person's voice or image violates an individual's publicity rights. For example, you can use a public figure's likeness or voice as long as you use it truthfully and don't imply that the individual whose voice or likeness you're using is somehow endorsing you or your show. But it gets complex, as most legal issues do. In some states—California, for instance—you could be found in violation of publicity rights laws if you used the individual's likeness or voice for advertising, sales, or solicitation.

Other states have different provisions; publicity rights laws are in the jurisdiction of states, not the federal government.

Trademark

Companies whose products are well-recognized go to great lengths to protect those brands so unscrupulous businesspeople don't market their own products under the same name. Trademark laws were created for consumers' protection so nobody could deliberately confuse them about the source or a product. But it's the trademark owners that fiercely protect those trademarks, notably because failure to do so in one instance will mitigate against the trademark holder when they try to protect it in another case. A couple of brands that are trademarked and protected by the companies that own them include Barbie, Coke, and iPod.

Does that mean your podcast could be violating trademark if you mention an iPod? (For that matter, could this book be in jeopardy because we mentioned the iPod?) Not really. Violating trademark means you have either *infringed* on the trademark or *diluted* it. Infringement occurs when you create confusion among the product's consumers. Thus, if you called your podcast, *The iPod Show*, it might lead many listeners and prospective listeners to think that Apple Computers was the official sponsor of a show about its product. That kind of confusion represents a violation of trademark, while saying, "I listen to podcasts on my iPod" does not. (In fact, the original podcatching software was called *iPodder* until Apple's lawyers issued a cease-and-desist letter, leading the software creators to change the application's name to *Juice*.)

You can also be sued if you *dilute* the value of the trademark. Mattel Toys issued a cease-and-desist letter to a photographer who had posted a series of photographs online depicting the company's signature doll in suggestive poses. While nobody would have been confused by these pictures, thinking that perhaps Mattel was behind them, the nature of the photos created an unwanted association that could tarnish the doll brand's reputation. Another trademark violation would occur if Mattel could show that the line between the photos and the brand had blurred, leaving people thinking that the doll routinely modeled in sexually suggestive poses.

These rules noted, it's equally important to know you generally don't need permission to make an editorial use of a trademark. That is, you can talk about Barbie, iPods, and Coke all day long if you're talking about the kind of business the brands did last quarter, analyzing advertising campaigns, reviewing the latest product line, or other such informational or "nominative" references. You can also use trademarks without identifying them as registered trademarks. You could, for instance, have a segment of your podcast called "Google This!" that discusses search engine techniques and be safe from any accusations that you have violated trademark.

Defamation and Right to Privacy

The next legal category to discuss is defamation, which is the same in a podcast as it is in printed (libel) or spoken (slander) instances. Basically, you cannot defame somebody in your podcasts without risking a lawsuit.

Libel and slander are both covered under the idea of defamation. Libel refers to the written word while slander accounts for what is spoken. In both cases, you defame somebody when you make a false and unprivileged statement that can harm the reputation of the person you're talking about. It's defamation whether you made the statement with malice or out of negligence.

A

In the United States, a statement must pass three tests to be considered defamation:

- The statement was published to somebody other than the individual the statement was about. If you send a letter or e-mail just to the individual you're talking about, it's not defamation. Publishing the same statement in a blog, though, clearly satisfies this requirement.

- The statement is false.

- It's clear that the statement was about the individual claiming to have been defamed and tends to be harmful to that individual.

If a statement must be false in order to be defamatory, then truth is an absolute defense against a defamation claim. Even then, however, you could be in for some trouble because proving what is true could be a challenge. Also, you're entitled to state your opinion, but it takes a lawyer to separate what is a genuine opinion from statements that were simply labeled as opinion. Courts tend to use the "reasonable" standard: Would a reasonable person hearing the statement think it was opinion or a statement that claimed to present a "verifiable fact" (one that can be proved true or false)? The difference can be seen in these examples:

Opinion: "I can't stand anything Jackie Collins writes."

Verifiable fact: "In my opinion, CEO John Smith has been looting Acme Inc.'s pension fund."

There is an exception to the definition of defamation. A public figure has to prove that you actually *wanted* to harm him when you defamed him, while a private figure need only prove that you acted negligently. This higher standard is harder to prove.

One issue that is still in limbo as of this writing is whether you, the blogger, are liable for defamatory comments somebody else posts to your blog. A case was in litigation as this book was being written over precisely this issue. It is generally agreed, though, that you are more likely to be held liable if you monitor your comments—that is, you read them before authorizing them to appear on your blog.

Closely related to defamation is another category worth mentioning: right to privacy. In the United States, the right to privacy is held very dear. As far as the law is concerned, a "private fact" is simply one that an individual hasn't made public. If you "out" somebody on a blog post, disclosing that he or she is gay, that qualifies as an intrusion into seclusion—you have violated that individual's privacy. As soon as the individual him or herself discloses that fact, though, it moves into the public domain and you won't get into any trouble for writing about it—at least, not from the law!

Not all states allow someone to sue for publication of a private fact, and those that do are not consistent in how the law is addressed. California, for example, requires four facts be shown before a lawsuit is merited: *public disclosure* of a *private fact* that is *offensive to a reasonable person* and which is *not a legitimate matter of public concern*. That last criterion is important, because if a private fact is newsworthy, then California allows it.

The question, thus, becomes: What is newsworthy?

As you might expect by now, the courts leave this to the "reasonable person" standard. It's newsworthy, therefore, if some reasonable members of the community could find a legitimate interest in the information.

There is one additional dimension of privacy to cover: intrusion into seclusion. This occurs when you intrude into the privacy or seclusion or his private affairs or concerns (again, assuming a reasonable person would find the intrusion offensive).

Your Rights as a Podcaster

Just as anybody who produced content you want to use in your podcast has certain rights associated with the content, you have rights as a podcaster yourself. The podcast you create is yours; the mere fact that it was "fixed" as an MP3 file means it has been copyrighted. It is entirely up to you how you exercise those rights.

Some podcasters—notably those who are repurposing mainstream media content into podcasts—hold their rights very close to the vest. But for most podcasters, they are more interested in spreading their podcasts around than protecting their copyrights. The social media space is populated mainly by people with more altruistic views of the world and are happy, with some restrictions and conditions, to share their work. This is true both of blogs *and* podcasts.

Shel recalls hearing Dave Slusher, the host of the *Evil Genius Chronicles* podcast, say something on his show that Shel wished he could play as a soundbite on *For Immediate Release*. So Shel sent an e-mail to Dave asking permission. The response came back from Slusher: There was no need to ask. Just looking at his site, we could have found a link that explained the rights he was offering.

In nearly every case, these rights are explained in a license that the podcaster (or blogger) has developed through a free service called "Creative Commons." Innovated by Stanford law school Constitutional professor Lawrence Lessig,

Creative Commons allows users to select the kind of content they are offering and the rights they are willing to relinquish. For example, the following is the set of rights we have established for *For Immediate Release*:

Attribution-NonCommercial 2.0

You are free:

to Share — to copy, distribute and transmit the work

to Remix — to adapt the work

Under the following conditions:

Attribution. You must attribute the work in the manner specified by the author or licensor (but not in any way that suggests that they endorse you or your use of the work).

Noncommercial. You may not use this work for commercial purposes.

- For any reuse or distribution, you must make clear to others the license terms of this work. The best way to do this is with a link to this web page.
- Any of the above conditions can be waived if you get permission from the copyright holder.
- Nothing in this license impairs or restricts the author's moral rights.

A **new version** of this license is available. You should use it for new works, and you may want to relicense existing works under it. No works are *automatically* put under the new license, however.

In this list of rights, we have let people know that they are free to do whatever they like with our work as long as (a) they give us credit for it, and (b) they do not make any money from it. We also ask that they apply the same terms to any redistribution of the podcast.

When you visit the Creative Commons web site and create your license, you'll get a "badge" you can put on your site that looks like the following:

This should appear on the site where your podcast is housed in order for your license to be "express," which means that you have expressly outlined the terms of your license in a tangible way people can see. There are, of course, other types of express licenses. Including a simple "All Rights Reserved" notification, which you can establish with the copyright symbol, followed by your name (or your business name) and the year, like this:

© Neville Hobson and Shel Holtz, 2006

Finally, if your podcast is hosted by a service like Podshow, you should make sure their terms of service are consistent with the kind of copyright you want to offer.

The alternative to an express license is an "implied" license, which suggests that you have extended a license to anyone who wants to use your podcast but you haven't spelled it out in writing. We don't suggest using an implied license for your entire podcast, but to instead apply it in its most common applications. This would include, for instance, paying somebody to produce a musical bumper or opening segment for your show. Even though the vendor did not give you a written statement assigning you the rights to use the work, the fact that you paid for it and that the artist knew what you were using it for suggests that such a license was implied.

Where to Get More Information

We strongly suggest, as we did at the beginning of this document, that you consult with an attorney on any legal issues. We also strongly suggest you download a copy of the *Podcasting Legal Guide*, offered by Creative Commons in conjunction with The Berkman Center's Clinical Program in Cyberlaw at Harvard Law School. Co-written by Colette Bogele, Esq. and Mia Garlick of the Stanford Center for Internet and Society, this document covers only U.S. law, but is comprehensive and served as the resource for much of what we have written here. You can obtain a copy at http://wiki.creativecommons.org/Podcasting_Legal_Guide.

Appendix B

A Guide to Podcasting Resources

Throughout this book, we have referenced a variety of products and services of which podcasters can avail themselves. What a hassle it would be if you had to thumb through the book to try to remember where we wrote about that *one* resource you really need. Fortunately, you don't have to. We've assembled them all right here.

Podcast Retrieval Software (Podcatchers)

- Juice (Windows, Mac, Linux) – http://juicereceiver.sourceforge.net
- Nimiq (Windows) – http://www.nimiq.nl
- Doppler (Windows) – http://www.dopplerradio.net
- iPodderX (Mac) – http://ipodderx.com
- iTunes (Windows, Mac) – www.apple.com/itunes

Podcast Directories

- Apple iTunes (download required) – http://www.apple.com/itunes
- Podcast Alley – http://www.podcastalley.com
- Podcast Pickle – http://www.podcastpickle.com
- Yahoo – http://podcasts.yahoo.com

Podcast Hosting Services

- LibSyn – http://www.libsyn.com
- Switchpod – http://www.switchpod.com
- Podlot – http://www.podlot.com
- Hipcast – http://www.hipcast.com
- Odeo – http://www.odeo.com
- Our Media – http://www.ourmedia.org

Podcasting Resources on the Web

- iLounge – http://www.ipodlounge.com
- Podcast 411 – http://www.podcast411.com
- Podcast Expert – http://www.podcastexpert.com
- Podcast Rigs – http://www.podcastrigs.com
- Podcasting Optimization – http://www.podcastoptimization.com
- Podcasting News – http://www.podcastingnews.com

Remote Recording Services

- Gabcast – http://www.gabcast.com
- Phoneblogz – http://www.phoneblogz.com
- Gcast – http://www.gcast.com

Promo Hosting

- Podcast Promos – http://www.podcastpromos.com
- Podcast Spots – http://podcastspots.com/Add-Podcast-Promo.aspx
- Podshow Promos – http://promos.podshow.com
- Promo Picker – http://www.promopicker.com

Podcasts Mentioned in the Book

- Accident Hash – http://www.accidenthash.com
- Across the Sound – http://www.acrossthesound.net
- American Copywriter – http://www.wehatesheep.com/americancopywriter
- Barbecue Secrets – http://barbecuesecrets.libsyn.com

B

- BiddyCast – http://www.biddycast.com

- The Cystic Fibrosis Podcast – http://www.jerrycahill.com

- Dawn and Drew Show – http://dawnanddrew.podshow.com

- Digital Flotsam – http://digitalflotsam.podshow.com

- Endurance Planet – http://www.enduranceplanet.com

- Evil Genius Chronicles – http://www.evilgeniuschronicles.com

- For Immediate Release – http://www.forimmediatereleaes.biz

- National Public Radio podcasts – http://www.npr.org/rss/podcast/podcast_directory.php

- Adam Curry's "Daily Source Code" – http://www.dailysourcecode.com

- High Orbit – http://www.matthewebel.com/podcast

- John & Elizabeth Edwards' Podcast – http://www.oneamericacommittee.com

- The Gillmor Gang – http://gillmorgang.podshow.com

- Manager Tools – http://www.manager-tools.com

- Podcast NYC – http://www.podcastnyc.net

- The Ricky Gervais Podcast – http://www.guardian.co.uk/rickygervais

- The Official ABC *Lost* Podcast – http://abc.go.com/primetime/lost/podcasts.html

- Podcast 411 – http://www.podcast411.com

- Podcast Brothers – http://www.podcastbrothers.com

- Podictionary – http://www.podictionary.com

- Rock 'N Roll Geek Show – http://www.rocknrollgeek.com

- Reel Reviews– http://www.reelreviewsradio.com

- This Week in Tech – http://twit.tv

- Geek News Central – http://www.geeknewscentral.com

- U-Turn Café – http://www.uturncafe.com

- Your Jewish Neighborhood – http://www.yourjewishneighborhood.org

Business Podcasts

- Speedo "Make Waves" Podcast – http://www.thenewpr.com/wiki/pmwiki.php?pagename=Resources.BusinessPodcastList

- BMC Software – http://talk.bmc.com/podcasts/simpleblog_view

- BMW – http://podcast.bmw.com/en

- Disney Resorts – http://disneyland.disney.go.com/disneyland/en_US/calendar/specialEvents/detail?name=PodcastingSpecialEventDetailPageGold&bhcp=1

- General Motors *Fastlane* Podcast – http://fastlane.gmblogs.com/archives/podcasts/index.html

- IBM and the Future Of… – http://www.ibm.com/investor/viewpoint/index.phtml

- iPressRoom's *On the Record Online* – http://www.ipressroom.com/pr/corporate/info/Podcast-Center.asp

- McDonald's Podcast – http://www.mcdonalds.com/corp/podcasts.html

- Purina's Podcasts – http://www.purina.com/downloads/Podcast.aspx?DCMP=RAC-PUR-Podcasts&HQS=Home

- Sprint's *Communication Insider* – http://podcast.sprint.com

- U.S. Air Force podcast – http://www.af.mil/podcast

- U.S. Department of Defense *Pentagon Channels* podcast – http://www.pentagonchannel.mil/podcast.asp

- Virgin Atlantic's Podcast Destinations – http://virginatlantic.loudish.com/destinations.html

- Whirlpool's American Family – http://www.mayitpleasethecourt.com/journal.asp

Podsafe Music Resources

- Internet Archive – http://www.archive.org/audio
- The Podsafe Music Network – http://music.podshow.com

B

- PodsafeAudio – http://www.podsafeaudio.com
- Garage Band[1] – http://www.garageband.com

Sound Effects Resources

- A1 Free Sound Effects – http://www.a1freesoundeffects.com
- Sound Effects Library – http://www.sound-effects-library.com
- Sound Dogs – http://www.sounddogs.com
- Partners in Rhyme – http://www.partnersinrhyme.com
- Sound Effects CD Libraries – http://soundfx.com/sfxcategories.htm
- FindSounds – http://www.findsounds.com

Voiceover Services

- Interactive Voices – http://www.interactivevoices.com
- Radio Daddy – http://www.radiodaddy.com
- Voice123 – http://www.voice123.com
- Audiobag – http://www.audiobag.com

RSS Resources

RSS Newsreaders that Support Podcasts

- FeedDemon (Windows) – http://www.newsgator.com/NGOLProduct. aspx?ProdID=FeedDemon
- NetNewsWire (Mac) – http://www.newsgator.com/NGOLProduct. aspx?ProdID=NetNewsWire

---

[1] Not all music on Garage Band is podsafe; check each artist to see if they allow you to use their music without requesting permission from them.

RSS Tutorials

- RSS tutorial from mnot.net – http://www.mnot.net/rss/tutorial/#Versions
- RSS – A primer for Publishers and Content Providers – http://www.techxtra.ac.uk/rss_primer
- RSS tutorial from Wizard Creek Consulting – http://www.wizard-creek.com/rss/tutorial/index.htm

RSS Services

- Feedburner – http://www.feedburner.com
- Feed2Podcast – http://www.feed2podcast.com

RSS Code Editors

- Feed for All – http://www.feedforall.com
- Feed Editor – http://www.extralabs.net/feed-editor.htm
- RSS Editor – http://www.rss-info.com/en_rsseditor.html

Feed Validators

- Feed Validator – http://feedvalidator.org
- Smoothouse Podcast Validator – http://www.smoothouse.com/podcast/validator.php
- Check for iTunes compatibility – http://www.nobodylikesonions.com/feedcheck

Voice Over IP Resources

- Skype – http://www.skype.com
- Skype Journal – http://www.skypejournal.com

B

- The Gizmo Project – http://www.gizmoproject.com
- Recording Skype with Virtual Audio Cables – http://www.henshall.com/docs/Skype%20Recording%20WinXp%2012202004.pdf
- HotRecorder – http://www.hotrecorder.com

Podcast Networks

- Association of Music Podcasters – http://www.musicpodcasting.org
- Podcaster News Network – http://www.podcasternews.com
- BluBrry – http://www.blubrry.com
- Odeo – http://www.odeo.com
- Podshow Plus – http://www.podshow.com

Audio Hardware

Microphone Manufacturers

- Audio Technica – http://www.audiotechnica.com
- Beyerdeynamic – http://www.beyerdynamic.com
- Heil Sound – http://www.heilsound.com
- Kel Audio – http://www.kelaudio.com
- Neumann – http://www.neumannusa.com
- Rode – http://www.rode.com.au
- Samson Technologies – http://www.samsontech.com
- Sennheiser – http://www.sennheiserusa.com
- Shure – http://www.shure.com
- Studio Projects – http://www.studioprojects.com/b1.html

Mixers

- Alexis – http://www.alesis.com

- Behringer – http://www.behringer.com

- Mackie – http://www.mackie.com

- Yamaha – http://www.yamaha.com

Digital Recorders

Compact Recorders

- M-Audio Microtrack 24/96 – http://www.m-audio.com/products/en_us/MicroTrack2496-main.html

- Edirol R-09 – http://www.edirol.net/products/en/R-09

Portable Recorders

- Marantz digital recorders – http://www.d-mpro.com/users/folder.asp?FolderID=3507

- Edirol R-1 – http://www.edirol.net/products/en/R-1/index.html

Headphones

- Sony MDR-7506 stereo headphones – http://bssc.sel.sony.com/BroadcastandBusiness/DisplayModel?m=0&p=10&sp=79&id=52568

Telephone Recording Inline Patches

- JK Audio – http://www.jkaudio.com

- Radio Shack – http://www.radioshack.com

- Telecom Audio – http://www.telecomaudio.com

- Telos – http://www.telos-systems.com/?/one/default.htm

B

Software

Recording and Editing Software

- Audio Hijack Pro (Mac) – http://www.rogueamoeba.com/audiohijackpro
- Audacity (Windows, Mac, Linux) – http://audacity.sourceforge.net
- Adobe Audition (Windows) – http://www.adobe.com/products/audition/index.html
- DSP Quattro Pro – http://www.d-soundpro.com
- Sony Sourceforge –http://www.sonymediasoftware.com/Products/ShowProduct.asp?PID=961
- Steinberg Cubase – http://www.steinberg.net
- WavePad – http://www.nch.com.au/wavepad
- SoundSoap – http://www.bias-inc.com/products/soundsoap
- Waxmail – http://www.waxmail.com
- Skylook – http://www.skylook.biz

All-in-One Podcast Packages

- Podcast Station – www.podcaststation.com
- Mixcast Live – www.mixcastlive.com
- Castblaster – www.castblaster.com

MP3 Software

- Daily MP3 – http://www.dailymp3.com

Flash-based Audio Players

- Dew Player – http://www.estvideo.com/dew/index/2005/02/16/370-player-flash-mp3-leger-comme-une-plume
- Wimpy Player – www.wimpyplayer.com

Local Podcasting Meetups

- New Jersey Podcasters Association – http://www.njpodcasters.org
- Hawaii Association of Podcasters – http://www.hawaiipodcasting.com
- New York City Podcasting Association – http://podcasting.meetup.com/33
- Utah Podcasters Association – http://www.utahpodcasters.com
- Greater Houston Podcasting Association – http://www.houstonpodcasting.com
- Los Angeles Podcasters – http://lapodcasters.com
- Kansas City (MO) Podcasting Meetup Group – http://podcasting.meetup.com/15
- New England Podcasters – http://newenglandpodcasting.com
- Chicago Podcasters – http://chicagopodcasters.org
- Orange County (CA) Podcasters – http://www.ocpodcasters.com
- San Diego (CA) Podcasters – http://podcasting.meetup.com/14
- San Francisco Podcasters – http://podcasting.meetup.com/20
- Detroit Podcasters Network – http://www.detroitpodcasters.net
- Miami Podcasting Meetup Group – http://podcasting.meetup.com/59
- Phoenix/Scottsdale Podcasting Meetup Group – http://podcasting.meetup.com/67
- Portland (OR) Podcasting – http://www.portlandpodcasting.org
- The Seattle Podcasting Network – http://www.seattlepodcasting.net
- The Indianapolis Podcaster's Guild – http://www.indypodcasters.com
- The Nashville Podcasters Meetup Group – http://podcasting.meetup.com/44

Blogging Resources

- Blogger – http://www.blogger.com
- Typepad – http://www.typepad.com

B

- WordPress – http://www.wordpress.org
- WordPress podcast plugin – http://digitalpodcast.com/podcastnews/index. php/2006/03/02/podpress_a_podcasting_plugin_for_wordpre

Audio Engineering Message Boards

- Music and Technology: Resources for the Recording Musician – http:// www.music-tech.com/cgi-bin/yabb/YaBB.cgi
- ProSoundWeb – http://www.prosoundweb.com/forums
- Audio Forums – http://www.audioforums.com

Other Resources

- Creative Commons – http://www.creativecommons.net
- K7.net – http://www.k7.net
- Frappr – http://www.frappr.com
- Café Press – http://www.cafepress.com
- Podzinger Audio Search – http://www.podzinger.com

Appendix C   Podcasting Glossary

As you delve deeper into podcasting, you are likely to hear terms with which you have passing familiarity or have never heard before. The definitions that follow cover the most frequently referenced terms used in podcasting and recording circles. Many of these terms were covered in the body of this book.

AAC   Advanced Audio Coding; a format for an audio file embraced by Apple for use in its iTunes service and iPod device. Apple has enabled bookmarks or chapters within AAC files.

Aggregator   Software that collects and displays RSS feeds. Also known as a "newsreader." Some aggregators are able to retrieve and play podcasts; others do not have this capability.

AIFF   Audio Interchange File Format; a common Macintosh audio file format.

Amplitude   In physics, the extent of a movement measured from the starting point. In audio, amplitude is a technical term referring to volume or loudness as measured by the vibrations created by sound and displayed as a waveform (*see* Waveform). The louder the audio, the greater the amplitude.

ASCAP   American Society of Composers, Authors, and Publishers; a collection society that ensures creators of music collect appropriate fees as compensation for performance of their work (*see also* BMI).

ATOM   A web feed format that offers an alternative to RSS (*see* RSS). ATOM was developed as a means of overcoming perceived shortcomings to RSS.

Backsell   In radio, the announcement of the title and artist of a song after the song has been played.

Badge   A graphic that podcasters can provide for listeners to display on their blogs or web pages with a link back to the podcast site. A means of promoting the podcast.

Bed   Audio that plays continuously, usually softly, in the background; typically music is used, but sometimes other audio effects are employed.

Bit Rate   The number of bits that are processed per unit of time. In audio, the bit rate refers to the number of bits stored per unit of time in a recording. The more bits stored per second, the better the audio fidelity and the larger the resulting file.

Blog   *See* weblog.

BMI   Broadcast Music Incorporated; a nonprofit performing rights society that collects fees on behalf of artists as compensation for performance of the music they created; established by broadcasters as an alternative to ASCAP (*see also* ASCAP).

Board   Mixing board or mixer; hardware used to combine, or "mix," multiple audio sources into a single signal for recording.

Bumper   A prerecorded audio element consisting of voiceover music that acts as a transition to or from one element of a show to another.

Bumper Music   Short music clips used to transition between one element of programming to another.

Clipping   A form of distortion that occurs when a signal exceeds its limits. In a waveform, the normal peak that appears at the apex of a sound appears plateaued or flattened. This occurs because the amplifier will only amplify the signal to its maximum capacity, and thus cuts or "clips" the rest of the signal.

Codec   A program that encodes or decodes, as in encoding an MP3 file from a WAV file. The name is shortened from "compressor-decompressor."

Compression   Also known as dynamic range compression, this is the process that manipulates the dynamic range of an audio signal in order to improve the perceived sound of the signal. Compression reduces the dynamic range of the signal if its amplitude exceeds a user-defined threshold.

CPC   Cost per click.

CPM   Cost per thousand.

Creative Commons   A nonprofit organization that provides online content creators with the ability to assign rights to their intellectual property as part of an effort to expand the amount of creative work available for others to legally use for their own purposes.

Crossfade   A technique where the sound between two sources is mixed by fading one down while simultaneously increasing the volume of the other.

dB   Decibel; the measure of the ratio between two quantities. In audio, dB is used to measure sound levels relative to 0 dB. For example, the noise inside an office or a restaurant is usually around 60 dB.

DNS   *See* Domain Name.

Domain Name   An alphabetical name assigned to an IP address. Internet addresses are numerical (for example, 201.247.173.45). Since most people would not be able to associate sites with numbers, the domain name system (DNS) was established, allowing site owners to give their sites names like podcast.com, harvard.edu, and redcross.org. The DNS associates the name with the IP address and directs traffic to the appropriate server.

Drops   Sound bites lifted from mainstream media (such as TV shows or movies); used to accentuate or emphasize content.

DSP   Digital signal processing; actions taken to improve the overall quality of a digital signal, such as noise removal, equalization, and compression.

EQ   Equalization; manipulation of high-, mid-, and low-range frequencies, akin to adjusting the treble and bass on a stereo system.

Enclosures   A technique for linking to multimedia files within an RSS 2.0 newsfeed. Podcatchers and some aggregators recognize enclosures in RSS feeds and automatically retrieve the indicated multimedia file.

Feed   An XML file—usually RSS or ATOM—containing headlines, descriptions, and often multimedia enclosures to which people can subscribe in order to have updated content delivered directly to them. Feed "enclosures" allow for the distribution of multimedia content through feed subscriptions, enabling podcasting.

Frequency   The measurement of the number of times a repeated event occurs per unit of time.

FTP   File Transfer Protocol; the means by which content, from multimedia files to web pages, is transferred from an individual's computer (client) to a server and vice versa. FTP can be used with a direct connection or with an FTP client (software that creates a user-friendly interface between client and server).

Harry Fox Agency   One of the primary agencies for collecting and distributing license fees on behalf of music publishers.

Hz   Hertz; under the International System of Units, a unit of frequency, usually referring to one per second (100 Hz refers to 100 per second).

ID3 Tag   Metadata contained within an MP3 file that is displayed on the screen of a portable digital media player or in the media player software on a computer. Developed for commercial music, ID3 tags include artist, album, track, year, and genre, among other fields.

Ident   Before the introductory music or the introduction, the brief voice announcement of the episode number and/or date of the episode. Also used at other points during radio broadcasts to inform listeners about what they are listening to in the event they tuned in after the show began.

Imaging   The term for using audio effects, spoken phrases, or music to create an "image" or brand for a radio station or show.

Intro   The introductory portion of a podcast, usually used to welcome listeners and provide basic information such as the names of the hosts, the nature of the content to follow, and recognition of sponsors or advertisers.

IP   Internet Protocol.

iPod   The most popular portable media digital player, manufactured by Apple Computers Inc., and the source of the "pod" in the word "podcast."

ISP   Internet Service Provider; a business that hosts Internet content for a fee.

iTunes   The digital media distribution service launched by Apple, Inc. When iTunes introduced podcasts in mid-2005, awareness of, and subscriptions to, podcasts skyrocketed.

kHz   Kilohertz; 1000 hertz (*see* Hz).

LAME   A standalone MP3 encoder that is often required by other applications in order to convert native audio file formats (such as WAV and AIFF) into MP3.

Latency   The amount of time it takes an audio signal to travel through a system. The term usually refers to the delay between the time the audio signal is introduced and the time it arrives at its ultimate destination.

Lossless   A compression technique that does not result in the loss of any data from an audio file.

Lossy   A compression technique that removes data from an audio file in order to reduce the overall file size without significant degradation to the quality of the music. MP3 is a lossy compression format.

Mastering   The production of the final audio output.

Mixer   Mixing board or board; hardware used to combine, or "mix," multiple audio sources into a single signal for recording.

MP3   MPEG-1 Audio Layer 3; a compression technique used to create small audio files that contain nearly faithful reproductions of the original music file. The most common format for music on the Internet and the default format for podcasts.

Newsfeed   A collection of news or story highlights made available on the Internet in a standard format, usually RSS 2.0. Newsfeeds are used to publish information about podcasts. Podcast clients can subscribe to podcast newsfeeds, and use their information to find new shows and download them.

Newsreader   *See* aggregator.

C

OGG   A patent-free format for streaming and compressing audio files.

Outro   The final part of a podcast or radio show in which the host wraps up the episode.

PHP   Hypertext Pre-Processor; a server-side, HTML-embedded scripting language used to create dynamic Web content. PHP scripts can be embedded in HTML code. Most blogging applications are written in PHP.

Playlist   In radio, the official list of songs a station is playing during any given week. In a podcast, playlists can represent the songs to be played on any given music-focused show, or the topics to be covered in a nonmusic episode.

Plosive   Also known as a "stop" or "occlusive," a plosive is a consonant sound that is produced by an abrupt stop to the airflow in the vocal tract. The most common plosives occur with the consonants p, k, and t. Microphones can accentuate these sounds. Many podcasters and other audio performers use pop filters to soften or reduce plosives (*see* Pop Filter).

Podcast   Audio files published to the World Wide Web and/or intranets, usually episodic in nature, that are accessible through a web feed allowing audiences to subscribe and retrieve the files using aggregators or podcatchers in addition to downloading or streaming the files. Podcasts can be played on a computer or transferred to a portable digital media player.

Podcasting   The process of producing and publishing podcasts (*see* Podcast).

Podcatcher   A term for programs used to subscribe to and download podcasts.

Podroll   A list of podcasts appearing on a podcast web site or blog. Usually, this is a list of other podcasts to which the podcaster listens, and serves as a means of telling listeners, "If you like my podcast, you'll probably like these, too." Podcasts listed on a podroll generally address the same theme as the podcast that hosts it; podcasts on a music podroll will point to similar music podcasts.

Pop Filter   A shield that resides in front of a microphone that softens or reduces popping and hissing sounds. Generally constructed of semi-transparent material like woven nylon and stretched over a circular frame that clamps to a microphone stand (*see* Plosive, Sibilant).

Promo   A brief audio file promoting a podcast; meant to be played on other podcasts.

RMS   Root Mean Square; the square root of the arithmetic mean (average) of the square's set of values. A reasonably accurate method of describing an amplifier's power output. Many experts recommend the RMS for a podcast at –12 dB with a peak setting of 0.2 dB.

RSS   Really Simple Syndication; this is the most popular news feed syndication format. RSS 2.0 is the de facto feed format for podcasting. (*See also* ATOM.)

Sample   A sound stored digitally in a computer, synthesizer, or sampler.

Sample Rate   The frequency at which a sound is recorded (or "sampled") and converted into digital data. A sample rate of 44,100kHz was recorded at 41,000 samples per second.

SESAC   Society of European Stage Authors and Composers; small for-profit Performing Rights Agency that collects fees for performance of licensed work in order to compensate artists for the use of their licensed material.

Sibilant   A consonant that makes a hissing sound, like s, f, sh, z, and th (when used in words like "thin" and "then"). Podcasters and other audio performers often use pop filters to reduce or soften sibilants (*see* Pop Filter).

Shout-out   A brief vocal audio soundbite that recognizes someone. Shout-outs can come from listeners praising the show (for example, "This is John Doe, and you're listening to *The Podsafe Music Podcast*, the best darned music podcast on the Net") or from the podcaster to somebody else (for instance, "I'd like to send a shout-out to John Doe, who put in a lot of time and effort to create a new logo for us").

Skype   An Internet telephony service that lets you make calls via an Internet connection.

Soundbite   A snippet of audio obtained from another source such as an interview, which is then inserted into a news or feature story.

Stinger   A sound or musical effect that punctuates a punchline or emphasizes a thought.

Stream   The ability to play an audio file over the Net without waiting for it to download by sending the data over a data link in a single operation.

Sweeper   An audio clip (voice, voiceover music, or sound effects) that bridges two other audio elements together, such as two songs or an announcement and a song.

URI   Uniform Resource Identifier; an address for a resource accessible over the Internet (*see also* URL).

URL   Uniform Resource Locator; an address that specifies a specific file on the Internet; a URL is one example of a URI (*see* URI).

C

Vidcast   *See* Video Podcast.

Video Podcast   A podcast produced with video files instead of audio files and included in an RSS enclosure so audience members can retrieve them and watch them on their computers or portable media devices.

Vlog   *See* Video Podcast.

WAV   A common audio file format that dominates the Microsoft Windows world and used routinely as the format for recording onto CD because of its uncompressed sound.

Waveform   A graphic representation of the shape of a sound wave that displays amplitude variations over time. Waveforms are used for editing audio in recording and editing software.

Weblog   A web site constructed with the use of lightweight content management software that incorporates certain standard elements such as comments. Items appear in reverse chronological order (newest item first).

XML   eXtensible Markup Language; the scripting language that is the foundation for RSS (*see* RSS).

Index

C